SEP 1986

You Were Marvellous

by James Fenton

TERMINAL MORAINE
THE MEMORY OF WAR

You Were Marvellous

Theatre reviews from the *Sunday Times*

by James Fenton

JONATHAN CAPE
THIRTY BEDFORD SQUARE LONDON

First published 1983
Text copyright © 1979, 1980, 1981 by James Fenton
'The Right to be Wrong' copyright © 1982 by *Plays and Players*
Introduction copyright © 1983 by James Fenton

Jonathan Cape Ltd, 30 Bedford Square, London WC1

British Library Cataloguing in Publication Data
Fenton, James
    You were marvellous.
    1. Drama – History and criticism
    I Title   II. Sunday Times
    809.2   PN1721

    ISBN 0-224-01995-3

Typeset by Oxford Verbatim Limited
Printed in Great Britain by
St Edmundsbury Press
Bury St Edmunds, Suffolk

To Nicholas Garland

Contents

Contents

Contents

Contents

10

Contents

Acknowledgments

The reviews contained in this book first appeared in the *Sunday Times* between November 1979 and December 1981. The Postscript, 'The Right to be Wrong', first appeared in the February 1982 issue of *Plays and Players*, whom I wish to thank for permission to reprint it here. The letter on p. 33 appeared in the *Sunday Times* of 3 January 1980 and is reprinted by courtesy of William H. Honan.

I would also like to thank John Whitley, John Peter, Sarah Foreman and Robert Hewison for their help.

J. F.

Introduction

I offer this selection of reviews to the general reader with two purposes in mind: as a record of recent work in our theatres, and as an account of my own critical interests and preoccupations. As far as the first purpose is concerned, I have no doubts as to the value of the exercise. We live in a period of intense, exciting and clamorous theatrical activity. The quantity of work produced far exceeds that of all other ages. If I am deceived as to the quality, it must be that we are deceived as to the permanent value of the classical repertoire, since that repertoire is on display as never before. It may be that in an age when productions of, for instance, Chekhov's plays were few and far between, there was an excitement attendant upon these occasions which we cannot imagine. It may be that, say, the post-war productions at the Old Vic have a significance in the experiences of those who saw them, a significance not to be reproduced on the modern stage. It may be. If those experiences were unique, it would be pointless to reach back into history and try to steal their uniqueness from them. The greatness of past actors is their inalienable right. A man may challenge Newton, or Darwin, or Einstein. No one can challenge Garrick.

What we may compare, on the other hand, is the over-all activity of the stage, and the freedom and opportunities of the theatrical audience over the years. In such a comparison, the ghosts of past witnesses would be loud in our favour. Those who asked for freedom of expression would envy us our freedom. Those who asked for a National Theatre would envy us our two national theatres with their seven auditoriums. Those who observed their contemporary repertoire with impatience and despair would be astonished at what has been achieved. For our part, if we turn to the critics of the past, it is hard not to pity them for the wretchedness of their fare. What did Shaw see? What did Beerbohm have to sit through? They wrote at length. I should say, rather, they embroidered at length. I wish that Providence had allowed them my miserable 1,200 words a week, and set me loose on their pleasant acres of good paper.

When the *Sunday Times* theatre critic, James Agate, collected his pieces for the volume *Red Letter Nights* (published by Jonathan Cape in 1944), he chose to divide his survey of the years 1921 to 1943 into such categories as 'Restoration Plays', 'Ibsen' and 'Foreign Plays'. He could offer an almost complete record of the first two categories during the period mentioned. He had sought out, and even in his youth helped to finance, Ibsen productions. He loved the affront given by the Restoration dramatists to the gentility of his own day. But during those twenty-two years he had seen only nine Restoration plays, and only fourteen productions of Ibsen.

Harold Hobson began work as Agate's assistant in 1946, and in the next year took over the job of chief drama critic. His first three years' work are recorded in diary form in the volumes *Theatre* and *Theatre 2*. In 1948 he records six Shakespearian productions (three of them revivals of *Hamlet*) and ten other pieces from the classical repertoire: *The Relapse*, *The Government Inspector*, *Dandy Dick* (I am stretching the definition of a classic), *Medea*, *Doctor Faustus*, *Le Misanthrope*, *The Way of the World*, *The Wild Duck*, *The Cherry Orchard* and *The Father*. The average week seems to have involved three or perhaps four nights' work. Very little of the new writing of that year has retained any interest, although the actors and actresses who led the field in those days have kept an unrivalled prestige.

When Hobson retired in 1976 (he was knighted in the following year), the artistic, intellectual and political ethos of the theatre had been completely transformed. The commercial West End was in rivalry with the Royal Shakespeare Company and the National Theatre. The Fringe had grown into an institution. Censorship had been abolished. The glamour of the first night had gone. High society had deserted the theatres in favour of the opera. In every way, the theatre was more demanding, and the job of the critic had been transformed.

Sir Harold's successor, Bernard Levin, combined his work

with a frequent column in *The Times*, and appears very much to have kept up with opera and classical music. How he managed this regime I do not know. He had two writing years followed by eleven months of silence, during the dispute which closed down the Times group of papers. In November 1979 he signed off, with the admission: 'The brutal truth is that I couldn't stand it any longer.' This had been Levin's second stint as a drama critic (between 1959 and 1966 he had worked on the *Daily Express* and the *Daily Mail*) and in the opinion of his colleagues he had been unprepared for the change that had taken place in the theatre. Levin himself, while welcoming the disappearance of a certain kind of fatuous West End comedy, claimed that the intolerable part of the job had been the new writing, and in particular what he identified as the 'relentless negativity' of the Fringe. Here is Levin's list of the kind of play he could not stand:

> *The Love of a Good Man* by Howard Barker; *Plenty* by David Hare; *Sisters* by David Storey; *A & R* by Pete Atkin; *Laughter* by the jonsonicidal Peter Barnes; *Savage Amusement* by Peter Flannery; *Shout Across the River* by Stephen Poliakoff; *Lost Worlds* by Wilson John Haire; and *Deeds* by Trevor Griffiths, David Hare, Howard Brenton and Ken Campbell.

The reader might have concluded from such a list that Levin was out of sympathy with a whole generation of playwrights. But a generation is a short time in the theatre, and I think that, if this type of play was indeed what drove Levin to quit, he despaired too soon.

I'm glad he did despair, though, since at the time of his desperation I had only one ambition in journalism, which was to work as a theatre critic on a weekly paper. One might imagine that this would be a very common ambition among journalists. Oddly enough, it isn't, particularly when the details of the job are explained: you are likely to be working five nights a week. You can't smoke, and you'd be exceedingly unwise (in most theatres) to drink. Your social life on weekdays is not destroyed exactly, but it tends to be conducted on a 'one-to-one' basis. On top of that, there are all those plays

15

. . . People I meet often say, 'What a wonderful life you must lead,' only to add, after a moment's thought: 'I couldn't stand it.'

The secret of survival is to recognise at an early stage that you have a full-time job, and that your day's routine has been turned on its head. This means that you must liberate yourself from any nagging guilt about, for instance, staying in bed late, wandering around the shops or putting your feet up when decent folk are at work. You must not consider it sinful to drop in on mid-week matinées of films – although you may find it impossible to walk out of a cinema and into a theatre. Aesthetically, you must learn to pace yourself, so that you do not exhaust your capacity to respond to the evening's drama.

The plays come at you with bewildering speed. When I began work on the *Sunday Times*, it was like trying to cross a road with very heavy traffic: bearing down on you all the time are the articulated trucks of world literature; you wait for an Ibsen to pass, unaware of the Chekhov in the middle distance; zipping along in the outside lane is a Shakespeare problem-play, spattering everything in its wake; and look, here comes the entire corpus of Greek Tragedy, in a convoy, their head-lights blazing and their CB radios crackling with activity; deftly weaving through the traffic comes a Pinter with darkened windows, a Frayn with the new registration, a filthy Brenton, a chauffeur-driven Shaffer, a souped-up Neil Simon with a Colonel Bogie klaxon. You wish there were traffic lights. You yearn for a friendly lollipop man. But the lollipop men have been laid off . . . and this image has probably outlived its usefulness.

Alarming though the rate of work might be, it did quell any possible fears that the job might turn out to be something of a bore. On the whole (although it is obviously unwise to write this) the boring nights in the theatre come as a bit of a relief. If an evening's work can be written off, at least it does not *have* to be written up. There is space for something else. Who knows? one might even be able to afford a first paragraph. (The critics of the past used to wiggle their toes in the water during the first paragraph, insert a foot in the second, get their knees wet in the third; pages later they were to be observed in an ecstasy of shivers as the water lapped around their bathing-trunks. The modern critic is obliged to dive in at the sound of the whistle. I can't dive. Hence the technique of leaping hectically into the air, clasping your knees to your chest and bobbing up seconds later with a nose full of chlorine.) In the past two years I can remember hardly a single week when I was stuck for a subject – however much I may have failed to rise to the occasion.

And failure to rise to the occasion is always the besetting fear. The critics of the past, when they approached a new *Hamlet*, appear to have allowed themselves a leisurely preparation. They would discuss previous *Hamlets*, *Hamlets* they had never seen but about which they would love to chat, in the way that Renaissance writers used to discuss the merits of Classical Greek painters, not one of whose works had survived. In order to make this kind of causerie possible, there would be frequent recourse to the authorities, to the apostolic succession of critics and witnesses whose accounts of past performances were a kind of legal precedent for the theatre of their day. Agate's ambition was to line his shelves with reviews which would account for every decade of the nineteenth century and beyond, as far as he could go. Thus equipped, he could floor anyone who ventured to disagree with a judgement by a cunning use of precedent.

All this would seem to contradict what I said earlier, that the greatness of past actors is their inalienable right. And indeed it would contradict it, if this argument from precedent were much employed today. But it has lost its vogue and its meaning. In 1947, reviewing Peter Brook's *Romeo and Juliet*, Hobson finds himself enthusiastic about Tybalt (Myles Eason) but unable to praise Lawrence Payne's Romeo. He concludes on the remark that 'Irving also failed in the part'. A correspondent is immediately provoked:

Irving's Romeo was before my time, but having seen him constantly since 1895 till the time of his death I believe I should have liked his Romeo. No doubt it was awkward and angular *outside*, but I think he must have suggested the poetry and the beauty of the lines more fully than any of the Romeos I have seen, including Forbes-Robertson.

Challenged thus, Hobson is obliged to consider the various possible merits of Irving, Forbes-Robertson and William Terriss as Romeo. Criticism, it would appear, never gave up in those days, and people were passionate advocates of performances they had never seen. This strikes the modern reader as quaint. But there was a measure of reality to the tradition. When Hobson asks himself what Shaw would have thought of the various performances he mentions he is asking a pertinent question, since Shaw, we discover, has had a direct influence on the Brook production. Brook had asked Shaw about *Romeo and Juliet*, and had received the advice to concentrate 'on young lovers and hard fighting'. This advice had been closely followed.

Here is a striking example of theatrical continuity. And yet, despite the great love of tradition in the theatre, it does seem to me that in the post-war years it is the discontinuity, the theatrical revolution, which is more important than the tradition. One may read Hobson or Tynan or their contemporaries with enlightenment. Their predecessors, however eminent, are less useful. They are talking about a different kind of theatre, and the approach they employ has rather little in common with modern criticism. I enjoy building up a library of past critics, but to be quite frank I do not often feel impelled to consult it. The period which would be most useful, that is to say the past two decades, is horribly incomplete. Hobson's diary was discontinued. Tynan covers only a very small proportion of what one wants to know. There are other collections, but there is no possibility of systematically reading through the reviews without recourse to a newspaper library.

This state of affairs is paradoxical. In an age which has invented so many means of storing and transmitting information, we run the risk that whole areas of our experience will be lost for future generations. No doubt the Special Branch will bequeath fascinating details of the private lives and telephone traffic of our left-wing playwrights (just as the FBI assembled useful information on the private life of Brecht during his stay in America, information which came in very handy for a recent scholarly book), but it is rather more important that someone should record what their plays were like in performance. The same goes, of course, for the right-wing playwrights, if they exist.

The trouble is that under the present dispensation the critics are just not up to the performance of this task. There are few papers. It is hard to find a decent theatrical magazine. The publishing of books about major productions is a rarity. For the nightly reviewer, the more space he is allowed the less time he has to compose his thoughts. For the weekly critic, it is impossible to do justice to five productions in the space allotted.

For this reason, I sympathise with those writers and directors who throw up their hands in despair at the treatment they get from the press. At least, I sympathise with those who are involved in complex and considered work which gets praised or panned in at best a few hundred words. It is true that, as a profession, we do not in general rise to the occasion. The chief problem is that the economics of the industry do not permit us to do so. An ideal newspaper would treat the reviewing of theatre in much the same way as the reviewing of books. It would not be expected that one person (or one plus occasional assistant) should review all new productions. There would be a team of reviewers, with a range of specialised expertise. The overnight notice would be banned as an anachronism. The critic would be expected to undergo a preparation commensurate with the production in question, and to give a full and reasoned account of what he has seen.

I doubt if such a system would be generally welcomed, if it could be financed. At least, I doubt if it would be welcomed by the theatrical community. It would raise the standard of reviewing, but it would inevitably raise the standards required from the theatres. It would mean that the dramaturgical side of a company's work (that is to say, the literary preparation for a production, the work on text and programme notes) would come under closer scrutiny. But few of our companies can afford any equivalent of a *Dramaturg*. If the ideal theatre page, or the ideal theatre magazine, existed, it would make demands far beyond the capacity of our theatres, as they are now run.

There are in fact two distinct worlds of reviewing: there are the literary reviewers, who include full-time writers and academics drawn from the humanities faculties; and there is the theatre world, with a very few full-time critics whose terms of reference are set to a large extent by the traditions established by playwrights and directors. The values of these two worlds are very different, and there are precious few areas of overlap. In recent years the *Times Literary Supplement* has pioneered, through its Commentary pages, the kind of criticism which attempts to cross this divide; but while the results may have had an impact on the literary world, I do not see a tremendous number of copies of the *TLS* floating around the theatres. In general, theatre people do not seem to yearn for a more exacting kind of review. What they want is more enthusiastic notices.

For my own part, starting work as a theatre reviewer was very much like embarking on an assignment as a foreign correspondent. My background in the subject was minimal. As a child I had had the luck to visit Stratford and Nottingham quite often during the 1960s. In the early 1970s, beginning on the *New Statesman* in political and literary journalism, I would enjoy the opportunity of seeing London theatre; but my chief preoccupation in those years was with work in the revolutionary Left (I was a member of what later became the SWP). Political work took precedence over the political theatre. For most of the period 1973–5 I was in Indochina as a freelance correspondent. In the subsequent years, the Callaghan years, I had a job in Westminster which involved, as far as I recall, getting drunk with the nicer members of the Tribune Group and their friends in the press. A year or so in Germany left me painfully aware of my short-comings as a foreign correspondent. I decided to give up journalism for good.

There was nothing odd about this. Most journalists spend all their time deciding to give up journalism for good – just as soon as they have made a little nest-egg. In this respect, as in so many others, we are like prostitutes, with our sad, fantastic plans for our retirement. When the time is ripe we will get out,

write a novel, open a hairdresser's, start a restaurant specialis-
ing in the sort of food we like to eat, or retire to the kind of
cottage we imagine we would like to live in. These are the
illusions by which we like to live, and I do not think we should
be mocked for our illusions.

My last assignment was a fiasco. I was to write an article
about Budapest, a city which I know slightly, and which I very
much like. I went to Budapest in great hopes. I met people. I
walked around the city. I put myself as much as possible in the
way of experience. I was confident that in the course of time I
would have a theme, and some experience to back it up. But
as the time allotted drew to a close, I knew that I had no
material at all. Budapest had defeated me. I had nothing
whatever to say on the matter, and I would observe my
typewriter with a blind terror.

From Budapest I took a train to Vienna, acutely depressed.
Sitting opposite me was a powerfully-constructed peasant in
wide breeches and a thick jacket, eyeing a bottle of fruit juice
he had bought on the station, and wondering how to tackle
the screw top. It was a simple contraption with a perforated
seal. A single twist would have solved the man's problem.
Instead, he produced a gigantic jack-knife and proceeded to
peel the metal away. He looked extremely happy. Clearly he
was congratulating himself on his foresight in coming thus
armed.

There was no question of not talking. He was extremely
happy to tell everything about his life and his opinions, and in
a short while I became sufficiently accustomed to his dialect to
understand a proportion of what he was saying. He had been a
soldier in both world wars, fighting on both occasions on the
Russian front. In the First World War he had been taken
prisoner and had gone to live in Siberia, where he had worked
as a carpenter. The local women had a penchant for bearded
men, and he had followed the fashion. He had not been,
apparently, very much *au courant*: when I asked him about
the Bolshevik revolution he said, well, he had heard
something about it, but it had really not affected his life. I
think it was in 1920 that a German-speaker arrived in the
village and he asked him how the war was going. To his

21

surprise, he found that the war was over and that he was able to return home. When he did so, his mother, who had gone into mourning on his account, refused to have him in the house, or to be left alone anywhere near him. It wasn't till he shaved off the beard that she began to admit that he might be her son.

I thought: God has delivered you into my first paragraph. But a little further reflection convinced me that it was all too late. If the train had been travelling in the opposite direction, if this man had been on his way to visit his Hungarian in-laws, as opposed to returning home to Austria, all would have been well. I should have arrived in Budapest with my senses sharpened and my work already under way. Old people are fascinating when they reach that stage of not caring what they say. This man's disquisition on Hitler's good and bad points was causing acute embarrassment elsewhere in the compartment, but it fell like music on my ears. He was saying what he thought, what he had thought over the decades. He was talking without circumspection.

The music continued, but it was like the music in *Antony and Cleopatra*, when hautboys are heard under the stage. A soldier asks: 'It signs well, does it not?' But the explanation comes: 'Tis the god Hercules, whom Antony lov'd, Now leaves him.' The more the old man talked, the more I knew that my luck as a journalist was out.

Vienna, for a journalist, is a good place to get lost. On my previous visit I had been asked by the *Guardian* to carry out a rather delicate assignment. For many years the paper had had a correspondent in the city, but in the last couple of years they had not heard from him, and they wondered vaguely what had happened. The foreign editor still had the old man's phone number, but was unwilling to try it in case . . . well, in case the fellow might have passed away. My job therefore was to enquire, 'as discreetly as possible', into our correspondent's ontological status. If he existed I was to give him lunch. If he did not exist, I was to report back – when, presumably, in a simple ceremony, his filing card would be torn up. Whatever happened, I was not to hold out the prospect of more work.

Well, he did exist. Indeed, he must have been sitting by the phone. We met. I gave him the lunch, which he seemed to enjoy, and I soon found myself answering a great number of detailed questions about the current state of Fleet Street. He was touched that the paper had thought of him, and he rather wondered what had happened to his career as a journalist. But he hadn't liked to ask, and so – only a week before – he had formally resigned from the press club. Now he was in complete retirement. On the other hand, if there *was* something he could do, he would be only too pleased. No? There wasn't? He thought as much. I paid the bill and set out with him to walk to his next appointment, at the Burgtheater.

We went by a very strange route, I thought, along back streets, turning around and around. It wasn't that he was lost. He told me a great deal about the places we passed. But I couldn't quite understand where we were bound for, until he chanced to say: 'You know, since they began the one-way system in Vienna, life has become very complicated.' At this point, we obeyed the last of the arrows and arrived in the theatre square.

Returning to Vienna on this occasion I felt a great deal in common with this fine man. But the route that I chose to the Burgtheater was rather more direct. A friend was directing a play there, and I had been invited to watch the proceedings. It turned out that there was a crisis on hand. The actors had been allowed just that little bit too much improvisation and had pushed the production towards a completely inappropriate neo-brutalist excess. There were quarrels among the cast. One of the chief performers had gone lame – like a horse, with no apparent prospect of recovery. The assistant director was all timidity and tact. The *Dramaturg* was all chain-smoking and evasion. The state of the production reminded me of a TV advert in which Columbus's ship suddenly finds itself about to fall off the edge of the world. The director was desperately turning the wheel and issuing orders to furl or unfurl this or that sail. There was a great deal of bead-telling and talisman-touching. The opening was a few days off, and the prospect of disaster seemed certain.

In the inspissated gloom of the Café Landtmann, in the garden-restaurants of the outlying hills, I would try to distract the director's mind with an account of my own woes. These woes were easily upstaged by the immediate problems on hand. Indeed, it was not long before they began to lose their significance in my own eyes. I had never had the opportunity of observing theatrical work behind the scenes, and the more I saw, the more fascinated I became. I realised that, if there was one thing I wanted to do in the future, it was to work somehow in connection with the theatre. At the moment I realised this, the prospects for the production were at their most bleak. But this if anything was an attraction. These people lived dangerously. They worked with the whole personality. They put everything at risk. And in the following days the ship was wrenched away from the abyss at the edge of the world.

In the afterglow of this excitement I began to think how I might acquire some kind of theatrical work, but I had had no opportunity to acquire any credentials to this purpose when, on a visit to London, I learned that Levin was giving up his job and that a replacement was sought. Once again, I cursed Providence for creating this vacancy at precisely the wrong moment. I was favoured, however, by one circumstance – that the paper I wished to work for did not at that moment exist. For the last weeks of the stoppage I was able to work on probation, practising as it were on a mute keyboard. I very quickly saw around seventy productions as a critic, before publishing my first piece, but even by that stage I had not caught up with the whole London repertoire. And since that time I have learnt that one never does catch up.

Lark Rise, Candleford (COTTESLOE)

They talk of involving the audience, of the intimate theatre and the promenade style. Yet the truth is: the smaller the theatre, the more rigorously the spectator must be excluded from the actor's evident consideration. The large auditoriums resound to the pleadings of grand players: just look at this, admire that, see how I can roll my eyes to the back of my head, or deliver a scream like an emasculated civet. But in the studio theatres there is no appeal to the gallery. As often as not there is no gallery. And anyway, it is of the essence that the audience be ignored.

So here is the Cottesloe company, lined up for a day's reaping, a song on their lips and their scythes at the ready. And here stands the Cottesloe audience, uncomfortably aware that they are about to be reaped. Unblinkingly the actors advance. The scythes sweep. The nerve of the audience cracks, and they retreat before the encroaching blades. Seen from above, the spectators looked for a moment like wheat itself. One felt that if they had dawdled any longer they would certainly have been cut down.

That was in *Lark Rise*, Keith Dewhurst's adaptation from Flora Thompson's work, to which the same team, directed by Bill Bryden, added their *Candleford* this week. I watched both spectacles in one day, which means about five hours of watching, and for the first part I was somewhat sceptical of the project.

There is a way in which the National, having identified a certain area of middlebrow enthusiasm, holds on to it for dear life, like a plucky little terrier to a stick. And then there is a question of scale: the Thompson trilogy, for heaven's sake, is no Wagnerian epic; had it not become terribly overblown in the course of this transformation?

After an hour or so of *Candleford*, however, I could not deny that I was moved. The production is richer in incident and detail. There is a greater variation of pace and tone, and there is more to see than in *Lark Rise*. At one moment, a quite painful feeling of nostalgia hit me, when I remembered what it was that the set reminded me of. It was the Street in the museum at York, but animated. There is the post office, the domestic interior and the smithy faithfully copied from the late nineteenth century. There is mist in the air and fake snow on the ground.

The rest is teased from the imagination of the audience. When the hunt arrives, for instance, the gentry are borne aloft on the backs of the actors. That this device has its obvious political implications could not be denied. At the same moment, however, the sudden inrush of bright colour elicited from the audience just the sort of excitement that is created by the arrival of a hunt in a village.

Of the cast, Valerie Whittington bears the heat, or more accurately the chill of the day. She plays Laura, Flora Thompson's recreation of herself as a young girl, observing the country life of Oxfordshire at the moment when its traditions were being finally swept away by the machine age. For the rest, it is the company style that pleases, more than the individual performance. There is a reserve in the playing, a sense of dignity and privacy which is pleasing. I ought to add that there are moments when the actors have sufficient pity on the audience to allow them to sit for a while. I advise against reading the book too soon before the show or you will be distracted by the ingenuity of the adaptation.

18 November 1979

Rich and Rich
(NOTTINGHAM PLAYHOUSE)
The Caucasian Chalk Circle (RSC)

Brecht got Hitler wrong. He thought of Nazism as a simple ruse whereby the ruling class could distract attention from the difference between rich and poor – the true division within mankind. Hitler was called in by capitalism, as Angelo in *Measure for Measure* was called in by the Duke, to find a solution to a problem which had got out of hand. Once the revolutionary class had been defeated, the old ruling class would relieve the dictator of his post, and suppress the excesses of his time. Hitler's version of class war would never be allowed by a capitalist class to extend in a revolutionary direction as expropriation of the property-rich Jews, for instance . . .

Whether out of respect for the memory of those Jews, or out of kindness to its author, *Roundheads and Pointed Heads* has rarely been performed in Europe since the original production in Denmark in 1936. Now the Nottingham Playhouse has staged the British première, under the title *Rich and Rich*; this is a half-translation of the punning German title, *Reich und Reich gesellt sich gern*, or 'Rich and Reich keep good company'. The Nottingham translation, by Dietz and Brown, introduces material not to be found in the standard German version, most notably a large chunk of Shakespeare, an 'up-date' of the famous scene between Angelo and Isabella. Retranslated into English, in a version which replaces Brecht's Roundheads and Pointed Heads with two races called Krytes and Krinks, this scene yields some truly awful lines: 'What if an honest Krytish gentleman propositioned you, a Krinkish maid?'

There was one way open to an intelligent director, faced with the rightly obscure work. He could set out to evoke the original production, and thereby put the play's fatal errors in their historical context. Brecht could himself be shown, in that early and interesting period of his exile, as he scandalised the Danish Nazis and insulted Church and State. And the later Brecht could be ransacked for any number of quotations which recognise that things did not turn out in the manner predicted by this play.

Instead of working in such a direction, Geoffrey Reeves has adapted a wrong thesis about Germany in order to make a doubly-wrong point about Britain. The Hitler/Angelo figure is played by Christopher Ettridge, an actor who contrives to look just like Enoch Powell, and whose voice (one of the few voices in this production which actually carries) is obviously based on Powell's. When Angelo is relieved from office at the end of the play, he is sent over to Northern Ireland to sort things out over there.

Now I do not care two hoots about the insult to Powell in comparing him with Hitler. I do most strongly object, however, to the insult to the audience's intelligence. Powell was not called in by any ruling class in order to sort out their problems. On the contrary, he was excluded from power, quite deliberately stopped in his tracks. He did not go over to Northern Ireland after a job well done in England. He went there because that was the only political home left for him. One might add that his most significant contribution to British politics in the last few years has been to maintain the Callaghan government in office long after it was, to all intents and purposes, dead on its feet.

By all means let us have a political theatre – but not a theatre that treats us as morons. By all means let us see the plays of Brecht, but since most of those plays are designed as parables, since they are intended to evoke a critical response, let us treat them to the criticism they deserve. Since 1964 there has probably never been a moment during which *The Caucasian Chalk Circle* was not being rehearsed or performed, by amateurs or professionals, somewhere in Britain. Having just seen the RSC's travelling production in Surbiton, I have a question to ask about this most popular work. If you were a Caucasian peasant at the end of the Second World War, had been ordered off your land by the authorities, applied to return, and been fobbed off because a rival commune had better plans for the use of the territory, and if you were then treated to a parable by Brecht in which your claim to the land is compared with that of a vile Governor's wife to a baby she has deliberately abandoned and which she only now wants because there is money involved, would you take such an insult lying down? Would you applaud, or would you pelt the stage?

9 December 1979

Amadeus *(OLIVIER)*

Critic of my acquaintance – no names, no pack-drill – one of the few who strongly attacked Peter Shaffer's *Amadeus* (Olivier) in the British press, was due to review the thing for the *New York Times*. Found himself somewhat 'got at' by the National Theatre. Was asked whether he could not make it clear for the American public that *his* dislike of the play had been exceptional, and that in general the new Shaffer had been rapturously received by audience and critics alike. It had been slobber, slobber, all round – words to that effect.

Now there is nothing a critic likes less than to be asked to make out that his own views are somehow eccentric, and therefore to be – well, to be treated with caution. Why should it be eccentric to hold a minority position? For heaven's sake, does one not read critics precisely to learn the points they have the originality to make?

My colleague objected to being asked effectively to tone his comments down. But he is a fellow who, if he *have* a fault, is cursed with almost paralysing attacks of acute fairmindedness. When he came to write the American review, he did put in a phrase to the effect that *Amadeus* had been controversial.

He should not have bothered. A couple of days after the review had been accepted, a transatlantic call informed him that there had been a change of policy: not only would his piece be 'killed'; he was told that his services as a reviewer were no longer required.

Those of us who dislike *Amadeus*, those of us who think the play a perfectly nauseating load of – to use a word much loved by Peter Shaffer – shit, and those of us who are not impressed by Paul Scofield's acting as Salieri, still less by Peter Hall's production, have been feeling somewhat 'got at' recently. I am perfectly aware that the National Theatre does not like the fact that every time the play is due to be put on, I refer to it in my capsule review as 'appalling'.

In fact, I think 'appalling' is a somewhat generous word in

the circumstances, and I take the opportunity of a quiet week to discuss the play for the first time and defend my position and that of the minority.

Or is it a minority? Did my raving colleagues really like this play, in which the rival composer Salieri is imagined to have murdered Mozart? Or did they perceive something inevitable – something in the nature of a heavy truck with brake failure bearing down in their direction? Did they foresee a runaway commercial success, and did they simply get out of the way?

Certainly it is common to find that, in private, Peter Shaffer's public admirers are apt to make the most extraordinary qualifications of their praise: 'Oh, Peter can't *write* for toffee, but he does create such marvellous *theatre* . . .' Or: 'Ghastly, but what a wonderful *vehicle* for Scofield . . .'

If, as I suspect, a large number of critics felt incapacitated by the inevitable box-office success, there were others who praised out of obvious conviction. Among them, Bernard Levin in *The Times*. Levin believes in the same God as Peter Shaffer, a God for whose divine music Mozart was no more than a 'conduit'. They know – Levin and Shaffer – that God was actually speaking through Mozart, because in Mozart's manuscripts there are no crossings-out. Or so they say.

Well, I went to the British Museum to see for myself, and it is true that, in a couple of Mozart MS pages displayed, God has not bished more than twice. It is also true that Schubert's originals are a mass of crossings-out and revisions. If Mozart was God's conduit, what was Schubert? A blocked drain? And what was Beethoven? Why did he need to revise so much? Was he literally too deaf to pick up the messages of Levin's fatuous God?

Of course, a conduit is a passive thing. All that happens in the life of a conduit is that a certain amount of slime accumulates at the mouth; and this, to an extraordinary degree, is what has happened to Shaffer's Mozart. He talks foul; and it is difficult to object to the way Mozart talks without seeming to object to foul language in the theatre. I honestly couldn't care less about foul language. Pam Gems's Piaf talks foul from start to finish, and this seems perfectly right. Shaffer's Mozart is a different kettle of fish. Skip the next three paragraphs if

31

you are reading this over breakfast.

After a deal of squeak-squeaking and miaouw-miaouwing, Mozart and Constanze get down to a few endearments. Mozart: 'I think you're going to *shit* yourself! In a moment it's going to be on the floor.' Poor Felicity Kendal demurs. Mozart makes a fart noise and continues: 'All sticky and steamy on the floor!' 'Sssh!' says Constanze.

'What colour's it going to be?' pursues Simon Callow: 'Yellow. All sticky and yellow. Here it comes now! I can hear it coming . . .' Stage direction from the text: 'Another fart noise, slower. She is shocked and amused.' Mozart is just getting into his stride: 'Do you know what I'd really like to do now – this second? Shit on your nose and watch it run down your chin. Diddle-diddle-diddle-diddle-diddle!'

This final trochaic pentameter is a good example of the Shafferian invented language pioneered in *Amadeus*, a language if anything more irritating than Shafferian coprophemy. Here is a crucial exchange from later in the play: 'My big starling.' 'Yes.' 'Darling starling!' 'Stanzimanzi', 'Wolfi-polfi', 'Poopy-peepee!' Those lucky enough to have tickets for *Amadeus* are going to have to sit through a great deal more of this kind of talk.

For breakfast-time readers who have just rejoined this review, my argument is not that the historical Mozart did not talk foul. Let us leave the historical Mozart out of it (since however he talked, it was certainly not in the language of the Shaffer family nursery). The point is that Shaffer's Mozart is depicted with a dreadful and offensive banality.

There is all the difference in the world between a depiction of a boring character and a boring depiction of a character. The same goes for offensiveness. It will not do, as some critics have tried to argue, that Mozart is shown this way because he is seen through Salieri's eyes. No, Mozart is depicted in an offensive and banal way because he is seen through the eyes of a very, very bad dramatist indeed – perhaps the worst serious English dramatist since John Drinkwater.

As for Salieri, if the audience is impressed by the way Paul Scofield can change registers at will, when switching between the old and the younger man, or if they respond to all those poutings and pleadings, and if they imagine they are in the presence of great acting – let them do so. I would have more heart to attack Paul Scofield if he had really managed some-how to cover up the tawdriness of the great chunks of docu-mentary narrative he has to put across, if he had made con-vincing Salieri's challenge to God.

As it is, I call his depiction of mediocrity mediocre. But I have no great quarrel with it. With Peter Hall I have a great quarrel, but its elaboration must await another quiet week. Of the National productions I have seen this year, he has directed by far the best (*Betrayal*) and by far the worst. This indicates an unforgivable willingness to squander great talent.

One last point. Criticism does not stop where great art begins. We should not worship Mozart's music. Let those who want to worship, worship gods. Let them not imagine that, in the theatre or opera house, they are in church. God will not be deceived, we may be sure. Attendance at divine service is one thing, *Così fan tutte* is quite another. This may be incon-venient, but the distinction is vital.

23 December 1979

CRITIC NOT SILENCED – OFFICIAL

I wish to protest strongly at the inaccurate and unfair accusa-tion against The New York Times contained in James Fenton's review of Amadeus (The Arts, December 23), which has just come to my attention.

Mr Fenton states that a negative review of Amadeus by Benedict Nightingale was 'killed' and Mr Nightingale was fired by the Times after he 'found himself somewhat got at by the National Theatre' and had been asked by the National Theatre 'whether he could not make it clear for the American public that his dislike of the play had been exceptional.'

The conclusion which readers are deliberately led to draw is that the National Theatre failed to persuade Mr Nightingale to soften his review but somehow succeeded in getting at The

33

New York Times to have Mr Nightingale silenced. Even though the accusation is absurd it must be emphatically denied. We Americans greatly respect the National Theatre but have not yet conceded to it the powers once held by the Lord Chamberlain's office.

The facts in the case are as follows: as soon as I recognised how divided the British critics were over Peter Shaffer's play Amadeus – and this discovery dawned even before reading Mr Nightingale's review – I asked the editor who had been in touch with him to request that Mr Nightingale give us a report on the controversy rather than only his own view of the play, whatever that might be. Mr Nightingale obliged us with a fine report, which was promptly published and he remains a valued contributor to our pages.

Mr Nightingale's assignment was changed because controversy, when it develops, is always news – and more newsworthy than any one person's opinion. This is true in culture as well as in politics. In different circumstances, of course, one does crave opinion, and so naturally, whenever suitable in the future, we will invite Mr Nightingale, as well as other foreign critics, to write reviews for our pages.

William H. Honan

Editor, Arts and Leisure Section, The New York Times, New York

Sunday Times, 3 January 1980

Juno and the Paycock
(ABBEY THEATRE, DUBLIN)

Juno and the Paycock, among the boiled shirts and evening togs, in the gracious presence of the President of the Republic of Ireland, not to mention the Catholic Archbishop of Dublin, not to mention the Chaplain to the Archbish (the ADC to the AB of D)! Well might a fellow reach for an exclamation mark. Well might History raise an eyebrow, or two, or three.

Was it only twenty-one years ago that a former Primate, the Reverend John C. McQuaid, withdrew permission for a votive mass to celebrate the opening of the Dublin Festival, on the grounds that Joyce and O'Casey were to be featured? (The decision which caused O'Casey himself to put a ban on performances of his work in Ireland – a ban not shifted till 1964.) Indeed, a little more than a generation ago, in 1935, the Irish press was full of clamour against the Abbey Theatre ('It should be abolished'), against its director ('Mr Yeats is no literary leader for a Catholic country') and in favour of a law banning O'Casey's plays.

The history of the Abbey Theatre, as it emerges from Hugh Hunt's recent volume, *The Abbey, Ireland's National Theatre (1904–1979)*, has oscillated between violent controversy and turgid mediocrity, between periods of spectacular achievement (with Yeats, Synge and O'Casey as playwrights) and times when the company seemed, to all intents and purposes, dead on its feet. This week brought the theatre's 75th anniversary. Hence the dinner jackets.

Odd things, dinner jackets. They seem to alter the acoustics of an auditorium, taking the edge off passion and absorbing surplus pain. In serious theatres people ought to be ordered to leave their dinner jackets in the cloakroom, out of deference to the interests of those who are there to see the play.

But it was not simply a matter of dinner jackets and the formality of a gala night. It was not a question of production

35

or individual acting. There was a problem on Thursday night. The problem was the play.

It is a problem common to all works of art in the realist tradition – the particular way in which they age. Realism was born with a protest on its lips. Yet even the great realist paintings – those of Courbet, for instance – went through a process whereby they lost some of their original significance and impact, so that, without being in any visual way indecipherable, they became obscure.

Theatre people often compare a new production of a classic to the cleaning of an Old Master, in a way which implies that, once you have removed the varnish, you can see a picture as it used to be. But if you took a realist painting of the nineteenth century and restored its visibility, you would not suddenly be able to perceive the work as it appeared to a contemporary of the artist.

In the same way, a production which simply remains faithful to the tradition in which a play was originally rendered, a production like Joe Dowling's *Juno*, does not bring back a work to its former vitality. Certain elements are irretrievably lost. The nationalists are no longer outraged. The Archbishop's hackles remain limp. The audience doesn't see the piece as if for the first time. They see the sum of received wisdom about O'Casey. It is highly dangerous for a director to play so safe.

Suppose that 'Captain' Jack Boyle, the Paycock of the title (played by Philip O'Flynn), becomes simply a mildly engaging old drunk and fantasist, while Juno (Siobhan McKenna) is little more than the personification of long suffering. One might ask why, at the end of the play, the personification of long suffering decides to let her husband go to the dogs.

I realised afterwards that during the whole course of the play I had never taken Juno's warnings to her husband seriously. Nor did I believe the Paycock when he threatened to kill his pregnant daughter. But perhaps the drunken old man can actually be rather less pleasant than he was portrayed, just as Joxer Daly, his drinking companion and evil genius, can actually be evil.

Joxer (Eamon Morrissey) is one of the more compelling

figures in the production. Always on the balls of his feet, like an agile, stylish coward in a boxing ring, he watches the fortunes of the Boyle family as they suddenly rise, suddenly collapse. O'Casey deliberately clears the stage of Boyles, so that we may see Joxer delight in the prospect of their impoverishment behind their backs. The scale of this motiveless malignancy may be trivial enough, but its purpose is none the less evil.

Garrett Keogh plays Johnny Boyle, the Republican son of the family who must cry out:

Haven't I done enough for Ireland! I've lost me arm an' me hip's desthroyed so that I'll never be able to walk right agen! Good God, haven't I done enough for Ireland?

To which the Republican answer comes, 'Boyle, no man can do enough for Ireland!' A form of words which means: You will be killed.

Johnny Boyle's guilt (he has betrayed another Republican to an opposing gang) lies behind the whole action of the play and erupts from time to time, in the form of a hallucination, fits of temper, bitterness and whining self-pity. Mr Keogh twists his whole body into a suggestion of the effect of this guilt. His actions are powerful, nervous, spastic. One could easily imagine that the actor had taken a trip north, to study the effect on the participants of prolonged exposure to conflict. Certainly it is his performance that has the most contemporary feel, but this may partly be the result of the immediate interest of Johnny's predicament – the notorious difficulty of extracting oneself from a fanatical movement.

People found the evening long, but I must say I did not. What I did miss was definition in the performance of Emmer Bergin as Charles Bentham, the fortune-hunting Theosophist who has his evil way with Mary Boyle. Surely there is more comedy to this character's pretensions.

As for Mary herself (Fedelma Cullen), she reads – and derives from – Ibsen. O'Casey gives clear textual instructions as to how she should be played:

Two forces are working in her mind – one, through circumstances of her life, pulling her back; the other, through the
influence of books she has read, pushing her forward. The
opposing forces are apparent in her speech and her manners,
both of which are degraded by her environment, and improved by her acquaintance – slight though it may be – with
literature.

Yet it has to be admitted that there is not a great deal in her
speeches, as written, which helps to make this particular
conception evident.

Something extra was needed – something that would make
palatable the opposing forces at work. Just as something extra
was needed to take the place of that shock the Irish no longer
appear to feel at seeing the Irish realistically portrayed. So
much has happened to drama since this play was written – so
much of it, indeed, because this play was written. So much has
happened since the foundation of the Abbey Theatre, when it
seemed imperative to import actors from England. A whole
tradition is there, where seventy-five years ago there was
nothing. But tradition is not an unmixed blessing, as Thursday
night so clearly showed.

30 December 1979

The Long Voyage Home (COTTESLOE)

Do we value the American dramatists for their virtues or their faults? Do we see them as great and profound writers or as purveyors of 'good solid stuff'? Are they perhaps the beneficiaries of a residual English snobbery about the United States – in the sense that, because we do not expect great art from them, we applaud madly each time they seem to come within hailing distance of competence? As if they were chimpanzees, whose ability to hold a knife and fork was quite sufficiently admirable, even though the knife would never be used for cutting nor the fork raise a single morsel of food to the mouth.

I ask these questions because I have been reading Mary McCarthy's theatre criticism (*Sights and Spectacles*) and have found that the very qualities I had thought most appealing in American drama were those which, to an intelligent American, were the most depressing and frustrating. I *like* the transparent ambition of Tennessee Williams, the strivings of Arthur Miller, even the corniness of Eugene O'Neill. I like the very passages which McCarthy singles out for attack.

When the mother in *Death of a Salesman* makes her plea for attention, attention to be paid to her husband's plight, the voice is suddenly authorial, rather than that of a humble housewife. Great art would forbid the sudden and intrusive appearance of the author on stage. Yet I cannot find it in me to object to that speech.

McCarthy does not reject indiscriminately, or – at least in the case of Miller and O'Neill – absolutely. She has a telling comparison between the two playwrights:

'Those old Irish actors were exactly like that,' the man next to me said of Fredric March's performance in *A Long Day's Journey into Night*; this was a real testimonial to the performer and to the (now old-fashioned) solidity of O'Neill's play. On the contrary, the man who was quoted by *The*

New Yorker as saying, after *Death of a Salesman*, 'That damned New England territory never was any good' had committed a boner; he had missed the play's 'profundity' by trying to localise the trouble.

A distinction is being made here on behalf of realism, and the tribute is just. Not wishing to commit a 'boner', or to pay O'Neill the profound insult of admiring him for his faults, I must say that the four short plays currently being revived by the National at the start of their O'Neill season – under the joint title *The Long Voyage Home* – are pure corn.

They are worth seeing. On historical grounds, because they include *Bound East for Cardiff*, the first O'Neill to be staged. On critical grounds, since they will stand in contrast to the other two forthcoming Cottesloe productions, *Hughie* and *The Iceman Cometh*, not to mention Susan Tracy's admirable *Anna Christie* which the RSC are taking to Newcastle, and which will presumably come on to the Warehouse later in the season. If you want to get to know O'Neill this year, seven of his works are already on offer, which leaves a mere thirty-eight more to go.

The best reason, however, for seeing the Cottesloe revival is that the four plays of the sea are quite marvellously acted. Each impossible task set by the author is performed by the company with an almost unbearable seriousness and skill. Jack Shepherd, in *The Moon of the Caribees*, must get drunk (as people often must in bad plays) extremely fast and on very little rum, and all the time – as if that alone were not enough – must deliver lines to the effect that the native music is driving him crazy. Tony Haygarth, in *Bound East for Cardiff*, must die slowly, movingly and articulately, noticing a mist which has somehow got into the cabin and then realising that his sight is failing.

Think of the least good prentice work by Joseph Conrad – there is nothing in it to compare with these scenes for bullshit-artistry. As for *In the Zone* and the *The Long Voyage Home*, they bring us in contact with the word and style of the temperance melodrama. They whisk us off to the nineteenth-century stage. There should be footlights and grand gestures. Should we not hiss Gawn Grainger off the stage, as he makes his supple way towards the innocent sailor he intends to shanghai?

Yet all these actors triumph, as the director, Bill Bryden, triumphs, through their willingness to confront each of the grave problems set by O'Neill, and their obvious belief that realism in acting will conquer all. Realism at the Cottesloe does indeed produce some remarkable effects. Hayden Griffin's excellent design of the tramp steamer's deck is backed by a night sky, which moves gently up and down to suggest a slight swell. After a few minutes of watching this, I began to wonder what was in the coffee I had just drunk. Suddenly I realised I was actually feeling slightly seasick. They do not sell Kwells in the foyer. I recommend you take your own.

13 January 1980

Liberty Hall *(GREENWICH)*
Hughie *(COTTESLOE)*

Liberty Hall, Michael Frayn's new or newish play at Greenwich, belongs to the category of the Philosophical Farce – as odd a category when one comes to think of it, as the theological thriller which flowered in the middle of this century. In the Philosophical Farce, the trousers of an Idea are discovered around its ankles, a Notion is interrupted in bed with a Postulate, or a Proposition sets its foot on a banana skin. To adapt the standard definition: ordinary men are discovered in extraordinary situations because of an extraordinary reasoning.

The sort of reasoning, for instance, which brings Godfrey Winn, Warwick Deeping, Enid Blyton and Hugh Walpole to Balmoral in 1937, twenty years after the revolution which, missing Russia, struck England and turned it into a Stalinist state. A reasoning which eliminates Walpole, restores him catastrophically to reality, strikes him dead before our very eyes, pushes him callously into a laundry basket and sits on him for the rest of the play while a Scottish manservant (Rikki Fulton) gives an interview on his beliefs to a visiting Russian representative of the capitalist press. That sort of reasoning.

I enjoyed it. Alan Dossor's production was less funny than the play for the first part of the first act; perhaps we were all disoriented, unsure what sort of play we were watching. But once the course of action is at the mercy of Rikki Fulton's dour Scot, once the drink flows, the only problem is to take on board so many comic ideas. The cast features some fine farcical features: Julian Fellowes's features, for instance, as Godfrey Winn, Oliver Cotton as the Russian, and Jill Meager as his interpreter. The design is very much to the credit of Poppy Mitchell.

Realism in a set could hardly go much further than Hayden

Griffin takes it in the new production of O'Neill's *Hughie* at the Cottesloe. The elevator seems to work. The reception desk of the bum hotel has a well-used and battered look. I noticed the fingerprints on the wall, where hands had groped for the brass light-switch, the messages scrawled near the telephone, and – most realistic of all – the night clerk behind the desk was played by a real actor, Howard Goorney.

At least, for the majority of the piece, Howard Goorney is a part of the set, and when he finally springs to life, with a creaky enthusiasm, it is a sign that the action of the play is drawing to a creaky close. For the rest of the time, the stage belongs to Stacy Keach, the excellent American actor who has been imported to portray Erie Smith.

It is a performance which rivals the set for virtuoso detail. There is a good deal of 'business'. Erie Smith has lived off his wits, gambling and running shady errands for the big shots on Broadway, and his hands are made to indicate – through success or unsuccess at spinning and palming a coin – a great deal about the soundness of the hero's nerve. Two moments of business remain in my mind: the finding, and quiet pocketing, of the cigar in the sandbucket; and, many minutes later, the production of same cigar in a moment of celebration. One saw what people mean by a performance being 'well constructed', and why metaphors from building should be used to describe acting.

But even the best acting can only go so far with a text like *Hughie*, which was apparently never intended for performance and which suffers from one glaring fault: explicitness. There is nothing wrong with the conception of the relationship between Erie Smith and former night clerk, Hughie – the one boasting and lying about his exploits, the other providing the necessary admiration to keep them both going. What is wrong is that such a relationship should be so clearly understood and articulated by one of its participants. So much self-knowledge, one inevitably feels, would change a man's life, forcing him into either paralysis or improvement.

O'Neill mistrusted the ability of the reader to draw certain conclusions from the information given. In fact though, as an audience, we draw all the right conclusions fairly fast, only to find to our utter consternation – that the characters on stage have reached the same point of critical insight.

In caricature the action of the play is as follows. Erie Smith comes back to his cheap hotel after a bender. He tries to strike up a relationship with the new night clerk. No go. He redoubles his efforts. Still no go. He explains that he used to have this wonderful relationship with the old night clerk, which made both of their lives bearable. He describes exactly how it worked. He offers the same terms to the new incumbent. Still no go until, as a last throw, he breaks down. At this point, the night clerk dramatically gives in, and having done nothing all evening suddenly reveals a perfect grasp of the rules of the games. Conclusion: triumphant return to normality.

I don't believe in this, although I do believe in the psychology on which the play is based. Bill Bryden directs.

27 January 1980

Richard III (ROUND HOUSE)
Richard III (OLIVIER)

On one matter there is no doubt: the Rustaveli company have caused a sensation with their *Richard III* (Round House). It is hard for a small audience to maintain a standing ovation at Monday night's noise levels, and not to mean it, for ten minutes. On Wednesday night, when I returned, the ovation was similarly enthusiastic, if slightly shorter. It is easy to report great enthusiasm. Harder to reach an honest judgement.

To be quite frank, the critics have been bluffing like crazy. They have not all come as seriously unstuck as Mr Milton Shulman, whose gigantic self-regard permitted him to mock a certain lack of subtlety among the actors, while revealing the critic to be under the impression that the play was in Russian verse. It is in Georgian and the company interpreter assures me that it is in prose – 'although it does sometimes sound like poetry'.

Georgian, I gather, has a 10 per cent overlap with Basque, and zilch resemblance to owt else. How can one assess a performance in this language? The Georgians in the audience were appreciative but, as one of them said, 'I'm too much of a nationalist to say that I'm not enjoying it.' I asked later whether the cast were aware that their reception had been quite exceptional for an English audience. Oh yes, I was told, they don't normally get that response in Georgia either.

After watching the Rustaveli *Richard* twice in performance, and once in dress rehearsal, I am still not entirely sure how much of the play there is, and in what shape. Clarence's dream speech, for instance, appears to be delivered – but in curtailed form, and in the presence of Gloucester. Just before Clarence dies, he sees something which provokes him to smile – almost to laugh. It is obviously an important moment in the production, and may well be a moving one – if Clarence becomes reconciled to death or if he sees some point which provokes ironic laughter at the world. Very appropriate, say, for Webster. In Shakespeare, Clarence is urgently begging for his life when:

> SECOND MURDERER: Look behind you my lord.
> FIRST MURDERER (*Stabs him*): Take that, and that: if all
> this will not do,
> I'll drown you in the malmsey-butt within.

Death in the court of the Rustaveli is very much a part of life. How does Clarence die? By the mere passing of a hand across his eyes. He seems to have been told: this is the moment in the play when you die. And later on, Hastings is actually shown by Queen Margaret the place in the text where he is supposed to make his last speech. At first he reads the wrong line. Then he realises what is going on.

All this is part of the 'alienatory' or distancing style in which the play is presented. It goes with the elevation of Queen Margaret to chorus, the introduction of the jester in the last act (previously, the actor had been Edward IV and the Archbishop of Canterbury) and with the rather comical music (a theme-tune which sounds very much like 'Maybe it's because I'm a Londoner').

This tune is first played by a violinist who seems to have walked out of an early Chagall on to the stage, to witness the wooing of the Lady Anne over the coffin. It is an impressive wooing – that is to say that its various stages of repulsion and attraction have a certain balletic rhythm and vigour. It ends with Lady Anne drawn down on to the body of Gloucester, her skirt hitched up. Then the coffin rolls a little forward, in a manner which irresistibly suggests sexual penetration. At this moment the violin begins its jaunty tune.

It is the purpose of the alienatory style that it sacrifices empathy and illusion for a continuously *critical* response. But of course, with an impossible language barrier, that kind of criticism is sacrificed. We are left therefore with a vocabulary of symbolic gestures and facial expressions on which to form our judgement.

46

If, therefore, I decline to join other critics in calling the
Georgian *Richard*, and its director Robert Sturua, great, it is
not for lack of enthusiasm but rather for basic lack of information. A great performance of this play must tackle certain
enormous problems. The whole game can be lost (although
not won) in the opening scenes, in which we must be plunged
into a world of Elizabethan evil, with speeches reminiscent of
the earliest English poetry. There is no build-up, no gentle
introduction of the theme. The starting-pistol is fired, and if
the actor is not absolutely ready he is out of the race.

John Wood's performance at the Olivier bears all the signs of
an awareness that elimination, in this contest, can be decided
on the first round. He loses no time in building up a relationship with the audience which amounts, in my view, to com-
plicity. Writ large, the invited reaction seems to be 'Oooh,
you are awful', a nudge and a wink and a 'Whatever will he get
up to next?' What stays in my mind after a second viewing is
the moment over the coffin when the bleeding corpse is
revealed, Gloucester dips his finger in the blood and gingerly
tastes it.

The sheer unlikeliness and psychological vulgarity of this
detail infects one's apprehension of the rest of the performance, a performance which, if energy could be considered as
it were in the abstract, would be rated high on that single
count. What Christopher Morahan's production would be
like without such a central figure I dread to think, for the play
has been bled away. It drips from the Ralph Koltai set, it flows
into those silly gutters which ooze with brilliant gore – gore
which means nothing in the play because it has been sub-
sumed into the design. There is no sense of a court, no
articulation of the characters. They stand uncomfortably
around, prisoners in their grey suede, while the blood flows
meaninglessly by.

3 February 1980

The Greeks (RSC, ALDWYCH)

There came a dismaying moment on the first morning-noon-and-night of *The Greeks* at the Aldwych, when disaster struck, not at another member of the house of Atreus, but at the whole project itself. It was as if, after seeing a colossal piece of knitting taking shape before our eyes, we had been suddenly asked to stand by and watch the whole thing gleefully unravelled. Once the first thread had been pulled, there was no stopping it. The annihilation of the first two parts of John Barton's epic was all but complete, after the first few minutes of the third.

Janet Suzman had been chosen to give that fatal tug at the thread, and the choice could not have been more distressing. It is Miss Suzman's figure which dominates the whole cycle – and whatever the character represented, the figure remains vividly and compellingly Miss Suzman. So that the pink-robed Clytemnestra's beauty, made cruel by the sacrifice of her daughter, appears merely in a different aspect as the Illusory Helen, unscathed in her questionable, chryselephantine splendour among the ruins of Troy. Beauty lays Troy low. Beauty waits to avenge itself on the returning conqueror. And, in Part Three, the same beauty is seen, squeezing a pimple and adoring itself in the glass.

The first-night audience laughed heartily at Miss Suzman's farcical Helen – but the laughter expressed the accumulated tension of the cycle. All right, said the audience, we've been together all day, and if you assure us that the whole project is ludicrous, we'll take your word for it. When I returned to see the whole thing through again on successive nights, this sense of community had been dissipated. The audience hardly laughed at the 'Helen'. They seemed, as I was, puzzled and embarrassed.

The fact was, we felt our good-will had been betrayed. We had brought plenty of it with us, and had spent it occasionally in the first two parts, as if the good-will had been expressed in

48

little books of vouchers, and we had silently torn off a voucher every time a moment had been unintentionally ludicrous.

For instance, the Troy theme in Nick Bicât's score happens to be the advertising jingle for Fry's Turkish Delight. I spent one voucher every time it was played. There were occasional awkward rhymes in the script: 'They cut the meat, from the hands and feet, and gave it to my father, to eat . . .' That cost two vouchers at least.

Again, many people will have wondered whether the pony-tails of the Greek menfolk were not perhaps mildly funny. To say nothing of the black leather costumes worn by Achilles and Patroclus, which seemed to have been chosen by mail-order from some specialist magazine. But we did not laugh at these things. We had vouchers to spare, we reckoned.

But when the company began to send the whole project up, when for instance John Shrapnel appeared with nose-putty as Apollo, God of High Camp, our laughter had become lethal. The good-will vouchers had long ago lost their value as currency. Why not kill Helen? suggested Orestes' friend. We roared with laughter. Why not indeed? The more the merrier! Why not kill everybody and let us go home?

I said that annihilation of the first two parts was almost complete, but the operative word was almost. It cost Judy Buxton a few misplaced laughs, in the *Iphigenia in Tauris*, to bring the audience back to its original mood. This was the last play, and perhaps the most moving. One emerged from the theatre with a sense of bitterly frustrated respect for John Barton and the company's achievement.

What had gone wrong, and what had gone right? First, it was not at all a question of individual actors' limitations, even though these were sometimes cruelly displayed. Nor was it a flaw in the basic idea of putting Greek tragedy on the con-temporary stage. We are told that Trevor Nunn and Terry Hands warned John Barton off the idea, thought it was mad and that Greek plays are ghastly. But this is narrow-minded-ness on their part.

When Greek plays go wrong it is precisely because they offer us an experience all too familiar, as when the tasteful pillars of the set look like the window-dressing of a high-class florist's, or as when a row of women mourn the destruction of Ilium in the accents of Knightsbridge. That kind of familiarity is painful.

On the other hand, the *Antigone* has recently been performed in almost every theatre in West Germany, because, rightly or wrongly, there is an audience which identifies its own political dilemma as that of the heroine. As a matter of fact, I think the reasoning of these audiences is ludicrous. They were not forbidden to bury Andreas Baader. But they feel that they were forbidden. Greek tragedy has thus regained its political dimension. It lives.

Can it come alive in England? Can the RSC make it do so? There are, of course, great difficulties with the convention. In Greek tragedy there is a lot of past, in the shape of choruses and messenger speeches, and a lot of future, in the shape of prophecies and pronouncements from the gods. But there is very little present. There is no action – or when there is it takes place behind closed doors which should form a major feature of the stage architecture. That is a problem for modern taste, and the task is therefore to educate the taste.

Oddly enough, it is not the worst problem against which John Barton so painfully stubs his toe. The worst problem of *The Greeks* arises from the attempt to mix tragedy and comedy. In a sense, the problem revealed amounts to a theatrical discovery.

Think of Shakespearian tragedy. Think of what makes it distinctive. In the eighteenth and early nineteenth centuries, when Shakespeare was being edited, performed again, translated and propagated throughout Europe, one of the features which those brought up in the classical tradition found at first repellent was precisely this tendency to mix the genres. They could not believe that great tragedy could stoop in the way that Shakespeare stoops. They could not believe that a play might move laughter and tears at the same time.

But when the taste for Shakespeare triumphed and spread as far as Russia, was it not the very moments of this delicious mixture which became most cherished and imitated? Everyone loves Hamlet's scene with the gravedigger, the great locus of confrontation. Nor is it accidental that the knocking on the gate in *Macbeth* elicited from de Quincey the greatest single piece of Romantic Shakespeare criticism.

My point is that Shakespearian tragedy was not a mere successor to classical tragedy (its debt was only indirect); it was a vigorous alternative which the classicists rightly saw as inimical to their ideals. The dislike is mutual. Mr Barton cherished the idea of telling the whole story of the house of Atreus through the medium of the Greek tragedies. But when he came to do so, his allegiance to Shakespearianism proved too strong. He could not help but mar the plays. It was as if Shakespeare was the Fury, pursuing the director and punishing him for a temporary defection.

We think of the values of tragedy as eternal. We are wrong to do so, but the illusion is forgivable. Less forgivable is the idea that comedy is eternal – when comedy is so obviously specific to culture and period. What those who tried to warn John Barton should have said was: revive Greek tragedy by all means, but do not attempt at the same time to revive, or invent, Greek comedy. On its own, this task would be daunting. In tandem with the other task, impossible.

Praise, then, in conclusion: to the Chorus, whose prologue and epilogue and continued help provided the audience both with beautiful faces to see and beautiful voices for the poetry. People thought in advance that the project would founder on the chorus but it was often saved by them and there is no doubt that the first session's success owes much to the charm of the opening scene.

Eliza Ward as Hecuba and Billie Whitelaw as Andromache share the main burden of suffering womanhood. Miss Ward's voice sounds sometimes disturbingly flat and prosaic, and I could not decide whether this was a virtue or not. But her performance was exciting and never ridiculous, just as Miss Whitelaw manages to survive intact from the most ridiculous moment of Part Three (when she sings Fry's Turkish Delight over the picnic baskets full of dismembered body). Considering that she was one of the best actresses in the cast, it was a pity that Miss Whitelaw's major moments as Andromache came when the third evening was off the rails, just as it is a pity that Lynn Dearth's Electra fell during the Baader-Meinhof

51

period (the *Orestes* would have reminded us irresistibly of modern terrorism if it had not been played in such a way as to remind us of modern terrorism), and it was impossible to decide quite where the virtues of the performance ended and the vices of the conception began. Otherwise, Celia Gregory (Cassandra), Diana Berriman (Chrysothemis) and Judy Buxton (a stunningly beautiful Iphigenia) were notable.

Of the men, John Shrapnel gave a very convincing Agamemnon, a picture of moral cowardice in high office, and a perfectly ghastly Apollo. Tony Church's Menelaus was the fault of the production, while his Odysseus was too like his Menelaus. Mike Gwilym and Peter Woodward made more of their Orestes and friend act than of their previous roles as Achilles and Patroclus. More or less everybody else was played and well played by Edwin Richfield and Oliver Ford Davies.

To end, as I began, with Janet Suzman. She has a moment, as Clytemnestra, when her daughter is taken off for sacrifice, and she must weep. She does so in a short musical chant, which she will repeat at the most moving moment of the cycle – her death. This chant is in a way more a matter of singing than acting, but it is an inspired touch, and it remains in the memory as the best moment of her performance, the performance through which the triumphs and failures of the vast project are most poignantly expressed.

10 February 1980

Juristen
(ERNST-DEUTSCH-THEATER, HAMBURG)

On Thursday night, Rolf Hochhuth's remarkable new play, *Juristen*, was simultaneously premiered in Göttingen, Heidelberg and Hamburg. It was the first night for the play, but the last chapter of a great scandal – one which dominated the German press for many months, and caused heartache to the older generation of politicians.

Scandal and Hochhuth are not strangers. Scandal of international proportions attended the opening night of *The Representative* (1963), his first play, in which Pope Pius XII was taken to task for not speaking out against the Holocaust. Four years later there was a virulent debate about *Soldiers*, in which Churchill was depicted as implicated in a murder plot against General Sikorski. The banning of this play from the National was one of our own Lord Chamberlain's last flings.

The scandal on which Hochhuth's latest play is based may be simplest expressed in figures. During the First World War, German military courts found reason to condemn to death a total of forty-eight members of their own armed forces; during the Second World War, the number was somewhere around 30,000. The field judges of the Nazi period, 'intellectual Schweyks', in Hochhuth's phrase, made up for their unwillingness to fight for their country by lavishly condemning its soldiers to death. They did this even when soldiers were in desperately short supply. More amazingly, they continued to do so after the very defeat of Germany.

But the legal profession escaped with notorious impunity from the ruins of the Reich, and not one of these field judges had been brought to trial or even required to give an account of himself. Not one, that is, until a certain Dr Filbinger read, and objected to, an advance extract from *Juristen* in *Die Zeit*.

Dr Filbinger, who was then Prime Minister of Baden-Württemberg, had been a navy field judge during the latter part of the war, and had actually condemned a man to death three months after the extinction of Hitler. He objected to being described as a 'terrible jurist', and took Hochhuth to court. He was pushing his luck. He lost the case, and soon afterwards lost his premiership.

To the horror of his Christian Democrat colleagues (as I vividly recall from that period, during which I was working in Germany), Dr Filbinger became a byword – for his inability to remember an execution he must have witnessed, and for his expressed belief that 'what was justice in those days cannot be the opposite today'.

But he had always been notorious among the young, as one of the founders of the system whereby radical left-wingers have been excluded from public service in West Germany. At the time that Hochhuth brought about his downfall, Filbinger had been widely tipped as a future president of his country.

The main character in *Juristen* (played in the Hamburg version by Friedrich Schütter) is just such a man: a prominent minister due for the highest office, a stern upholder of the extirpation of radicals . . . and a man with his own 'radical' past as a military jurist. The play is set on 9 May 1978, the day that Aldo Moro's body was discovered.

The minister goes under armed escort to spend a quiet evening at the studio of his daughter Tina (Daniela Ziegler) and her boyfriend Dieter (Claus Wilcke). An old friend of the family, Klaus (Peter Zilles), has lost his job as a hospital doctor, because of his political past.

Aware that he is humiliating himself in asking for a private favour, but faced with the alternative of being excluded for ever from public hospital work, Klaus comes to the studio in order to try to get his job back. The minister, however, takes his usual stern line – so Klaus decides to turn the tables and confront the minister with what he happens to know about his past – facts of which even Tina is unaware.

The ensuing argument made a riveting spectacle. One cannot sit with a Hamburg audience of the haute bourgeoisie and watch such a brutally direct confrontation between old and young Germany without being intensely moved and disturbed. The audience applauded, but I noticed that the applause rolled down from the gallery into the stalls. The partisans were in the cheap seats. The faces in the stalls were uneasy.

The presentation is a mixture of realism and documentary reconstruction. During the early scenes in the studio, the detail was so true to contemporary German life that I sometimes had the illusion of being among old friends. When the past is to be evoked, the studio wall becomes a film-screen. The film roles are taken by the stage actors – so that the daughter sees herself as a woman about to face the guillotine, and the boyfriend is blindfolded and shot for desertion. When the minister is shown in his old uniform, the effect is particularly compelling. There is also a chronicler who interrupts the course of the play to give factual details. Every effort is made to keep the audience's mind on historical truth.

Hochhuth's strength in this play derives from what I would call his ethical realism – by which I mean that every moral issue is seen in terms of the particular experience of the particular people involved. No one is a cipher.

The minister may be representative of his generation, but he is also flesh and blood. When he seems to be ill, his daughter rushes to his aid, even though she knows by now that he is a monster. The discovery of his past causes her to loathe him – and loathe the grandchild she is due to bear him. She determines to abort the child – a decision which causes her father to say that she is 'the real Nazi'.

In the last moments of the play, Tina and her boyfriend are left alone together, still determined to go to Amsterdam for the abortion, him insistent that she will not allow the events of more than thirty years ago to decide the fate of their child. To fight against disgust at one's parenthood is depicted as the best protest currently available against the past. With a determined optimism of the will Hochhuth is arguing that the young should not allow their behaviour to be dictated by Nazism. In so doing, he implicitly attacks the point made forcibly by Tina (and widely believed throughout West Germany): that the state which allows such men as her father to walk free has in effect legitimised the terrorists of today.

17 February 1980

55

Duet for One *(BUSH)*

By the time that I went to see *Duet for One*, at the Bush Theatre, everyone involved – author, director, actors, audience – knew that the project had been an immense success. The notices were good. The West End was licking its lips. The last readjustments had been made to the production, and from the word Go the self-confidence of the acting put the audience at ease.

From time to time, remembering the purpose of my attendance as a critic, I would try to separate the virtues out: writing, acting, direction – who was responsible for what? But while this kind of separation may be possible when things are not going well, it becomes rather a distraction with a success.

Tom Kempinski had written the play for his wife, Frances de la Tour. The director was an old friend and WRP associate, Roger Smith. The second actor – television actor and voice-over expert David de Keyser – had been something of an unknown quantity. It was only after the first night had made clear his exceptional qualities that he slyly revealed to the company that he had not been on the London stage for twenty-two years.

Mr Kempinski first showed his script to the Hampstead Theatre. They were impressed but chary. The play was about a woman violinist with multiple sclerosis, who was faced with the end of her musical career and a crisis in her marriage to a famous composer. This all sounded too much like the story of Jacqueline Du Pré. Could Mr Kempinski not make a few changes? For instance, could the main character not be – say – a footballer?

Mr Kempinski thought not. It is true that his wife achieved her latest London success as Hamlet. If Hamlet, why not Kevin Keegan? Unfortunately a large part of the play was devoted to the analysis of what it is to be a *musician* – and somehow the substitution of a football for a violin did not make sense. Instead, Mr Kempinski sent the script to Miss Du

Pré asking if she would be offended by its performance. To her credit, she gave the go-ahead.

I have given all this background in the hopes of forestalling the reader's depression. Obviously a bad play about multiple sclerosis would be a depressing thing to watch, although not (for me) as depressing as a bad 'classic' English farce. But good writing and acting are not in the least depressing, however overwhelming they may be. Pretentiousness is depressing. Stage philistines are depressing. Art ain't.

Duet for One shows a series of sessions in which Miss Abrahams, the musician, explains and explores her predicament in the presence of Dr Feldman, the psychiatrist whose help she has unwillingly sought at her husband's request. At first the 'patient' refuses to see herself as such. Her manner is bright and competent. She is well turned out. Above all, she is aggressive and resentful of the whole notion of psychiatry and the unconscious. She has a great deal of hollow fun at the expense of the doctor.

In later sessions, resentfulness mounts, turning into passivity and squalid despair. The bright manner and neat turn-out yield place to filthiness both literal and verbal. At this stage the doctor acts in the way the patient least expected. In a long speech, he pays her back for all the puerile fun she has had at his expense and forces her to see her behaviour not so much in psychological as in ethical terms. Up to this moment, the play has been really Frances de la Tour's. But when David de Keyser strikes back, the effect is all the more devastating for its quality of surprise and contrast. In the last scene, the patient is changed and respectful – but she insists she must terminate the treatment. The doctor cannot know what her art meant to her. Therefore he cannot help.

But there is a twist – and I think a profound one. For it is precisely at the moment when she articulates most honestly the devastating character of her predicament, at the very moment when she says in effect, 'I respect you, you are a good doctor, but you can't help me, my loss is too great,' at *this* moment the cure can at least begin. And it is at this moment that the play ends, on a note of what I should call improved despair.

In Roger Smith's production, every moment tells, and the audience was positively craning to observe what would happen next. At one dramatic pause, I heard a spectator thinking out loud: 'She's fallen in love with him!' An intelligent guess, but frustrated at the next move.

Miss de la Tour's face reminds me how, if one is forced to cry against one's will, the moment is always accomplished by the unwelcome discovery of a facial muscle, where one had never suspected that such a thing existed. Her voice too is continually surprising in its modulations. Her performance was an exercise in unwitting self-revelation, while Mr de Keyser's was all practised self-concealment – a perfect match.

I never found myself asking whether the main character *could* actually be a great musician – and this must be in part a tribute to the writing. *Duet for One* is a first-rate play, clearly conceived and executed with a great deal of the art that conceals itself. It may be odd to respond with such pleasure to the depiction of an experience so distressing – but that is a fundamental paradox of art.

24 February 1980

Doctor Faustus *(LYRIC STUDIO)*
Rose *(DUKE OF YORK'S)*

A few weeks ago, the actor James Aubrey found himself in an odd predicament. He had a leading role, Marlowe's Doctor Faustus, and he had a theatre to play it in, the Lyric Studio at Hammersmith, but he had no director – Edward Petherbridge having been obliged to withdraw at the last moment. Mr Aubrey turned to his former teacher, Christopher Fettes of the Drama Centre, and Mr Fettes managed to assemble a company largely composed of his former pupils.

It took six weeks to put the production together, four of which were spent on rehearsals.

Mr Fettes clearly decided, in the face of the odds, to live dangerously. The result is a startling production, and one to which I could imagine violent exception being taken. But I really admired it on Monday, and have continued to do so since while munching my way through the academic criticism of this play, from which I discover that some of the most striking scenes in the production are those of which the critics almost unanimously disapprove.

For instance, the scene in Rome. In a brilliant piece of casting, Mr Fettes has given us the three-and-a-half-foot-tall David Rappaport as Pope, and in an authentic spirit of utter blasphemy has doubled his part with that of Beelzebub. It is in the latter role that Mr Rappaport first appears with James Griffin's Lucifer, and quite freezes the blood. On his return to the stage, wearing the triple crown, this tiny, infernal Pontiff relishes every moment of his victory, as he walks on the back of the defeated Bruno. Finally, when Faustus fetches him a box on the ear, he has to be picked up by an archbishop, and held in the arms like a bawling child.

The focus of this studio production is a library table, around which, as the play begins, a group of gowned students are seen at work. The drama derives from interaction between passionate adolescent minds and powerful books.

Mr Aubrey's Faustus is a young man – and he does not age during the twenty-four years of the play. When he is killed, it is on the same library table. I thought: but this is just like some school debagging that has got out of hand. Then I reflected that we were being returned to the original conception, in which Faustus was seen circling the table and picking up the various books in turn.

The good and bad angels' voices emanated from the mouths of the other students seen at work. You could imagine the whole play taking place in the hero's mind, in a single afternoon – in a mind, perhaps, where the impulse towards knowledge was impossible to distinguish from a general erotic disturbance. The programme note features Sartre: 'La jeunesse? C'est une maladie bourgeoise.'

I was vividly reminded of Robert Musil's frightening novel, *Young Törless*, in which the hero's experience of homosexuality at school becomes mixed up with an equally disturbing sense – the sense that mathematical theorems express probability rather than certainty. The intellectual coincides with the erotic crisis.

In the mind of this Faustus, what begins as the pursuit of knowledge ends in an erotic climax with a fellow student, Simon Cutter, who impersonates the Bad Angel, Lechery and Helen of Troy. Some critics suggest that the sin for which Faustus is put beyond the pale of redemption is demoniality (like bestiality, only with demons). Certainly the moment of union with Helen is given full weight in this production.

The main virtue, from which all others stem, is that the text itself is vividly present throughout – always audible, and even at its most obscure never slurred over. There is no fancy paragraphing of the verse, no meretricious 'rubato'. It is true that scansion goes by the board when modern pronunciation of a word clashes with the correct one. But that is the only objection I have to the delivery of the lines.

Patrick Magee plays Mephostophilis as a spirit in torment – bang right. G. H. Lewes objected to this character that 'the language he addressed to Faustus is such as would rather frighten than seduce him'. But this is precisely the point: it is

Faustus himself who chooses his path to perdition, while Mephostophilis warns him quite openly about the consequences. Mr Magee's suffering is most poignantly expressed through his large eyes, and a voice that seems to triumph over some strange, secret restriction.

James Aubrey's Faustus, equally beautiful to listen to, has an essential quality of likability. He is a naive enthusiast for knowledge – naive because while he sells his soul for knowledge it is precisely his knowledge which Lucifer will restrict. Faustus may go where he likes, have what he likes, but he may not know what he likes. This is his earliest discovery. He has sold his soul for the equivalent of the *Encyclopaedia Britannica*.

The company includes eight actors, the remainder being Garry Cooper as the sinister Wagner, Roger Frost and John Sommerville. The dumb-shows are strikingly staged by Sara van Beers. The design is by Kandis Cook. This is the best thing the Lyric has so far done. Let's have some more Marlowe from the same team.

The Duke of York's Theatre has reopened with Andrew Davies's *Rose*, in which Glenda Jackson plays a nice primary teacher, with bright ideas for improving school life, with a little more wit than she knows what to do with, and with a handful of problems. Getting on with mother isn't always easy. Her headmistress will not give her a good reference. Her husband's career is going to the dogs. If she wants a divorce, her husband will sue her for custody of the children.

This is certainly not a bad play, but it does go in for a bit too much fudging. I'm not in the least bit convinced that those bright ideas for improving school life would have survived very long in the classroom, but for the purposes of the play we are obliged to imagine the children responding well. Too much of what happens, inconvenient as it is for the heroine, is rather convenient for the playwright.

Miss Jackson's task, throughout the evening, is to make us forget nearly every other role she has played. She must lower herself gently into the part, in order to become the sort of character who admires a friend's ability to speak of kicking her husband out of the house. But do we really believe that

Miss Jackson cannot fend very well for herself, or that she would have got herself into the position in which we find her? Do we really fall for this portrayal of ordinariness? I think not. The play, with a good supporting cast and under Alan Dossor's direction, makes a pleasant enough evening. It is a modest study in the moral and theatrical virtues of self-restraint.

2 March 1980

The Iceman Cometh (COTTESLOE)
The Dresser
(ROYAL EXCHANGE, MANCHESTER)

Too long, repetitious, could be cut, blah–blah–blah – the criticisms levelled at *The Iceman Cometh* (Cottesloe) have been much more boring than the evening itself. I agree that the play, which forms the third part of the National Theatre's O'Neill season, has faults, but I hardly think that they could be eliminated with a little ingenious blue pencil.

The problem is that a large number of people are shown undergoing the same experience – they are depicted in turn, but their experience may be imagined as simultaneous. Now if you cut such a play, what happens? You simply end up with a smaller number of people undergoing the same experience. But perhaps the interest of the play derives from its breadth of characterisation. Perhaps the scale is vital to the work. Art is long, says the author, and so, by the way, is life. In this case then, to cut is to kill.

There is a much-reproduced attack on O'Neill by Eric Bentley, a passionate essay which concludes that, while remaining uncorrupted by Broadway money, the playwright was led astray by the Broadway intellectuals – it was the high esteem of the Algonquin set which did him in.

This sounds convincing until one thinks about the experience which led Bentley to his conclusion, that of producing *The Iceman Cometh* before a Swiss audience. To this end, Bentley cut back the play so far as to eliminate several characters. He also found that there was no satisfactory equivalent for the various accents and modes of speech of the international cast.

In other words, the linguistic texture of the play, the very quality which distinguishes one character from the next was obliterated along with a few characters. Not surprisingly, the Swiss were unimpressed with the result. Rather more surprisingly, Bentley found their boredom interesting.

63

The Cottesloe O'Neill productions (designer Hayden Griffin, director Bill Bryden) have all been executed in what looks like a spirit of blithe indifference to the playwright's faults; in my case, the blitheness proved infectious. I love above all to be able to see a play without feeling that the director is fussing around, worrying that at any moment the audience may get bored. Let the director not be bored. Let the cast not be bored. The audience does not *seek* boredom in the theatre, and if there is any interest around, it will root it out.

So on this shallow stage, with its realistic depiction of a seedy bar, the cast is presented in a frieze deliberately reminiscent of the Last Supper. As the eye takes in the initial composition, the somnolent figures waiting for Hickey to come and bring some cheer, one is introduced at once both to the scope of the play and to its limitations.

There are people here in plenty, but the conversational resources are restricted. Conversation is like a spiritual event – like speaking with tongues. It happens down at one end of the frieze. Then it moves away to the other end. It never seems to happen in two parts of the bar at the same time. Those who are not talking are either asleep or are frozen into some typical attitude.

Tony Haygarth has been got up – with scandalously malicious accuracy – to look like the drama critic Steve Grant; he spends the first act with his head on the table and his nose squashed flat. There is something very committed about this squashed nose. Very committed. Very Cottesloe.

Gawn Grainger, playing a drunken has-been journalist called (I say, steady on!) James Cameron, passes his time in a slowly smouldering mood of what looks like existential astonishment. Oscar James, the black gambler, is devastated by emotion, and brings the most potentially dangerous force on to the stage. J. G. Devlin, on the other hand, is a preternaturally washed-out 60-year-old, with an alarming habit of going quite grey and limp. James Grant is alternatively plausible and beyond the pale.

These are some of the stronger portrayals, which remain in the memory. The play is dominated in this production by three characters. Kevin McNally, as the young man who has betrayed his anarchist mother, brings his distress to lay at the feet of another former anarchist, Niall Toibin. The young man will not let the older go. The older man, evasive and dedicated to withdrawal and gradual self-destruction, is roused to life by the eventual arrival of Hickey the hero.

It is Hickey's transformation from drunkenness to improbably perfect self-adjustment which provides the intellectual teaser of the play. Jack Shepherd, an actor of great power, with eyes that suggest, at their most passionate, the deepest reserves of cowardice and terror, takes the part of Hickey. The evening develops into a struggle between Mr Toibin and Mr Shepherd. Both of them are destroyed in the outcome.

I began the O'Neill season determined not to be indulgent to the playwright's faults – since such indulgence is only a deep form of insult. I must say, however, that while the distance between the immature early plays and the later works is far too short for comfort, and while the faults are always visible, they are not easy either to excise or to use as an excuse for dismissal. The faults of O'Neill do indeed derive from striving – but striving is in itself an ambiguous quality. And a man may be forgiven for visibly striving, when his task is no less than to found American drama.

The new play by Ronald Harwood, *The Dresser* (Royal Exchange, Manchester) is excellent. Based in part on the author's experiences as dresser to Sir Donald Wolfit, and in part on research into the lost world of the provincial actor-managers of touring companies, it depicts the relationship between such an actor and his dressing-room assistant.

The year is 1942, the setting an English provincial theatre behind scenes. The grand old actor is played with tremendous charm and presence by Freddie Jones, while the role of the dresser is taken by Tom Courtenay, who mixes devotion and dangerousness, camp humour and genuine emotional turbulence.

The story is quite simple – the actor is in the midst of a terminal emotional crisis, and the question is, will he perform Lear that night? The task of the first act, then, is for Mr

Courtenay to get Mr Jones dressed, made up and ready to go ahead. It is fascinating to watch, partly because the details of backstage life simply are fascinating. One could tell that the audience was just as interested in how to make up for Lear as in the details of the psychology, well depicted though these are.

In the echoing spaces outside the theatre we glimpse (or those of us in the best seats can glimpse) a part of the *Lear* performance itself. It is faithful to period and to a style which is universally frowned on. Or rather, not quite universally. The audience did not laugh at this *Lear* (though they laughed a lot where they were invited to laugh) and nor does Mr Harwood laugh at what his heroes represent.

9 March 1980

Othello (OLIVIER)

By the time of the interval at the end of Act II in *Othello* (Olivier), I thought that there was everything still to win. There had been faults. John Bury's semi-existent design had not worked hard on behalf of the production, while Basil Henson's Brabantio yielded his daughter to the Moor with a grudging, almost indifferent spirit. One cannot believe that this match will be 'mortal to him' or that 'pure grief' will shear 'his old thread in twain'. Brabantio it is who, on relinquishing Desdemona, first implants the idea of infidelity in Othello's mind:

> Look to her, Moor, if thou hast eyes to see:
> She has deceived her father, and may thee.

A towering insult, publicly delivered. But in Peter Hall's production it passes almost unnoticed.

Now for the virtues: Michael Gambon, Michael Bryant, Felicity Kendal – the first remarkable for the pouches above his eyes, the second for the pouches beneath, the third for a hamster-like arrangement whereby she stores her winter provender in the base of her cheeks – Roderigo, Iago and Desdemona respectively. Add Stephen Moore's relatively unpouched Cassio and you have the core of the company – a company which works together here with no small success.

Roderigo: a curly wig above a face which looks as if it had just woken up, pale, puffed, comically slow of understanding, voice pitched at a height which just threatens hysteria. Iago: capable of unnerving merriness, the benevolently evil genius of the piece, who only loses his self-possession on confessing his fears that the Moor has cuckolded him.

Desdemona: an affectionate spirit, wrenched by her own courage and love from her naturally domestic setting. Hear her argue in Act III that, when she pleads on behalf of Cassio,

Tis as I should entreat you wear your gloves,
Or feed on nourishing dishes, or keep you warm . . .

This is a good handle for the character: one can well imagine
Miss Kendal begging her husband to wrap up well.

Cassio: a close relation of Hjalmar Ekdal, likable, led
astray. When Mr Moore mourned the loss of his reputation,
he gave us the first deeply moving moment of the evening. To
say which is not to argue that Paul Scofield's Othello had
already let us down. As I say, by the interval, I felt the contest
was still open. But I was not moved by Mr Scofield's account
of his wooing of Desdemona. I felt: this performance is largely
narcissistic, and, while narcissism does count as an interpretation of the part, it remained to be seen where self-love would
go from here.

Mr Scofield was certainly not in love with his wife, but he
had deep feelings for the audience, to whom he would regularly
appeal with looks that seemed to say: is this face of mine not
truly remarkable? this voice not unutterably profound? is not
the white of this eye the whitest thing you ever saw?

Remarkable it was, but I found the performance, as it
developed, quite incomprehensible. When it moved me, it
moved me to embarrassment, as when a word developed into
an extraordinary high-pitched whoop, which sounded like a
plane taking off. A voice with great depths, which slid directly
into falsetto, an accent which suggested – I couldn't tell what
race.

Most disconcertingly, a set of bodily gestures which defied
co-ordination. There was a vulgar sexual jutting of the hips.
There was a half-hearted abandonment in despair. There was
no heroic language of the limbs. If I call to mind Donald
Sinden's Othello at Stratford last year, what I immediately see
is an actor whose body falls naturally into postures suggestive
of old theatrical paintings and prints. Indeed, what I have in
my mind is an engraving of Mr Sinden. When I think of Mr
Scofield, I think of a face which seems to possess all the
traditional qualities of a great actor, set on a body which
refuses to speak in the conventional language of heroic acting.

This body is inarticulate, this voice is an unfortunate invention, an invention which tyrannises the performance, leaving it little by way of human scope. Everything about Mr Scofield's manner suggests a performance which has been worked up in front of a mirror, brought along to the stage door and then inserted into the production. The production is, for once, richly populated with human beings. What sets Mr Scofield apart is not his blackness but his acting.

Some final virtues. You get your money's worth in terms of an uncut text, which lasts over three and a half hours. I think this is absolutely right – a play of this scale should not be slished and slashed and hurried along. Peter Hall's production is never boring, and what it sacrifices in terms of dramatic speed is sacrificed in the cause of authenticity. There exists no better cause. Other virtues include a first-rate Bianca from Penelope Wilton. Peter Needham's Montano and Roger Gartland's Clown. If one were to seek out a single performance or moment, it would be Mr Bryant's Iago at the time of the exposure of his villainy. Sated with revenge, he succumbs to an attack of tertiary silliness. He is left with a lolling head and a pale idiotic smile, as if the badness has exhausted itself, leaving him genial and banal.

23 March 1980

Hamlet (ROYAL COURT)

A memorable *Hamlet* at the Royal Court. Jonathan Pryce plays it, Richard Eyre directs it, William Dudley designed it. We are in the studiolo of some Italianate palace, whose marquetry furnishings are devised so as to deceive the eyes. It looks as if lattice-work windows had been left ajar, revealing shelves on which symbolic objects had been placed: a skull, an hourglass, an open book. Here too is an opening door, behind which a marquety eavesdropper stands half revealed.

But these beautiful walls are false. These seeming doors are indeed, it turns out, doors. What they depict they also conceal. For the gravedigger scene they become a baroque ossuary, cupboards crammed with skulls, where – in flagrant but vivid violation of the text – the dead Ophelia will be laid on a hastily cleared shelf. Others of these doors will open on to stair-cases and corridors: when the whole palace is looking for Hamlet, the set will come alive with treacherous possibilities. Hamlet's usually defiant 'hide fox and all after' will be delivered at the moment of defeat, when all possible exits are bristling with arms. The possessed Prince will yield meekly to the straitjacket.

Possessed. If there is a moment that the eye will treasure more than any other, at the end of an evening rich in spectacle, composition and tone, it is the revelation of the play's key concept. There is no exterior ghost: Hamlet Senior speaks to us from the cellarage of his son's guts. The Prince perceives him in a pale light that shines from the Circle. When the voice erupts from the body, it seems to produce a quite different face in the speaker. We watch alarmed, not only at the extreme physical pain from which the Prince seems to be suffering, but also at the daring of the actor and director.

No ghost, then? This will take some getting used to. But there is no time for a rethink, either for us or for the Prince. The elimination of the ghost has all sorts of intellectual consequences – none of them more significant than the practical one that, whereas we might hitherto have thought we knew the play well, from now on the director and actor are in charge and we must follow where they lead.

Mr Pryce has been noted for his Modigliani face, with its dominant brow, and the negative deceleration curve of his cheeks. If it is an especially apt face for Hamlet, I believe the aptness derives from the face's tendency, in moments of suffering, to evoke a babyish quality. This actor is immensely forceful, can hold the attention of the house, can dominate the stage at will.

In the very dangerous-seeming fight with Simon Chandler's Laertes (directed by Malcolm Ranson), there was no question that this Prince could give as good as he got. All the more striking then was the ability of the face to betray – behind what was masculine, aristocratic, commanding – an aspect of infantility, a tendency to self-pity, vulnerability.

This is a tremendous *Hamlet*. I do not think it is the whole thing, but perhaps it has no pretensions to completeness. The production, in eliminating the first scene, seems also to squeeze out Horatio (Jarlath Conroy) wherever possible. One is not left with a profound sense of that friendship between the two men – rather, is this Prince more terribly alone than usual. I missed also that gear change, on the return of the Prince from the sea, which usually signals a mood of serenity before the catastrophe.

The cast is always interesting, if not always successful. I disliked the phrasing of Claudius's opening speech, as delivered by Michael Elphick, but came to admire the solid, realistic, sensual presence of the King, more so as the evening developed. Jill Bennett is Gertrude, and very striking too, as much to watch in response as in action. Harriet Walter, as Ophelia, finds her brother's advice impossible to take seriously, and shows herself full of spirit. In next to no time this spirit will go from her, and she will become pale and drained. One felt still that there was a lot to her as a character.

Geoffrey Chater plays Polonius, with a minimum of risibility. He is a nasty figure in a dangerous court. Christopher Logue suddenly appears on stage as the Player King and

71

delivers his own paraphrase of the Hecuba speech. I thought he acquitted himself well both as poet and as player. Richard Eyre's production is both exciting and intelligent. It demands to be seen.

6 April 1980

Three Sisters (WAREHOUSE)

Trevor Nunn's production of Chekhov's *Three Sisters* arrived at the Warehouse already sold out, and with its exceptional reputation long since firmly established. One of its chief strengths I remember from the Other Place at Stratford, where I saw this production last autumn, was the way in which the noise level ranged from extreme rowdiness to utter quiet. The transfer faces the serious problem of the Warehouse itself, in which it appears impossible to achieve total silence.

The quiet of Stratford is indeed a great boon. I recall the matinée audience, as the lights went up, and a particularly beautiful moment when each person discovered that his or her companion was in tears. At once people brushed away the tears or attempted to laugh through them. Then we issued forth into the dark evening. On these occasions, the dispersing theatre crowd is like one single, great volcanic argument that bursts forth into the night, red hot, and then makes its way, in little rivulets, towards pubs, coaches and parked cars.

And sometimes the argument does not cool. It remains as a permanent disturbance in the mind. When I think of this production, I find myself first of all aroused to a general passion, and only afterwards able to point to specific details. I think of the sisters themselves: Janet Dale as Olga, learning with a reluctant horror that she is to become a headmistress, as if success at her job were a kind of martyrdom; Suzanne Bertish as Masha, hearing Vershinin nearby humming a snatch of *Onegin*, and deciding, without a word, on infidelity; and Emily Richard as Irina, warding off the realisation that the man she does not love has been killed for her sake.

This is the moment at which the romanticism of Bob Peck's Soliony, a kind of bitter egotism learned from Lermontov, deals the fatal blow to the more novelettish romanticism of Irina, leaving the three sisters to face reality as they cannot help but perceive it – not simply in its grim immediacy, but in a grim immediacy perceived from the point of view of history. It

73

is the tendency of Chekhov's characters to project themselves into the future, and then to look back in horror at the triviality of the present moment. This is the chief source of their malady.

Those who do not share the malady are the victims of self-deception. Timothy Spall's Andrei, the once-promising brother who was to have become a professor in Moscow, descends gradually from diffidence into aggressive self-defence. He has become a member of the local council – is that not enough, for heaven's sake? One sees him condemned for ever to pushing a pram, as if his odious offspring were the stone of Sisyphus.

Then there is the pernicious success of Natasha, at first the despised outsider, the common girl with bad dress-sense who marries Andrei and gradually triumphs in getting rid of the sisters from the house. This part is played by Susan Tracy, and appears to have been deliberately toned down since Stratford. On two occasions then she really screamed at the household, first when she wanted to get rid of the old Nanny (Rose Hill), and second when, at the end, she discovers a fork on a garden bench.

There was something utterly terrifying about this performance, a portrayal of vindictiveness that has allowed itself time to work its way, and will not stint itself in its triumph. With what falsely innocent glee does she announce that her first act, when Irina has left the house, will be to cut down the row of fir trees – an act which, even though we know nothing of these trees, we immediately perceive as a kind of murder.

Yet the sisters are not entirely nice; they *are*, to a certain degree, snobbish and exclusive. Some of what they get they deserve.

Suzanne Bertish's Masha, for instance, may excite our admiration with its spiritedness and intelligence, and its intense elegance. But it is set side by side with Patrick Godfrey's portrayal of her teacher husband, a portrayal which refuses the temptation to play the utter fool. This man is a pedant, yes, but the actor insists that the pedant is also a man of some judgement and worthy of our sympathy. He realises, in a dramatic moment of unspoken panic, what is going on between Masha and the handsome battery commander Vershinin (Edward Petherbridge), but he does not later seize upon the opportunity to triumph over Masha in her loss. He accepts what has happened and wants to make his marriage survive it. If we are forced to sympathise with him, we must therefore divide our loyalty to Masha. Miss Bertish seems aware of this, and aware, despite her repugnance, of her husband's merits.

In the same way, although Chekhov's way of introducing us to the Baron is through a comic characteristic – his nervous insistence that despite his name, Tusenbach, he really is Russian through and through – we come to sympathise just as much with Roger Rees as he sues for Irina's hand as with Emily Richard, who seems almost more culpable in accepting than in rejecting him. We love Mr Rees because, despite his obvious worth, he is continually rebuffed on stage, while Mr Petherbridge, who has not been on stage two minutes before he has charmed the company, comes in for some quiet censure in our minds. Is he not perhaps amusing himself with Masha – while she is certainly not amusing herself with him, but in real earnest?

The most powerful moment I recall from the Stratford performance was the scene in which Bob Peck warns Irina that he will not allow her to make any rival happy. Mr Peck's Soliony is very quiet, very reserved. His tendency to make idiotic remarks seems to stem from a contained passion rather than from, say, idiocy.

This is a marvellous company, and a great production.

13 April 1980

A Typical Week

In Southampton, at the National Student Drama Festival, I heard Timothy West bemoaning in a speech the state of British theatre. Not much was happening. The managements were playing safe. People had run out of ideas. We were in the doldrums. Returning to these doldrums at the end of last week, I found myself caught up in the following events:

Saturday. The penultimate night of Eleanor Bron's show, *On Her Own*, at the Riverside Studios. Miss Bron avoids the straight cabaret routine, varying her programme between comic and serious, offering poems and extracts from larger works, in the spirit of an artist selecting a found object. Her face ranges from charming diffidence, through a radiant consciousness of its own beauty, and off into the grotesque distortions of the comic roles. She plans well. She does not have to signal frantically when she wishes to say: 'No, but seriously . . .' Each change of mood comes across clearly, and the total effect is both highly interesting and highly entertaining.

If I have a criticism (which I do not), it is this: Miss Bron should not fear her great talents or consider them as leading to a terrible destiny or trap. To be uniquely beautiful, funny, and affecting as an actress – is this not something? Something to be going on with, at least.

Sunday. The cast of Strindberg's *Creditors* have clubbed together to bring their Leicester production to the New End Theatre, Hampstead. An amazing play, illuminated with the brilliant light of paranoia. Strindberg seems to have said: 'One day, I shall simply die of a broken heart, and then they'll be sorry. Then they'll understand – and it will be too late.' It is his mad clarity which allows the characters to reveal themselves and each other with absolutely none of the customary indirectness of realist drama. As they perceive something, they are at once enabled to express their perception.

Heather Sears, as long as she is on stage, ensures that the

emotional temperature is kept high. Malcolm Rennie and Philip Brown are less completely achieved, and sometimes seem not to understand the full force of their lines. But this is a striking production, and absolutely appropriate for the tiny theatre.

Monday. In Manchester, the Royal Exchange Theatre has a new play by Gerard McLarnon, *Blood, Black, and Gold,* a fantastic confection of Irish religion and folklore. My objection to this kind of writing is that, while the individual elements may be genuine and interesting enough, put together they turn bogus. Tinkers, priests, slaughterhouse managers, fairground workers, witches, and so forth – every part is too extraordinary. The verbal imagery is powerful, and controlled, but the plot over-reaches itself. If someone dies, and is raised from the dead in Act One, what is left to happen in Act Two? Braham Murray's production shows off the resources of the theatre, including a slaughterhouse version of a Chinese dragon. The designs are by Johanna Bryant.

Tuesday. Back in London for David Storey's *Early Days* at the Cottesloe. What a dreary play. A failed politician is going senile and behaving badly. But we are not asked to be interested in him as a politician. He is attended by a companion, a daughter, a son-in-law, a granddaughter, and the granddaughter's poet-fiancé. But we are not asked to be interested in these characters either. We must concentrate on a brief passage of childhood memory, cornily reiterated, which comes to obsess the main character in what we take to be his last moments. But this little memory has no significance for us unless the character himself has some interest, and some past history. Mr Storey does not provide this. Ralph Richardson does. He gives us Old Ekdal, his last role at the Olivier.

This is very amusing, and well worth seeing again, but it hardly amounts to a new performance in a new play by David Storey. Lindsay Anderson's production is very bad indeed: it gives the remaining cast absolutely nothing to do except watch Sir Ralph having a good time.

Wednesday. Anton Lesser steps out of the discotheque straight into Ron Daniels's production of *Romeo and Juliet* (Stratford), his feet still tapping. He is a quicksilver Romeo, with a generally passionate disposition, who happens to bump into the lovely Judy Buxton, and of necessity falls in love.

During the fast action of the play, there is no chance to test this passion against time. That is not the purpose either of the play or of this production. We are quite at liberty to doubt Romeo's seriousness. What we may not doubt is the force of his emotions. When roused to fight, he is quite palpably able and willing to take on more than one opponent and, under Peter Woodward's guidance, shows himself an accurate and angry swordsman.

This Romeo is both funny and heroic, a blend of the obviously modern and the historical – a blend which is reflected in the rest of the production. Judy Buxton's approach would fit equally into a more traditional staging – it is straight, powerful, and very good-looking. Miss Buxton's Iphigenia was one of the best things in *The Greeks*. This is of the same quality.

On the other hand, Chris Hunter's Tybalt and Jonathan Hyde's Mercutio belong without question to the world of punk and rock. They set the pace for the street life of the play, a pace which will prove tragic for them both. I admired these, as I admired David Toguri's choreography, and some of Stephen Oliver's music. But Ralph Koltai's abstract set of screens proved distracting and apparently dangerous to shift.

Thursday. Richard Cottrell's production of Marlowe's *Edward II* takes place in the Studio Theatre of the New Vic, which has been fitted out with a steel-faced stage for the purpose. The designer is John McMurray. The costumes are individually elegant and collectively splendid, and the general presentation is convincing.

I have strong reservations about the casting of Robert O'Mahoney and Clive Wood as Edward and his lover, Gaveston; at least their relationship seems to be expressed entirely through a kind of mental imbalance on the king's part. Gaveston was too reserved in his performance, too inert, while Edward put himself beyond the range of sympathy at too early a stage. But there was a strong company, including Stuart Wilson as the young Mortimer and Ian Reddington as Kent. The play was brought to a cruel, impressive, and explicit conclusion, which many of the audience found some difficulty in watching.

Friday. Had none of the previous productions been visible, I would have had at least three strong contenders for reviewing: a major production of *All My Sons* at Bristol, *Love On The Dole*, at Manchester, and in London, the transfer of *Make and Break* to the Haymarket.

This last, Michael Frayn's new play, was enthusiastically reviewed by John Peter when it opened at the Lyric, Hammersmith, and where I later saw it. It contains two admirably funny and original performances, by Leonard Rossiter and Prunella Scales, and is written with great wit and skill. There is neither time nor space to say more. If only these doldrums calm down a little, perhaps I shall be able to return to the theme.

27 April 1980

The Hothouse (HAMPSTEAD)
The Dresser (QUEEN'S)
Hamlet (ROUND HOUSE)

Reading through the early plays of Harold Pinter, I realised that the qualities I most admired in them were those which I strongly believe to be fundamental to poetry on the one hand and drama on the other. When the two get together, we have something called poetic drama, which has not, in this century, been an entirely happy experience.

I conceive of poetry, however, as the activity which underlies all creative writing. Lyrical verse is one manifestation of poetry, prose can be another, dramatic writing a third. If it is objected that poetry thus becomes everything, I reply that that is precisely my intention.

What, then, are these poetic qualities? I mean: a fierce independence of spirit – this art does not put itself at the service either of criticism or of ideology. It aims for something irreducible, something untranslatable into any other terms. The critic can go so far, but not further, in his investigation of such art. He will reach a moment at which all he can do is stand still, point with his index finger and say, 'Over there is the thing that I want you to look at.'

To the extent that Pinter achieves this irreducibility, he becomes an exemplary poet. The other virtues of his plays are secondary to this prime virtue. It is quite appropriate that Noel Coward should have admired and praised Pinter, since the two authors share a genius for the flat humour of common speech. Pinter's humour in the last twenty years has been deeply influential.

Pinter was born in 1930. The early plays were written in the following order: *The Room*, *The Birthday Party* and *The Dumb Waiter* belong to 1957. *A Slight Ache* followed in 1959, and in the subsequent year, *A Night Out* and *The Caretaker*. This list omits *The Hothouse* which came after *A Slight Ache*, but which its author put aside and until last year rejected. Now he directs it himself at the Hampstead Theatre, an occasion of historical and dramatic interest.

It is a two-hour play, set in what is referred to as a rest home but what appears to be a government-run experimental laboratory. The establishment is haunted by the sound of an express train, followed by mysterious voices, which are considered to be ominous. And indeed they prove ominous, since the climax involves a supposed uprising of the inmates, followed by a bloody reckoning.

The action of the piece amounts to a struggle between the director of the establishment (Derek Newark) and his assistant (James Grant). The former is an ex-colonel, with a complexion and a temper to match. The latter is the living embodiment of the dead-pan. It is his extremely reserved manner alone which indicates to his colleagues the passionate nature of the struggle in which he is involved.

The colleagues include a promiscuous Angela Pleasance, a suave, blackmailing type in Roger East, and a helpful doomed innocent in Roger Davidson. Michael Forrest and Edward de Souza complete the cast, who all act with assuredness of style and a complete understanding of the text. I have never seen Pinter direct better.

One is naturally interested to speculate both as to why the author rejected the play in the first place and why he resurrects it now. The second part is easily answered: it is a work full of comic invention, which clearly occupies an important transitional role in the development of the writer.

As to the first question, I return to the point about poetry and the irreducible. The faults of *The Hothouse* derive from a laxity of conception. There is too much here which yields, or seems about to yield, to the more intrusive spirit of criticism. At the centre is the struggle between the two men, but at the periphery there are distracting figures and scenes waving to attract our attention. I guess that what Pinter most disliked about the play in 1958 was the knowledge that he could already do much better. In his programme note, he says: 'I then went on to write "The Caretaker".' That puts it in a nutshell – irreducibly.

At Ronald Harwood's *The Dresser*, which has arrived at the Queen's Theatre from Manchester, I bitterly regretted an electric light bulb on Freddie Jones's dressing-room mirror, which blocked out 50 per cent of this marvellous actor's performance. It would not be cruel to have this light bulb taken out, and shot.

For Mr Jones's performance is worth seeing, as a study of a grand old actor quite corrupted by his grandness. What stays with me vividly from Manchester is a series of sudden transitions, when Mr Jones, although apparently in the depths of gloom, would hear a certain trigger-word (full-house, for instance) and immediately be back on the ball. He has a great gift for abruptly turning on a bogus and irresistible charm.

Tom Courtenay plays the dresser of the title, a case of unrewarded devotion. Here is a stand-up comedy act which at the same time is a study of nervousness, viciousness, self-pity and real affection. In the scene where he warns off an ambitious young actress from having anything further to do with 'Sir', the old actor, he shows a nastiness of almost melodramatic proportions. I liked it very much indeed. Part of the great interest in this play is to observe two well-matched actors contesting for the main laurels of the evening. It is a battle which, for the play to work properly, Mr Courtenay must win. I think he does so, but only after Mr Jones has been physically eliminated.

I have as strong a prejudice in favour of Steven Berkoff's style of acting as I have against his writing. In *Hamlet*, at the Round House, there are moments when he shows off this style at its best. It involves a set of limbs trained to evoke character or action with tremendous speed and utter precision. It involves a total consistency and discipline.

But the trouble is that, whereas in France this kind of bodily discipline would be coupled with a style of heroic delivery of verse, a style which England has simply thrown away, in Mr Berkoff's company, they just don't have it, and to judge by this *Hamlet* they don't want it. This is a foolish production, which sets up gigantic inverted commas around the text whenever it is uncertain what to do.

I'm not squeamish about Shakespeare, and I do not give up when the gravedigger bursts into strains of 'My old man's a dustman'. I merely stop taking Mr Berkoff seriously as a director. This production is conscious that its considerable merits might lead to it being genuinely admired. Whenever such a danger looms close, it puts a revolver to its head and pulls the trigger.

4 May 1980

The Merry Wives of Windsor
(RSC, ALDWYCH)

There is no such thing as an eternal preoccupation. The motives of Shakespeare's characters may become dated. Their interest may fade. For instance, we are not, as a culture, particularly obsessed with revenge. Sexual jealousy may be just as powerful as it ever was, but the conception of personal honour and reputation has entirely altered. In consequence, an important aspect of the character of Iago has faded, and we begin to find him hard to read.

Comedy tends to fade more rapidly than tragedy. All those jokes about cuckoldry, when the word itself would not survive in our vocabulary, were it not for the prestige of literature; all those plays in which the greatest source of humour is the humiliation of a single character – modern comedy tends to reject such a formula; jokes against doddering old men with young wives; jokes about slaves and their masters. Somebody ought to build homes for such old jokes to retire to. They deserve a good rest.

The Merry Wives of Windsor, which the RSC have brought to the Aldwych in a production by Trevor Nunn and John Caird, is of all Shakespearian plays the most Elizabethan in feeling and lack of feeling. Many of the jokes can only be guessed at through scholarly reconstruction, since they seem to refer to contemporary figures about whom we know next to nothing.

The production, designed by John Napier, is broadly Elizabethan in look. But it is significant that when Ben Kingsley, who plays Ford, disguises himself in order to discover Falstaff's intentions *vis-à-vis* his wife, he puts on a many-gusseted version of a raincoat and a hat that looks distinctly like a squashed bowler. He steps, quite deliberately, out of period and out of the production, and scores his success as a time-traveller on the set. It is a performance which obeys no rule to which the audience is privy. It seems to have come

84

perhaps from central Europe, from the 1920s, or 1930s. He emits extraordinary noises indicative of powerful emotions forcibly contained so that only a strangulated whine gives evidence of the turmoil within.

One wishes that a little more of the central European spirit had invaded the rest of this production. Not that it lacked fine actors and sharply differentiated performances. What it does lack, in the broadest sense, is design. The set is cluttered and unlovely. The costumes are fine, but the idiom with which they are associated is insufficiently lively to carry off the whole evening. That bowler hat proves subversive to the total effect.

The London contingent is represented by John Woodvine as a gigantically bloated Falstaff, practically incapable of raising himself off the bed, but conducting a continual conversation with the audience through the medium of his great grey eyebrows. John McEnery, Teddy Kempner and Norman Tyrrell provide variously shaped versions of violence and delinquency as Pistol, Nym and Bardolph respectively.

Nicholas Gecks, to whom the majority of the play's small amount of poetry is allotted, takes the straight romantic role of Fenton, to which he brings a mildly exotic quality. The Gloucestershire trio are led by Patrick Godfrey as Justice Shallow, a cross between the doddering and the dangerous, and an extremely effective piece of acting. David Threlfall, whose offbeat Mark Antony I particularly admired at Stratford last year, couples ineffectiveness and timidity with continual nervous activity to put across the character of Abraham Slender, while Timothy Spall has created out of nothing a moronic and highly noticeable Peter Simple.

Of the citizens of Windsor, we have Bob Peck at his most genial and unflappable as the pipe-smoking George Page, with Jane Downes as his wife and Cathryn Harrison in the somewhat thinly written part of the daughter. Mistress Ford is played by Susan Tracy, with only the ghost of a fault, namely that when she pretends to be exceedingly upset at the imminent return of her husband, she sometimes forgets that she is supposed to be acting badly, and makes the whole performance unconvincingly convincing.

11 May 1980

Nicholas Nickleby *(RSC, ALDWYCH)*

Roger Rees, the star of the RSC's *Nicholas Nickleby* (Aldwych) is not the sort of actor whose personality vanishes into the role he is playing. If I think of him as Tusenbach in *Three Sisters*, or as Semyon in *The Suicide*, or now as Nicholas, varied though these current roles are, what comes to my mind is not what differentiates the performances, but what they have in common. The personality of Mr Rees seems to have been schooled in the expectation of imminent disaster. The nervous activity of face and limbs is evidence of an extreme attentiveness to whatever may be happening around him. In other people, such an attentiveness might indicate something self-seeking, In the case of Mr Rees, it smacks rather of self-protection. Experience has taught him that all is not going to be well. Indeed, I can think of few actors who are better at conveying, through facial expression alone, a frank acquaintance with grief.

It was a good move to cast such an engaging actor in the part of young Nickleby, not because his personality closely resembles that of the Dickens hero, but because a striking character was required to add savour to the original. Dickens's writing bears a close affinity to a kind of satirical drawing in which the artist is fully at ease when depicting a specifically evil type, or a comic type, but hard-put to delineate a good or admirable character. It is easy to find the face which will express the quality of greed, or cruelty, or pride. It is hard to draw loyalty, or truthfulness, or general uprightness.

What then is the character of Nicholas, as depicted by Dickens? I should say little more than uprightness, tempered with a forgivable hotness of youthful disposition (for which the author later apologised in a Foreword). Let uprightness set off on the road, accompanied by innocent suffering in the shape of young Smike, and you have the framework of Dickens's novel. Put the thing on stage and you may well find the story sagging in the middle, because of the conventionality of its central figures.

This, I take it, was the most serious danger in Trevor Nunn and John Caird's vast directional enterprise, and it was well solved. Not only does Mr Rees prove well worth watching for eight and a half hours solid; David Threlfall too, by means of an extraordinarily faithful and detailed clinical observation, turns the portrayal of Smike into a theatrical tour de force. This is the most dangerous piece of acting in the show. It is one thing to play the comic simpleton in an incidental role (Abraham Slender in the *Merry Wives*). It is quite another to play a spastic youth at the very centre of attention.

Smike, with his trailing limbs and his grotesquely sunken eyes, is the symbol of all that is profound in the play – of everything that prevents it becoming (what it occasionally threatens to become) simply a gigantic and enjoyable romp. Smike is Ralph Nickleby's sin made flesh. He is the representative victim of the huge and various society portrayed on the stage.

The hugeness of the society is a great source of theatrical interest. Normally, when directors wish to vary the conventions of contemporary theatre, they tend naturally to scale down, rather than up. The reasons are partly economic and partly puritanical. There is a feeling that what is purely theatrical – essential theatre – must be created out of extremely limited resources. You stand up and make a speech. I throw a rotten egg. The essential theatre meets the essential critic.

But of course this kind of essential theatre is one of many competing brands. It is essential for a certain kind of musical that it should have a large chorus and magnificent costumes – otherwise it doesn't work. It was deemed essential in dramatising *Nicholas Nickleby* that as much as possible of the original should remain. In other words, the scope of the book was taken as an essential feature, and was preserved in David Edgar's really excellent adaptation.

The result is that after a while one begins to be reminded of opera. Quite apart from the fact that the play actually contains, in addition to a long scene from a happy version of

Romeo and Juliet, a cod Italian opera and several musical numbers written by Stephen Oliver, there is a grandeur of conception and a breadth of movement which most plays just do not achieve. It takes some time, at the start, to become used to the scale of the piece. One feels at first that too much explanation is being offered. Then one reflects that one way or another there is a great deal of explaining to be done. Then one relaxes, settles back, and has a good time.

If occasionally the style undergoes an abrupt change, or some striking innovation in group movement and mime interrupts the flow, one has to remember that, the scale being such, there is plenty of time for the prevailing idiom to reassert itself. For instance, the *Romeo and Juliet* sequence does indeed, as has been objected, go on rather a long time. But who cares? Say it's five minutes too long – what's five minutes out of five hundred? The scale permits it.

Unfortunately, my own scale does not permit me to go into further detail about the major performances from John Woodvine, Edward Petherbridge, Susan Littler, Janet Dale, Bob Peck, Suzanne Bertish, Graham Crowden, Lila Kaye, and vast numbers more. It is worth seeing both parts of the play. It is foolish to see them in the wrong order, but probably wise to go on different nights. It is a marvellous show and a very valuable experiment.

29 June 1980

Hamlet (STRATFORD)
The Fool (STRATFORD, OTHER PLACE)

Think of what has sometimes let Michael Pennington down as an actor, and one finds a fault which the new Stratford *Hamlet* deploys as a virtue. This is a certain prunish quality which lies in ambush for his better moments. Mr Pennington knows that his great strength derives from an ability to deliver lines softly, with exquisite accuracy and at the same time with force. Poetry is safe in his hands – safer than in any other Stratford hands. He will not drop it. If I picture this actor in a typical moment, I imagine the eyes downcast and the voice lowered rather than raised for emphasis. The ambush, at such moments, comes from a subversive smile which tends to threaten the lower region of the face. It is not narcissism, although it is reflexive. All too easily it can turn, for instance, compassion into condescension, or human warmth into a cold display of virtue.

Now here we have the third *Hamlet* of the year – Hamlet, Prune of Denmark. Where other productions tend to imply that the hero used to be basically an awfully good chap and a hell-raiser before these latest difficulties overcame him, John Barton's production, from the word Go, sets the Prince at a considerable distance from his friends. It is typical that the line to Horatio, 'We'll teach you to drink deep ere you depart,' is delivered with bitter irony. Hamlet is not saying, 'We'll go off and get smashed.' He is saying: 'You'll find us a court full of drunks.'

This is a consistent reading. It is consistent with the Prince's later attack on the habits of the court, and consistent with his moralising in the direction of Ophelia and his mother. But there is a price paid in terms of the sympathy of the audience, when part of what would establish some intimacy with the Prince, through the medium of Horatio (Tom Wilkinson), is carefully laid aside. In place of the back-slapping good fellow, there are moments in the soliloquies when the Prince shows a touchingly desperate awareness of his own deficiencies. We sympathise with the man in his solitude more than in company. Perhaps we do not sympathise enough, but if so what we lose in engagement is compensated in terms of clarity. From his first speech to his mother, Hamlet makes it clear that he wants everything he says to be absolutely understood. Mr Pennington faces the famous bits head on, and is right to do so. This is a distinguished performance.

But I wish there was more to support it from the production. The greatest single failing of the RSC at the moment is design. I don't think this is necessarily the designer's fault: the directors, as far as I can make out, are in love with music, and couldn't care less about the visual side of a production. Here, Ralph Koltai supplies a square stage on which the action takes place, and a few old props for background. The design derives from a conception of the production (emphasised by a programme note) in which *Hamlet* becomes very much a play about acting.

This is all very well, but the vacancy of the stage forbids the imagination to construct Elsinore. There is no palace life going on around Hamlet. There is no sense of a court. The castle does not exist, for the audience, from the battlements to the cellarage, in the way that it did in the Royal Court production. There are no great exits, and the only great entrances are through the trap. No, come to think of it, there is one great entrance which seems to have been borrowed from ballet, when Mr Pennington leaps in from the wings, lands in the centre of stage and exclaims: 'To be or not to be. That is the question!' Then he pauses a moment as if to say: There, I've said it!

At The Other Place, the other half of the Stratford company is giving Edward Bond's play, *The Fool*. This work insinuates that John Clare's poetic voice was silenced by incipient capitalism, which first drove him mad and then had him locked up. I doubt this very much. I do not think capitalism destroyed Clare as a writer, just as I do not think that socialism (or whatever it is supposed to be) will ever turn Edward Bond into anything other than an execrable poet. I don't deny that there are some arresting scenes in this play (particularly as directed by Howard Davies) – but the conception of the piece is so banal, and its working out so predictable, that as a piece of writing it bored me rigid.

James Hazeldine takes its main part, to which he brings a relaxed manner and a frankness of sexuality which is always convincing. I liked Domini Blythe's gypsy performance, Edwin Richfield's personation of the wicked Lord Milton, and Anton Lesser as the peasant rebel and victim. There is a very good fight (much better than the duel in the *Hamlet*) between Timothy Walker and Abraham Osuagwu.

6 July 1980

A Lesson from Aloes *(COTTESLOE)*
One Fine Day *(RIVERSIDE)*
Shakespeare's Sonnets *(OLIVIER)*

Betrayal is the theme of *A Lesson from Aloes*, which Athol Fugard wrote, and which he directs at the Cottesloe. There is the treachery which sabotages a great cause, and the treachery which abandons it. Both demand to be understood. Mr Fugard's great strength in this work derives from an intimate knowledge of defeat and the consequences of defeat. At least, it seems to me that those who really know what defeat is are in a better position to lead their companions to victory.

At one stage, the Afrikaner hero makes a plain distinction between a natural disaster, like drought, and a man-made catastrophe, like the political system in South Africa. Nothing can be done about the first. Everything can, and must, be done about the second. The optimistic credo is plainly set forth, and then tested against the experience of the three characters.

The Afrikaner, originally a farmer, is now living in double isolation, because of his espousal of the black cause, and because his political colleagues imagine that he has in fact been a police informer all along. His wife, a study in neurotic determination, has never embraced the cause, but has had her life destroyed by it nevertheless. Thirdly, there is the coloured activist, whose example first drew the Afrikaner hero into politics. His will has at last been broken, and he is about to leave South Africa for England.

What emerges most strikingly from the interaction of the three is the sense of an experience shared between black and white, protester and non-protester. It is like the experience shared by front-line soldiers of opposing sides in a war, an experience which paradoxically binds them, since no one could possibly understand what they have suffered. The aloes which provide the metaphor exist in innumerable varieties, but the harsh climate in which they must survive is one and the same.

The intense interest in watching the Market Theatre Company, who have brought the play from Johannesburg to the National, derives in great measure from non-theatrical considerations. There is nothing illusory here. This is not a play about protest so much as a genuine act of political protest taking place before one's eyes and, in the presence of such articulate courage, criticism does well to confine itself to applause. It is impressive to reflect that the conventions within which this play is written were established by realist drama around a century ago. Realism still thrives in the theatre, as in no other art. It thrives where courage is required, in societies where it is still the practice that the messenger is punished for the bad news that he brings.

At the Riverside Studios, Nicholas Wright's *One Fine Day* opens a season of five plays featuring predominantly black actors. This first play is set in an African people's republic loosely based on Tanzania. It shows an English polytechnic lecturer, a man who, while priding himself on his having outgrown the attitudes of imperialism, manages to exhibit the exact equivalent of those attitudes in a modern socialist form. Nothing can shake the lecturer's sense of justification, even when events around him rapidly demonstrate that the society with which he is meddling is much more complex than he can grasp.

It is a funny play, and terribly interesting. It shows you the mechanics of an African village economy, and the concomitant racism in the relations between Indians and Blacks. It manages to suggest very swiftly and convincingly a society living on entirely different lines from those of the all-too-recognisable lecturer. And yet the playwright does not abandon his Englishman to the mercies and laughter of the audience. Some lingering respect for him preserves him alive, up to a highly touching and ambiguous final scene.

At the National again, but this time in the Olivier Theatre,

Simon Callow gave a dramatic reading of the more-or-less complete Sonnets of Shakespeare. The point was to test the theories of a man called John Padel, which involved a new order for the sonnets, and the providing of a background story based on Mr Padel's research, but presented as if it were bare fact.

As it happened, the 'facts' offered made very little sense, beyond what one already knew from the sonnets as they stand in the 1609 Quarto, and there were occasions when the whole presentation seemed cranky, not to say bonkers. Whether this crankiness is entirely the fault of Mr Padel, I rather doubt. I think a great deal of the blame can be attributed to a conspiracy between the vanities of the director, Michael Kustow, and the actor Mr Callow.

Vanity in actors is a necessary quality – no one would act without a touch of the peacock. But vanity in directors is an absolute menace. Mr Kustow has plenty of experience in poetry readings, and he should know that an audience's capacity to absorb concentrated verse is strictly limited. A very few of Shakespeare's sonnets can be understood on first reading, but most require a second or third examination, plus some expert elucidation, before appreciation can even begin.

What I objected to, after a few hours of listening to Mr Callow, was that once the brain had given up trying to follow the precise sense of the sonnets themselves, one was left simply with the fictional Shakespeare of Mr Kustow and the grotesque ordeal of Mr Callow. The latter was wildly applauded at the end – but not by me. If he had spent his time with a ferret down his trousers, or stuffing his face with hard-boiled eggs, I might have been impressed.

As it was, he had been sometimes reciting, sometimes reading, sometimes forgetting, and very often mangling Shakespeare. It was not a pretty sight. When he really went off-course, it was usually in the most famous sonnets. 'That time of year thou mayst in me behold' was the worst victim. Then there was a moment at which it seemed as if rough buds were about to shake the darling winds of May.

But worse than this was the deliberate device of running the sonnets together in order to make 'poems' out of three or four of them. That the sonnets sometimes fall into a sequence is news to no one. But they remain sonnets nevertheless. They are individual poems, and each one ends with a couplet, a characteristically Shakespearian device which tends to emphasise finality. To pretend that these couplets do not exist, to slur through them, or introduce specious ligatures between one sonnet and the next is simply crass. It is to advertise a distrust of the poet one is pretending to promote.

Finally, it must be said that Mr Callow, engaging though he can be, does not have anything like the range required to sustain a solo performance for over three hours. His voice is at its most natural in the upper register. All its colouring and best effects stem from a kind of exasperation, which is the feeling through which the actor typically chooses to indicate all other feelings. He is like an artist who paints only in sepia, or draws only in red chalk. In his chosen medium, he is a master. Outside of it, he becomes affected.

13 July 1980

The Elephant Man *(LYTTELTON)*
A Dying Business *(RIVERSIDE STUDIOS)*
Scrape Off The Black
(RIVERSIDE STUDIOS)

The Elephant Man by Bernard Pomerance arrives at the National with success in Hampstead and on Broadway already to its credit, but there's many a slip in the transition between small and large theatre, and there was no guarantee that this transfer would be successful. In fact, from the start, I felt that the production sat easily on the Lyttelton stage, which had been appropriately encased in a set reminiscent of a white-tiled hospital interior. There was no sense of a gap between audience and players. Quite the reverse. Tanya McCallin's settings and Roland Rees's production worked smoothly and without question.

What an odd experience it is. There is a fascination which derives from the subject matter itself. A man of unbelievable deformity, of unparalleled physical repulsiveness, is discovered in a freak show. He is saved from the miseries of fairground existence in order to become a friend of Victorian high society. He becomes, as it were, a superior brand of freak. He receives his Royal Warrant.

Stage three in the process is provided by the author of this play, who rescues the Elephant Man from the misery of historical relegation to the London Hospital Museum. He is brought to a small booth in Swiss Cottage known as the Hampstead Theatre, where critical attention assures him a livelihood on Broadway and later on the South Bank. We see the original photographs of the naked hero, and beside them a naked actor shows us how a normally constituted body can give a quite astonishing imitation of deformity.

This is immensely effective as theatre, although the more I thought about the play afterwards, the less I was convinced by

96

its profundity of message. The central theme is the relationship between the superficially deformed Merrick (David Schofield) and the 'superficially' normal and benevolent surgeon, Treves (Peter McEnery). We are supposed to examine Treves and the values of the society to which he belongs, and to find them in their own way grotesque and freakish.

It is at this stage that I fail to be convinced by Mr Pomerance. Any number of accusations against Victorian society can be established with ease, but I fail to see precisely what was supposed to be wrong with the ethos of the London Hospital. The progress of Victorian medical science strikes me as quite simply progress. It was not a case, as Mr Pomerance implies, of trying to prune and crop and pollard people in order to fit in with a conception of an ordered world. It was a question of saving their lives. I can't see what's wrong with this.

But one doesn't have to go to the National for Mr Pomerance's message. One goes for the intrinsic interest of the story told, and for fine performances, such as Mr McEnery's as Treves, and that of the beautiful and clear-voiced Jennie Stoller as Mrs Kendal. Above all, there is Mr Schofield's personation of the Elephant Man himself, which is uniquely affecting, and quite unlike anything one has ever seen anywhere before.

The Riverside Studios have brought in two more works under their 'Plays Umbrella'. In *A Dying Business*, by Mustapha Matura, Malcolm Fredericks plays a young Trinidadian returned from London with a sense of his own newly-acquired sophistication, and a bright idea for turning his father's funeral into a profitable racket. The notion is to induce the local hoorays to outbid each other in contributions to a bogus memorial fund. London education is thus pitted against local know-how in the pursuit of dollars.

It makes a pleasant, light comedy, although I felt that Michael Joyce's direction must be somewhere at fault when quite funny lines failed to induce laughter. It is true that, as often happens in dialect plays, the audience was divided between those with, and those without, the lingo. What made

London chuckle was not necessarily the same as what had Trinidad rolling in the left aisle. And perhaps Mr Matura had not entirely made up his mind as to whom he was going to amuse. For instance, it was noticeable that a sudden injection of bawdy in the last scene proved highly effective with Trinidad. Perhaps there should have been more of this.

Lucia Lijertwood was the great attraction of the show, in her role as the dead man's former hot water bottle, and now professional mourner. She displayed a marvellous inability to sit down in her tight skirt without revealing great lengths of best underwear. Her mood was always her own, whatever was happening around her, and the final impression was that of a clearly-conceived and believable character. Joe Marcell, bright-eyed and with a keen interest in the misfortunes of his friends, vied with Rudolph Walker, the local conspicuous consumption specialist.

The play could have been better edited (for instance, it seemed at one point to end, and afterwards was somewhat heavily explanatory); the same goes for Tunde Ikoli's *Scrape Off The Black*, a one-act study of half-caste existence in London. This was directed by Peter Gill, and I am quite certain it would have been better directed if Mr Gill had set out in a more critical spirit, less sentimentally convinced of the worth of the piece in question.

Consider what the play was about. It established that it was ghastly to have a totally selfish mother who behaved like a pig, and it went on to show that if, in addition, you were half-caste, and had no hope in life beyond a series of abysmal jobs, life was even more ghastly.

With all respect, these points can be quickly understood. They do not need laborious proof. If we are told that the mother spends all day, every day at bingo, we recognise, with all the speed of cliché, what sort of mother she is going to be. We do not need to hear all that much more about the matter. Mr Gill's directorial style seemed to have far too high an opinion of the play's, and the actors', ability to survive merciless exposure to the elements. A great play about claustrophobia might survive on the wide-open Riverside stage. A more humble work, depicting a colourless existence in a wretched apartment, would be helped by being set within three walls.

But here one comes up against the theatrical ideology of these productions, where the word 'spare' is considered automatically to have great value, where simplicity equals virtue. I say, a fig for simplicity, if the result of simplification is the pointing-up of the faults rather than the virtues of the play. Alison Chitty's designs at the Riverside have elegance and finish. They are not always built to the best specifications.

An exception is her design for *One Fine Day*, which manages to reproduce on a large scale all the freshness and vitality of a notebook sketch, a swift jotting. The pleasure of sketchbooks is the pleasure of reading the artist's pure handwriting. In this case, one sensed the spontaneous personality of the designer. It is a good personality to have on stage. It adds to the total sum of enjoyment. I wish in general that directors would not consider designs to be a necessary evil, or as something theatrically inauthentic. One wants to see designers do more than merely laying out elegant floors.

20 July 1980

Sisterly Feelings *(OLIVIER)*
The Browning Version, Harlequinade
(LYTTELTON)

An unusually light week provided a welcome opportunity to catch up with two of the National Theatre's productions and in particular to see the work of a favourite actress, Penelope Wilton. Since recently moving to Oxford, I have developed a new scientific measure of theatrical excellence: something about the play, production or performance must last at least as far as Didcot. These nightly journeys home can be unlovely experiences, and one requires the companionship of a pleasant impression. Your average performance will seem pretty insignificant at Paddington, let alone Pangbourne. Miss Wilton, on the other hand, not only stays with you as far as Didcot: she sees to it that you make your connection.

How is this effect achieved? I suppose that her greatest talent is for suggesting the unspoken, unscripted inner turmoil of a character. One thinks of her quietly boiling with rage at the edge of the action, waiting for an appropriate entrée. Or one thinks of her, in Alan Ayckbourn's *Sisterly Feelings* (Olivier), conceiving a passion for Stephen Moore, and then seeing to it that a minimum of time should elapse between requital and consummation. One thinks of certain tricks: there is a way she has of dropping her jaw without opening her mouth, thereby distorting the line of her lips in a manner indicative of a suppressed but powerful emotion.

This serves in tragedy – in *Othello* she turns a minor low-life character into a considerable stage presence. In comedy, it provides the base-line for the performance. She sees to it that we know what she is thinking before she opens her mouth. Then she is at liberty to surprise us with false sweetness, or in some other way to play off what she says against what we know she feels. The voice is natural and unaffected, but quick as a flash with an insinuation or with mockery or with false or

100

with real charm. Real charm, I guess, must by definition elude definition, since false charm always gives itself away through self-consciousness.

If charm is one of the qualities which lasts as far as Didcot, it is always charm as evinced by a character of great passion and will-power. Perhaps will-power is the quality upon which Miss Wilton's other virtues depend.

The Ayckbourn play, in the version I saw on Tuesday, shows Miss Wilton desperate to steal her sister's boyfriend, an amiable athlete played by Mr Moore. In due course, Miss Wilton convinced Mr Moore that there was much more to her than there was to her sister, much more by way of, as she insinuated, spiritual ambition of a kind which might lead to all manner of exciting and enlarging experiences. Having set up this promising situation, the playwright then proceeds, in his equable fashion, to expose not only the limitations of the boyfriend but also the shallowness of the heroine's spirituality. It is rare, we are reminded, that passion survives a night under canvas in quite the same form. Indeed at the end of the play the two sisters are agreed that Mr Moore was the kind which passes like ships in the night. He was without significance.

And that, one might say, applies to this comedy. It is without significance, not because it fails to achieve significance but because significance is placidly ruled out by the author. There is enough – but only just enough – to keep one happy to the end of the evening. I must say though that the idea of going back in order to see how events might have gone differently with another spin of the coin, when the play is perfectly clear about its own triviality, seems to me quite out of the question.

The Rattigan double bill at the Lyttelton is supposed to give you one profound and one pleasant experience: one must weep and then have a good roll in the aisles. But just as this seems a somewhat schematic division, so, as it turns out, Rattigan over-directs the emotions in *The Browning Version*, and under-directs them in *Harlequinade*. The sentimentality of the first play is manifested as much in its harshness as its softness. There are perhaps more evil women than Mrs Crocker-Harris to be found in Strindberg, but the world in which they move is made consistently more evil with them. It is sentimental to imagine that the husband and lover of a woman so evil can extract themselves, finally, with so little difficulty and upon such gentle prompting. A man who has been fool enough to fall initially into such clutches would be stuck.

The gentle prompting comes in the famous moment when the schoolboy Taplow gives his old schoolmaster the Browning version as a farewell present. The schoolmaster breaks down at the thought that somebody in the place actually likes him, the wife seeks to discredit Taplow's motives in order to wound her husband, the lover is appalled at the wife's behaviour, the marriage and the affair dissolve at one and the same time. All this places a pretty insufferable burden on the single gesture of Taplow – although, by making the boy's motives somewhat ambiguous, Rattigan does pull the trick off. It is, is it not, a most committedly homosexual play? What's wrong with public school life, it says, is the presence of these terrible women. The rest of the world might have imagined that it was the absence of women which caused the trouble.

27 July 1980

Hedda *(ROUND HOUSE)*

In the first dumb-show we see General Gabler bringing his daughter to heel. In the next it is Hedda's turn to mount her father's back and whip him round the stage. Ejlert Loevborg drops in at Mademoiselle Diana's brothel for some comfort at the mouth of the proprietress; but the face that resurfaces after attending to his midriff is that of Hedda. Another client of the establishment is the old general himself in his silver Lurex uniform. His daughter is not slow to meet his requirements.

For this is, or should have been re-entitled, Hedda Gobbler, the 'free adaptation' of Ibsen's classic at the Round House, written and directed by Charles Marowitz. He is a queer sort of director, Mr Marowitz. His last production in London, *Ubu*, was one of the least funny things I have ever seen. His *Hedda*, on the other hand, is a hoot.

Sometimes the laughter was on the same side as the director. Sometimes it was against him, as when the spectacular entrance of General Gabler's enormous pistol, big enough for the heroine to mount, was greeted by an indulgent titter. A director should be worried when his most striking effects are greeted with a laugh which seems to say: Dear old Charles, he will have his fun and games.

The way Ibsen wrote this play, it is shocking. After a course in anabolic steroids from Mr Marowitz, it is merely grotesque. To give a famous example, when Hedda burns the manuscript, whispering, 'Now I am burning your child, Thea. You with your curly hair. Your child and Ejlert Loevborg's. I am burning it – burning your child.' This sudden insight into mad passionate and truly murderous hatred must be shocking, excepting to the most jaded theatrical appetite. But in a version which pretends to uncover throughout the hidden psychology and the emotional mechanics of the play, every moment aspires to be as shocking as this. With fatal consequences.

One does not see the play. One sees the interpretation. That is, Mr Marowitz's reading is dramatised throughout. But the reading itself is not only remorselessly unambiguous, and therefore insulting to the intelligence of the audience; it is also pitiably wide of the mark. It falls for the idea that the rivalry between Hedda's husband Tesman and Loevborg is important on a deeper than academic level. But the most shocking thing about Hedda's action in burning Loevborg's manuscript is that it is directed solely against Loevborg and Thea. There is no element of protectiveness towards her husband. Hedda could not care less about her husband's career. She has no conception of it.

In order to enact his reading, Mr Marowitz has doubled the size of the cast. The theatrical profession will thank him for this, but the fans might pause to wonder at the effect. So much that is characteristic of Ibsen has already been lost (the subtlety, the play between hidden motivation and superficial explanation) that it may seem a trivial point to mourn over.

Nevertheless it is worth mentioning that the smallness of the cast (six in the original) was one of the striking modern features of the play in Ibsen's time, and one of the cleverest technical innovations; the old general, the aunt who dies unseen and unvisited by Hedda, the scarlet woman whom Loevborg goes to see and in whose personal description Hedda takes a brief but sharp interest – all these invisible characters are indeed vital, but they are part of the vivid off-stage world which the play creates.

Ibsen's chief rival, Björnstjerne Björnson, had an explanation for this innovation, which he confided to the Munich publisher, Korfiz Holm: 'Holm, have you ever observed how the refined little apothecary, which is what he [Ibsen] is, in every new play that he writes, only puts five or six people on the stage, because he knows very well that there isn't one theatre in the world that has more than five or six really excellent actors. But as for me, when I write my plays, I of course cannot let my inspiration be restricted by such cold calculations – what?'

I need hardly add that time has been kinder to the cold calculations, if that is what they were, of the apothecary, than it has to the free and untrammelled inspiration of Björnstjerne Björnson. But the wisdom of Mr Marowitz has chosen to follow the later genius. He has the help of two excellent actresses in Jenny Agutter and Kathryn Pogson. Miss Agutter in particular, with her way of tilting her head forward and gazing upwards, reminds one of a turn-of-the-century Symbolist representation of sinful sensuality. She is beautiful, horrible and alive.

The cast is striking, the design by Timian Alsaker is strong, and Mark Henderson's lighting is fine. The production is speedy and always attractively grouped. It reminds one, with its bright costumes, of a ballet. But the reading it represents, the interpretation, is irredeemably second-rate and displays Mr Marowitz as a vainglorious bore.

10 August 1980

Galileo *(OLIVIER)*
Baal *(WAREHOUSE)*
Othello *(RSC, ALDWYCH)*

When we first see Galileo he is handed to us, as it were, on an enormous tray, from the vast depths of the Olivier Theatre. He is a heavily built man in his prime. He is just about to consume a large breakfast. And when we last see him, he is tucking in to an extra dinner, sensual as ever but by now broken with age. He arrives ever so slowly at the beginning, and his withdrawal is ever so slow, as if he were coming towards us out of history itself, and as if at the end it were history and the now measurable universe swallowing him up.

I do not know when it was, exactly, that this production established itself in my mind as a great work of art. I was not expecting to be so terribly moved – I have an intense dislike for the majority of Brecht's work, a dislike which extends to plays which many theatregoers find perfectly palatable. *The Caucasian Chalk Circle*, for instance, strikes me as an epic casuistry, gratuitously offered by art for the comfort of Stalinism. But *The Life of Galileo* is not like that. It is both profound and terrible.

Howard Brenton, in the complacent introduction he provides to his sometimes inept translation, considers the play to be Communism's answer to *Paradise Lost*. But the theme of *Galileo* is reason and justice; it is up to the audience to decide how far these are qualities represented by Communism. Galileo considers that he has betrayed science; if we think of him as to some extent a self-portrait of Brecht, one might well say that Brecht betrayed the truth by his silence about Stalinism. But the experience of Galileo, submission of the integrity to temporal powers, is universal; it was the shared experience of the German opposition to Hitler, whether in exile or at home. Even exile represented a kind of submission.

106

One should not think of this play as an allegory. One should think of it literally, in terms of the story it tells. That is the primary interest, but the great resonance of the story derives from the way it reflects the 'intellectual disgrace' of the mid-century. When Galileo's former pupil (played by Michael Thomas) returns to his old master, and must conduct a conversation in front of an old priest and embittered daughter, and must therefore hear Galileo saying the opposite of what he thinks, that is the prelude to the great climax, and that is the central humiliation of the play.

The production is by far the best thing now showing in London. The design, by Jocelyn Herbert, gets to grips architecturally with the whole of the space available, a space unparalleled in our theatres, but one which has proved very difficult to manage. John Dexter directs, the lighting is by Andy Phillips, and together these three show off the Olivier as a marvellous theatre, as opposed to a concrete white elephant. Mr Dexter's production has splendour of scale, economy or lavishness of means where appropriate. It fixes in the mind a series of stage pictures, of which the last two – Galileo's study and the typically Brechtian scene of common life on the epic scale – are the most beautifully thought out, while the robing of the Pope is the most splendid.

But, of course, this is the great triumph of Michael Gambon, who plays Galileo. One had always thought of Mr Gambon as a man with a secret – whether in light comedy, or when indicating the prolonged pain of an unhappy affair; in *Galileo* the secret is projected on to the large screen. It proves crippling. The virtues of the performance I find impossible to analyse, partly because they are not the kind of virtues, like tricks, which draw attention to themselves; partly because what happens to Mr Gambon seems to happen between scenes. Suddenly he is much older, his face is distorted, his body becomes painful, he is transformed. But this is not a question of make-up. It is a question of quite superb portrayal, as the hero staggers under the weight of his own silence, his disappointment at his personal shortcoming in view of the greatness of his genius.

To see where Brecht started out from, I recommend the

RSC's production of his first play *Baal* (Warehouse), an anarchic portrayal of the sinister side of the romantic poet as hero, lawless genius on the rampage in the forest. This is the pre-political Brecht and it is in many ways hard to fathom. The translation by Peter Tegel is rotten, which doesn't help. But it is compellingly and quite rebarbatively acted by Ben Kingsley, excellently directed by David Jones and designed by Ralph Koltai.

Macaulay once suggested, in his essay on Machiavelli, that to an Italian audience in the fifteenth century the conduct of Othello would have inspired nothing but detestation and contempt. However, 'the conduct of Iago they would have assuredly condemned; but they would have condemned it as we condemn that of his victim. Something of interest and respect would have mingled with their disapprobation. The readiness of the traitor's wit, the clearness of his judgment, the skill with which he penetrates the dispositions of others and conceals his own, would have ensured to him a certain portion of their esteem.'

The northern audience always sympathised with the Moor. The southern, Macaulay suggests, would have been on the side of his ensign. I think that in a contemporary theatre the house must always divide its sympathies; the leading player must struggle to avoid our condemnation, while Iago must take care that he does not, through an excess of bravura, bring the whole play crashing down around his ears. In the days of the one-star company, the days conjured up by Ronald Harwood's *The Dresser*, there would have been a way of dealing with the obstreperousness of Bob Peck.

Contemporary ideology, however, insists that Iago should have his say. So, in Ronald Eyre's strong production at the Aldwych, Donald Sinden must fight, in every moment at his disposal, to gain our northern respect; while, as soon as his back is turned, and Mr Peck has the audience to himself again, our southern sympathies are once more brought into play. It is worth going a long way to see this *Othello*, which is more than a contest between two men – it is a contest between two styles of acting. Mr Sinden, by his upturned face alone and his heroic bearing, reminds us of the great theatre of the past. Where he fails is where the effort shows, where the voice is observed too obviously being put through its paces. Such striving seems completely unnecessary. Mr Sinden is built on a different gauge from the other members of the cast. We know very well that, if provoked, he could blast them off the stage. He should rest more securely in this knowledge.

Mr Peck, unless I am imagining things, has toned down the comic aspect of his Iago, which was verging on the destructive in Stratford last year. The result is to improve even further on the sardonic nastiness of this performance. The character is admirably, and credibly, motivated: one believed that this Iago believed that he had been cuckolded by Othello. There is a moment in Act IV when Emilia (Susan Tracy, first-rate) innocently reminds Iago of the rumour of her infidelity. It caught Mr Peck on the raw. Suzanne Bertish plays an almost over-competent Desdemona; one finds it difficult to see how she could have got herself into this scrape. Gareth Thomas is an honest and innocent Cassio; John McEnery is most striking as Roderigo.

17 August 1980

Edinburgh Festival 1980 (I)

I arrived at the Festival a few minutes late – that is to say, at the split second when Eve sank her teeth into the apple 'whose mortal taste brought death into the world'. The band struck a note of horror. The serpent recoiled in triumph. I peered down from the balcony at an exotic and wonderful scene.

The first impression of the Assembly Hall was of smoky orange gloom, through which a thousand vague lights flickered, as the souls of the dead were once supposed to flicker in Hades. But when the eye grew accustomed to wander to the ceiling, it became apparent that these flickering lights were encased in the strangest of shades. There were aluminium cheese graters, perforated milk churns and dustbins, with railway lanterns and hurricane lamps – hundreds and hundreds of them. And weaving his way through this monstrous universe came the Almighty All-in Wrestler Himself – Brian Glover as God.

This was Bill Bryden's production of *The Passion*, designed by William Dudley. Part One is new, Part Two is a revival. Part One is derived from a selection of York and Wakefield Mystery Plays, Part Two comes entirely from York. On first viewing I strongly preferred Part One. There is more charm in the poetry, partly because a great deal of it is in rhymed stanzas (of a kind which was employed years later by Robert Burns) rather than alliterative measure. It is hard to listen for long to alliterative poetry without becoming tired of what seems to modern ears its constant striving for effect. There also seemed to be much more dubious updating in the translation of Part Two than in Part One.

But the whole production, with its unending surprises and inventions, constituted a very successful revival of medieval drama. It has a feeling for what is impressive in the simplicity of the original material, both in the poetry and in the stage-craft. Because it aims to re-create an atmosphere of natural

110

piety, it avoids any tone of voice that might be redolent of the piousness of the modern Church. Both in design and in rendition, it is full of reminders of contemporary working-class life. One might be forgiven for thinking that the ultimate object of worship was not God but the modern working man. Christ (Philip Donaghy) is crucified in a boiler-suit. There is no resurrection.

The next item on the official agenda was a Canadian tribute to the Royal Flying Corps's most decorated pilot in World War One: *Billy Bishop Goes to War* (Moray House Gymnasium). From the opening lines ('They were off to fight the Hun, they would shoot him with a gun') it was clear that we were embarking on some very bad poetry indeed, together with some pretty banal and bloody sentiments. I see from my programme that I have noted down the line 'the only way to learn survival is to survive', an example of the play's banal wisdom. As for bloodiness, there was a song which rhymed 'The first Hun I see is the first to die', with the thrown-away observation that 'they burn with a sound like bacon on the fry'.

Some critics have treated this play (which was written, composed and directed by John Gray, who played the piano and sang, in collaboration with Eric Petersen, who did all the acting) as a part-critical, part-sympathetic account of the brutalisation of the hero. I must say that it never occurred to me that it was anything so grand as critical in spirit. I thought it enthusiastically partook of the nauseating thoughtlessness it represented. There were occasional sentimental meditations on the human cost of the war, when such a note seemed conveniently to suit the tempo of the moment. But the overall effect was a shrewd exploitation of the worst blimpery. Mr Petersen's acting was blandly professional enough, although I found the oral flatulence of his aircraft imitations somewhat tedious and repetitive. Mr Gray's piano-playing amounted to a vile percussion. All in all, a ghastly evening.

At the Traverse Theatre Club, I saw the Lyric Hammersmith production of Barry Collins's *The Ice Chimney*: this was a two-hour monologue delivered by Chris Ettridge in the role of Maurice Wilson, an ex-First World War Tommy who tried to

111

climb Everest in the 1930s. Mr Collins has a great deal of ambition but no sense of artistic scale. It is impossible to listen to two hours of stream-of-consciousness prose without tiring very quickly. A much greater degree of organisation (or indeed dramatisation) is needed. Then there is that fatal tendency of Mr Collins to draw attention to all the possible interpretations, in advance of providing the audience with the material on which it might base its own judgements. So we are shown Maurice Wilson as representing the embittered working class of his day in its struggle against its rulers: the spiritual hero engaged in a contest with God: and, most insistently, the sexually inadequate man sublimating his urges through mountaineering.

This last interpretation, once signalled, was quickly grasped, and once grasped rapidly began to lose its interest. It has already been explored (much more profoundly) by Auden and Isherwood in *The Ascent of F6*. But if one interpretation of a hero has insufficient interest, it simply will not do to chuck in a couple more interpretations for good measure. The artist would do much better to retreat from the level of interpretation altogether, and to make sure instead that the reality of his character will survive the act of interpretation. Much better also to ensure that if the audience is to stay with one for two solid hours there is some indication of progression from A to B. We like to feel our efforts are advancing us. In the first few minutes of this play we got to know all about the sexual problems of Maurice Wilson. In the last few minutes we discovered that he was carrying his lover's underwear in his rucksack. But this discovery did not constitute dénouement. It simply underlined, implausibly, what we had already been told. After that, the hero gradually froze to death. The audience, I fancy, had been bored to death long since.

Elsewhere, Ian McKellen and Sheila Allen gave a reading from the writings of D. H. Lawrence and his wife Frieda – a reading which was all sweetness and light until at the very end Frieda referred with some passion to the great fight there had been for the two of them to establish a true relationship. We had neither seen nor heard anything of this fight, and Lawrence himself came over as a totally amicable, quizzical old feller with a heart of gold and a twinkle in his eye.

Meanwhile, at the Military Tattoo, the heights of Edinburgh Castle were descended by hordes of screaming and hitherto invincible Afghan tribesmen, who were duly conquered and slaughtered by our brave lads, in the pouring rain and from a theatrically impossible disadvantage. This was fascinating to behold, and I hope the Russian Embassy have already sent their observers.

24 August 1980

Edinburgh Festival 1980 (II)

Tadeusz Kantor sees the room in which he spent his childhood not as the sunlit idyll of literary convention, but as 'a dead room for corpses'. And this is what he presents in *Wielopole-Wielopole*, which was at Edinburgh last week.

The room of this extraordinary director's memory fills the stage with a clutter of relatives, and a human montage of dead conscripts, dressed in grey uniforms and with faces painted grey. These soldiers exist in a different dimension from the relatives, a dimension of death from which they are again and again to be rescued, and into which they will inevitably slip back. Active among the relatives is a gloating female body-washer, who doubles as group photographer, and whose large camera itself doubles as a machine-gun. People are mown down. People are dragged back to life. Existence is endlessly repetitive, and for ever disintegrating before our eyes.

A most persistent theme is that of the crucifixion of Uncle Jozef, the Priest. Sometimes the live man is crucified. Sometimes he is strung up in effigy. But whenever he undergoes this death, or whenever he is forced to witness his own execution, he seems to accept his fate with a thin smile of resignation, rather as if sainthood had become a dirty vice in which he could not help but indulge. The climax of the piece is a composition based on the Last Supper. It is achieved in the most apparently haphazard manner, with chairs being knocked over and the continual disturbance of unexpected new arrivals.

The composition is no sooner established than, like everything else, it disintegrates. But it lingers in the mind as evidence of Kantor's painterly education. Something of the High Renaissance has survived among the rubble and reconstruction of modern Poland. Inevitably a foreigner must concentrate on such visual aspects of this remarkable company's work. It may sound weird and off-putting. It is weird,

114

but it is also both memorable and convincing – as if Kantor had set himself the task 'Paint Memory, using only human beings as your pigments'.

The RSC arrived with Bill Alexander's travelling production of *Henry IV*, Parts I and II, in which Bernard Lloyd played the King. This was Shakespeare with no monkey business. Stuart Wilson first got things going with an engagingly eccentric Hotspur, a passionate soldier to whom communication of his thoughts did not always come easily. It was a performance which established a foothold in our affections by means of comedy. Hotspur kept a raw carrot in his wallet, from which, as the going got tough, he would occasionally cut off a bite-sized chunk. By the time of his duel with Prince Hal (a dangerous and exciting fight arranged by Malcolm Ranson) his humanity, nobility and vegetarianism were firmly established.

The Prince was gracefully portrayed by David Rintoul, who managed to establish around himself an aura of royalty, even during his unregenerate phase. In the deathbed scene both Mr Rintoul and Mr Lloyd put over their finest speeches with a beautiful clarity. Alfred Marks's performance as Falstaff seemed to come and go, as if the scrupulous avoidance of the stage cliché were involving the actor in too much sacrifice and uncertainty. But Mr Marks had his moments, and was strong on a kind of aggressive passivity with which he attended to what anyone else had to say. Among other performances, I admired very much Juliet Stevenson as Lady Percy, and the ability of Tearsheet to catch a somewhat unhinged manner common in prostitutes who have been on drugs (and presumably not inappropriate in a sack addict).

It was George Steiner's great-great-uncle, Franzos, who discovered the manuscript of Büchner's *Woyzeck* lying on an apothecary's floor, recognised the genius of the piece, and produced the first edition in 1875, forty years after Büchner's death. To him we owe not only the survival of the play and the mis-transcription of the name as *Wozzeck*, but also some interpolated lines. The moment when the child is told of his mother's death is the result of Franzos's touching-up. This provides Berg's opera with an effective final scene, but it should surely be cut out of any modern acting edition. It simply ain't Büchner.

Not that that would stop the National Arts Centre of Ottawa, whose production of *Woyzeck* amounted to a sentimental travesty of a great play. This was achieved with puppets taking the main roles, soldiers manipulating the puppets, and a royal audience providing the voices from an elaborate opera box. So the King (which king? I don't know, but they played 'Rule Britannia' in his honour) read the part of Woyzeck himself, while the King's soldiers pushed a gaunt effigy around the stage. This made no sense at all. Nothing made any sense. Michael Eagan's set looked as if it had been designed by at least three violent enemies, while directors Jean Herbiet and Felix Mirbt contrived to pass over most of the opportunities for pathos, and to provoke sniggers from the audience during the grandmother's sad fairy tale of disillusionment.

A programme note suggested the interpretation: 'the only way to defend oneself against . . . dehumanisation is to discover the ropes used by the "enemy" to manipulate people, the "puppet strings".' But while there are many themes in Büchner's play, there is no evidence of this cliché. In fact, it is hard to conceive of a less appropriate play for puppets to act. Woyzeck is the first hero of European literature to be seen in terms of his biology. In addition to everything else, he is an object of clinical investigation, a guinea-pig *avant la lettre*. Part of the business of being human (and this reflects on the theme of free will) is that, although he cannot stop himself pissing in the street when his bladder is full, he is unable to provide a specimen for the doctor on request. The fact that a man cannot piss at will may be of some scientific interest. The fact that a puppet cannot do so is of no interest at all.

I so loathed the Ottawa version of *Woyzeck* that I decided not to risk the company's second production (Strindberg's *Dream Play*). Instead I trespassed beyond the bounds of my responsibility, into the Scottish Opera's *Wozzeck*. Simply in terms of acting and production, this was a brilliant evocation of the age of expressionism. One saw, vividly, what that age had seen in Büchner. There was an atmosphere akin to that of

Doctor Caligari, but without any element of quaintness or
nostalgic reconstruction. And the acting was among the best
in Edinburgh.

31 August 1980

Timon of Athens
(STRATFORD, OTHER PLACE)

The new *Timon of Athens* at Stratford has been transplanted
from Athens to what looks very like the traditional world of
Japan – an inspired move, in my view, since it allows the
designer, Chris Dyer, a certain exotic freedom while it
emphasises those elements in the story which would be immediately comprehensible to a wide variety of periods and
cultures. Here is a nobleman ruined by his extravagance – a
spectacle familiar to any Japanese merchant of the last
century. And here is a philosopher who has embraced poverty
– the universal hero of the Orient. And here is a soldier
appearing at the gates of the city, to avenge a past wrong. Was
there ever, in the whole age of walled cities, a civilization for
which this experience would be unfamiliar or unthinkable?

Timon of Athens, this savage play which must seem, from
its rareness, more than usually problematical to us, is composed of elements which are as common around the world as
the counting-frame. Yet it appears that Shakespeare left the
work unfinished, and the Arden editor has produced two
speculative reasons. First, if the work is a study of shallow
nobility, then the shallowness of the generous Timon must
work against his ever achieving full tragic status. Secondly, if a
man removes himself entirely from society, where will the
play find its source of dramatic action?

That second reason is less convincing than it may at first
seem. Did not the early dramatists love stories in which the
hero was strapped to a remote crag, and was there not a play
in which the chief character was left behind on an island while
everybody else went off to fight a war? 'Dramatic action' was
not always as energetic – or indeed as active – as we sometimes
assume.

To the cynic Apemantus, the hero Timon is as despicable in
his glory as in his misery. In the days of his fortune, the

philosopher observes Timon among his flatterers. 'It grieves me', he says, 'to see so many dip their meat into one man's blood.' But when the flatterers are dispersed to the four winds, and the hero takes to the woods, the philosopher is pitiless in his mockery:

> What, think'st
> That the bleak air, thy boisterous chamberlain,
> Will put thy shirt on warm? Will these moist trees,
> That have outlived the eagle, page thy heels
> And skip when thou pointst out? Will the cold brook,
> Candied with ice, caudle thy morning taste
> To cure thy o'er-night's surfeit?

(That is: Will the trees follow you like page-boys, and will the brook offer you a hangover cure?) By this stage in the drama, Timon can give as good as he gets, and there follows a virtuoso exercise in ranting.

This is the great dramatic challenge of the play, and there is no getting round it. Timon must rant, but he must rant in such a way that he does not try the patience of the audience. The play works well in a small theatre because in a small theatre the actor need not, and indeed for the most part should not, shout. When Richard Pasco as Timon faced John Carlisle as Apemantus, it was noticeable that the most effective ranting was conducted at the lowest pitch. This was where the production's great love of the text shone forth, as in the following magnificent example of Shakespearian free verse.

Timon asks Apemantus if he would rather cease to be a man and become a beast. When the philosopher assents, Timon replies that this is a beastly ambition, since:

> If thou wert the lion, the fox would beguile thee; if thou wert the lamb, the fox would eat thee; if thou wert the fox, the lion would suspect thee; when peradventure thou wert accused by the ass; if thou wert the ass, thy dullness would torment thee, and still thou liv'dst but as a breakfast to the wolf; if thou wert the wolf, thy greediness would afflict thee, and oft thou shouldst hazard thy life for thy dinner;

119

wert thou the unicorn, pride and wrath would confound
thee and make thine own self the conquest of thy fury; wert
thou a bear, thou wouldst be killed by the horse; wert thou
a horse, thou wouldst be seized by the leopard; wert thou a
leopard, thou wert germane to the lion, and the spots of thy
kindred were jurors on thy life. All thy safety were re-
motion, and thy defence absence. What beast couldst thou
be that were not subject to a beast? And what beast art thou
already, that seest not thy loss in transformation!

I quote this at length in order to display the heraldic beauty
of its design. It is like a wonderful tapestry, which has retained
all its colours. Note the curious details – the horse with its
mortal hatred of the bear, the unicorn (which is at the mercy
of the lion in the branches because, in its fury, it rams the tree
and gets its horn stuck in the trunk). When people compli-
ment a production on doing justice to Shakespeare's poetry,
they are usually referring to what is conceived as a detachable
quality: the scansion of the verse. Thus they may talk about
ignoring the poetry and going for the meaning of the lines – a
pernicious distinction to make. The meaning is the poetry as
much as the sound is. The poetry of this passage derives from
its repetition with variations of an animal motif. It is a poetry
of pattern.

Now if one thinks of the poetry of a play in its broadest
sense, it is clear that a designer's work can contribute to a
realisation of the poetry, just as much as an actor's delivery of
the lines. The brightly coloured kimonos of these noblemen,
the contrasting costumes of scholar, merchant, judge and
particularly those of the warriors – all these came recognisably
from one society, a world with its own estates and ceremonies
equivalent to those of the world Shakespeare knew, but a
world historically (if not geographically) closer to our own.
The use of the abacus, the design of the furniture, the cere-
monial towels – all these touches had their significance.

This is Ron Daniels's production, and I presume that the
taste for bright colour is his. There is a splendid moment when
a long veil is whisked off a new arrival to reveal – a complete
surprise – Abraham Osuagwu as a magnificently plumed

Cupid, who seems to have found his way into the Orient via one of the more spectacular cultures of South America. Most of the acting was excellent. I would note particularly, besides first-rate classical performances from Mr Pasco and Mr Carlisle, James Hazeldine as Alcibiades and Arthur Kohn as the faithful steward.

It is the last mentioned who manages to penetrate the misanthropy of Timon, and to correct it. 'How fain would I have hated all mankind,' says Timon, 'and thou redeemst thyself.' But by this stage it is too late for the dying misanthrope to change his attitude effectually, and the hero's mantle passes from Timon to Alcibiades, whose clemency provides the climax of the piece. The production left me with a feeling of intense and abiding excitement, mingled with an indefinable frustration. Not an inappropriate response, as I afterwards reflected, to an unfinished work of Shakespeare.

14 September 1980

Watch on the Rhine *(LYTTELTON)*
The Duchess of Malfi
(ROYAL EXCHANGE, MANCHESTER)
Oklahoma! *(PALACE)*

Lillian Hellman's *Watch on the Rhine* (Lyttelton) brings the struggle against Fascism into the living room of a large country house near Washington. The year is 1940. The United States is not yet at war. What we see is a mortal combat between a German resistance leader, Kurt (played by David Burke), and a nasty Romanian aristocrat (Sandor Eles). At first, it seems to be a matter of bribery and blackmail. But in the fullness of time, we discover that Kurt's insouciance is a bluff. When the chance comes, he murders his opponent before our eyes.

I was reminded of Auden's 'conscious acceptance of guilt in the necessary murder', the phrase in *Spain* to which Orwell took exception. Orwell disliked the phrase because it could only have been used, he said, by one who had no experience of the sordid reality of murder itself. A similar objection might be levelled against Miss Hellman's murder, and its enactment at the National. It is glib; it's a stage murder. It is supposed to represent the intrusion of European political reality into an American household, but it has so little reality for the playwright that it does not for a moment affect the ability of the characters to indulge in the most sententious speechmaking. David Burke's performance, which could have been so distinguished, breaks down at precisely the point where he commits the murder. After this, he must drag the corpse out of doors and dispose of it, then return to the house, arrange his escape, and bid farewell to his family for ever.

Now a man who has been in mortal combat and subsequently endured the extreme physical exertion of carrying a body some distance would be bound to show the physical effects of the experience. His heart would be racing. He would be certain to tremble. Violent reaction would set in. But we neither saw nor felt that the murder had cost him any effort.

In these final scenes, Miss Hellman's play is as badly written as could be, and it is amazing to me that it was performed in this way without a little elementary revision. The piece could easily have been tidied up, but it could never have become anything other than very poorly constructed and conceived. Peggy Ashcroft's performance is unhappy. John Quayle exerts a generally benign influence, while Susan Engel is the single member of the cast who really touches the heart.

There is an exceedingly handsome set by Eileen Diss, and it is not the fault of Miss Diss that the actors behave on this set without doors as if they had no fear of being overheard, even though what they are discussing is highly secret. Some blame, however, must be shared between the author and the director, Mike Ockrent. This was a strange play to put on, and the production does not justify the choice.

At the Royal Exchange Theatre in Manchester, by contrast, murder became so real that the audience actually heaved and groaned in unison. By the end of *The Duchess of Malfi*, we were thoroughly revolted by the behaviour of the Italians. Antonio's son is introduced on to the corpse-strewn stage, and receives the obeisance of the few survivors of Webster's plot. The tiny child looks as if he fully shares the audience's revulsion, and in the final moments, he is seen looking up into the sunlight, as if questioning the sanity of the Almighty.

This made a splendid closing tableau to a really distinguished production by Adrian Noble. The lines are spoken very quietly, at times almost too quietly; but justice is done to the unbearable richness of the poetry. One admires the speed and daring of the plot; the Duchess has no sooner brought Antonio to her bed than she's had his child, and no sooner had his child than she's had three children by him. Helen Mirren takes this fertile part, which she plays with nervous energy and great attractiveness. Peter Postlethwaite is Antonio, the steward of the household who cannot believe his frightening good fortune at becoming the Duchess's lover. This was a moving performance although sometimes not quite audible. Mike Gwilym had all the raging to do, in the part of the sexually jealous brother who, on the lines:

> I'll go hunt the badger by owl-light;
> 'Tis a deed of darkness

begins to imagine himself to be a wolf. Bob Hoskins plays Bosola, the professional hit-man whose moral ambiguity provides the most interesting conundrum of the play. One is continually surprised and convinced by his performance.

Strange things happen in *Oklahoma!* (Palace Theatre). I have never quite understood, for instance, the surrealistic ambition of the chorus to 'sit at home and tock, and watch the hock making lazy circles in the sky'. The plot line becomes clear, however, when one sees that the villain is in fact the hero, and vice versa. Poor Jud Fry (Alfred Molina), the lonely and exploited farmhand (in two years of sweated labour, he has saved around 40 dollars), is going crazy for the love of Laurey (Rosamund Shelley), his employer. The supposedly sane world conspires to drive him completely round the twist. The plausible, blond hero, Curly (John Diedrichs), shows his truly villainous nature when he suggests in the best song of the musical that the proper course for Jud would be suicide.

This idea haunts our Woyzeck-style hero in his subsequent misfortunes. He is thwarted in love, and driven to the brink of distraction by the prevailing atmosphere of ruthless jollification. He is sacked without compensation by the woman he loves. Finally flipping his lid, he draws a knife in a duel he knows he cannot win. After his death, his killer is acquitted by a cynically-rigged court, with a speed shocking even to some members of the cast. Oklahoma, we are told, is to become a state where the lonely man must conform or die. We understand for the first time the full significance of that chilling phrase, 'plenty of room to swing a rope'. This is a musical about lynch law and mob justice. The first-night audience roared its approval.

21 September 1980

Translations *(GUILDHALL, DERRY)*
Duet for One *(DUKE OF YORK'S)*

An Englishman who prided himself upon his country's long tradition of classical education would be deeply affronted by Brian Friel's new play, *Translations*, which opened in Derry last week. For here we were presented with a picture of nineteenth-century Ireland, in which the peasant in the Hedge School was easily conversant with Latin and Greek literature and mythology, while the English officers were unable to translate, let alone distinguish between, the classical languages and Gaelic.

It was a deeply romantic and charming society which Mr Friel depicted, a country where education was conducted informally, at the end of a day's sweated labour, and where familiarity with classical learning was considered part of normal peasant life. I would have believed more readily in the historical accuracy of the picture had the English officers been less oafishly unlatined. As it was I took the piece as a vigorous example of corrective propaganda: immensely enjoyable as theatre if, like much else in Ireland, gleamingly tendentious.

But propaganda for what? The audience at the Guildhall in Derry included most political viewpoints, and it was an official Unionist who initiated the standing ovation. Dubliners had turned out en masse, but the bulk of the response was local and without apparent sectarian bias. The excitement of the audience was palpable. Applause punctuated the speeches in a way that London only witnesses in opera houses. As a former political correspondent, I am a connoisseur of fake standing ovations. The ovation this production received was genuine.

It was the first production to be staged by the Field Day Theatre Company, which has been founded by Mr Friel and the actor Stephen Rea. Mr Friel comes from Derry, where he is known to his numerous former pupils as 'Scoby' Friel. Mr

Rea is from Belfast. Derry was chosen for the opening night since it no longer has a regular theatre. The peasant house of Consolata Boyle's set was placed on the Guildhall stage where it nestled snugly beneath the magnificent organ.

A great deal of the pleasure of the occasion derived from the sheer achievement of assembling a new company of Irish talent and staging a world première in such surroundings. Mr Rea, an actor for whom I have great admiration, played the role of the well-meaning anglophile involved with a military project of producing a new Ordnance Survey map of the district, a project which involves the fixing and translation of the local place names into forms palatable to the English.

This designing of new maps is taken as the play's chief metaphor for loss of authentic culture. In due course, the cartographic exercise turns into a military operation. Murder is committed. Mass punishment is to be exacted. The idyll is destroyed. From the impressive company I would single out Liam Neeson and Ann Hasson for their performances. The director is Art O'Briain.

Duet for One, the Bush production, has now settled at the Duke of York's, where I revisited it on Thursday.

This is Tom Kempinski's study of a violinist whose career is cut short by multiple sclerosis and who goes, albeit unwillingly, to seek psychiatric help. Opinions have diverged as to the implications of the play – in particular over the final scene. In my view, the presentation of the argument is both clear and profound.

The violinist (Frances de la Tour) arrives in a mood of defensive truculence: yes, her performing career is at an end, but she and her husband are intelligent people, they are able to face up to this sort of thing, and she will find plenty to occupy her now that she is a cripple. The psychiatrist (David de Keyser) can see that a crisis is looming, but he cannot begin to help until his patient admits the size of the problem – that is, until she really accepts that she is his patient.

The play depicts a series of gentle attempts by the psychiatrist to force that admission. When gentleness fails, a sudden access of anger succeeds in precipitating a crisis. In a moving and eloquent speech the violinist explains that playing music is not a job like any other, that for her to lose her art is to lose everything, that psychiatry cannot help her and that she wishes to thank the doctor and to conclude her treatment.

But the paradox of the piece is that in making this speech, in achieving this degree of self-awareness, she has put herself within reach of help. Psychiatry is not magic. It does not have the answer to all her problems. And it is true that nothing will replace music in her life. But psychiatry may help her live with her loss. The patient is right in what she says, but the doctor remains unperturbed. For the moment of her rejection is the moment of his triumph; and her surprised turn of her head, as the doctor suggests that they meet at the same time next week, indicates that she is impressed with his resilience and faith.

28 September 1980

Illuminations *(LYRIC, HAMMERSMITH)*

'Fuck off!' snaps the Labour Home Secretary in Peter Jenkins's new play, *Illuminations* (Lyric, Hammersmith), in reply to a perfectly reasonable inquiry from the *Sunday Times*. It was a moment of authenticity which brought vividly back to me my own days as a Lobby correspondent. I remembered the line as a favourite Denis Healey ploy, but it would do as well for Anthony Crosland, who is obviously the original for Mr Jenkins's Martin Gale. (The scene is Blackpool in Conference season.)

There are some interesting differences between the original and the copy. I shall never forget two dreadful interviews with Crosland shortly before his death. In the first he was quite shatteringly unpleasant, even ruder than the Home Secretary in the play. He thought that he had been fearfully mauled by the press. In fact no politician of recent times was ever treated with more consistent respect. I ventured to suggest that he had firm friends among such celebrated political columnists as Peter Jenkins. Crosland's reply was a venomous accusation of betrayal. (Mr Jenkins had recently dared to disagree with him in print.)

In the second interview, which was called in order to dispel the bad impression created by the first, Crosland apologised graciously but proceeded to ward off any serious question. He admitted that his masterwork, *The Future of Socialism*, had proved mistaken in various ways. When pressed for a reason, he replied with an irrelevant diatribe against the public schools. I thought: this argument is not serious; he is using the public schools as a substitute for an economic analysis. In *Illuminations* the very same accusation is made by the Crosland-figure against the left wing of the Labour Party.

There are moments when Mr Jenkins and Paul Eddington (who plays the Home Secretary) between them conjure up so accurate a picture of Crosland that the effect is startling. At

128

other times it is Mr Jenkins's inaccuracy as a dramatist which produces the astonishment. One should not be surprised when a political pundit fails to reproduce his expertise on stage. But when obvious mistakes are made about, for instance, the Representation of the People Act, this comes surprisingly from an expert.

The chief argument of the play, which I would have expected to be much better presented, is over the abolition of public schools. Henriques, the left wing Employment Secretary (Trevor Martin), favours immediate abolition and the expulsion of Labour Party members who educate their children privately. Gale, the Home Sec, is in favour of the eventual abolition of public schools, through economic attrition. This is not a good basis for an argument over freedom. The left-winger is in favour of an open execution (an honest policy at least), while the right-winger wants to make the death look like an accident.

The Home Sec's boy is in the custody of a divorced wife (this is where the plot bears no relation to the real circumstances of Crosland's life) who has placed the child at Charterhouse. There is no way the Home Sec can interfere with this arrangement, nor does he wish to. Quite so. All he has to do is explain the circumstances in public – but this he is loath to do, since it implies that the Party has a right to interfere in his private affairs. At this point there was still a chance that the play would have some substance – we were pointed in the direction of a psychological study in which the peculiar mixture of principle, arrogance and fastidiousness (a typically Crosland mixture) would prove the reef on which a career is wrecked.

Instead, the militant left were called in to break up a Young Fabian Tea, while the police were brought along to break up the militants. The Prime Minister was roped in to call a general election in two weeks' time (illegal), and a mob was called in to attack the resort's Grand Hotel and set it alight, while the cast sang a song to the effect that they would keep the red flag flying.

In other words, Mr Jenkins gave up writing his play and merely set a match to the story so far. The glaring fault of the work otherwise was the portrayal of Henriques, who bears no conceivable relation to any major Labour Party figure. A realistic hero cannot hold a discussion with a cardboard villain, and it is not surprising that the main debate develops into a third-rate slanging match. The effect of this shoddily constructed piece is to evince a total disgust with the Labour Party. In this sense, of course, Mr Jenkins does betray his old friend and hero, Crosland.

16 October 1980

Show People by Kenneth Tynan

'Most self-delighting and self-damned of men!' This was the judgement Clive James passed on the critic 'Ken Onan', in the poem 'Felicity Fark'. Why, you may ask, self-damned? The poet explains:

> Since Onan, of all people, knows full well
> The deepest hole and hottest seat in Hell
> Are set aside specifically to cater
> For him who to his Talent plays the traitor.

This attack was published in 1975. In the same year Tynan collected the best of his shorter reviews in *A View of the English Stage* (still available in Paladin, essential reading) and many of his best longer essays in *The Sound of Two Hands Clapping*. It was four years before the next volume, *Show People*, was published in the United States. This was the period in which its author failed to write his biography of Olivier (he could not secure his old hero's co-operation) and switched to his memoirs, on which he was at work when he died. If Mr James's judgement and unorthodox theology are right, then Tynan must now be suffering a punishment worse than Hitler's. Or did *Show People* secure his reprieve? Or is Mr James wrong?

What, first of all, was Tynan's talent? To Mr James it was clearly a talent to attack, to put the fear of God into the West End. To theatre people, on the other hand, and to Tynan himself (as is repeatedly made clear in his writings), the essential gift was that of admiration. It was his talent to praise that first set him apart from his elders in the critical profession. This talent is rare. Praise is difficult because the language of praise is very soon repetitive. The talent is rare because many of those with the necessary articulacy are too proud to praise. They think that some virtue is gone out of them when they

131

praise. At the other end of the spectrum – but suffering from the same delusion – are those who love praising precisely as a form of self-abasement (you know the syndrome: 'God, isn't Mozart wonderful, ergo, we must be worms'). When Tynan 'betrayed his talent' (i.e. wrote badly from time to time), it was through an access of untypical abjectness: 'I wept, and there is nothing harder in criticism than to convey one's gratitude for that.'

This opening line in Tynan's review of *South Pacific* (1951) makes me throw up. It is no business of the critic to be grateful, as if he had been hanging round the theatre waiting for a crust to be thrown in his direction, as if a good performance or a great play was something vouchsafed. Nor does the last sentence of the same review do anything to reprieve the author: '. . . I have nothing to do except thank Messrs Logan, Rodgers, and Hammerstein and climb up from my knees, a little cramped from the effort of typing in such an unusual position.'

This is ghastly. It misses the point of dramatic criticism, which is to find the virtues of a performance and make them public. How did Tynan found his career? By writing, in *He That Plays the King*, a better account of the theatre of the 1940s than any of the critics of the time had managed. But in so doing he was conferring virtue on that theatre. As Orson Welles wrote: 'It must be that the theatre is in better shape than we thought it was. Pray accept an old fellow's thanks for pointing this out.' Quite so. It was for the Welleses, and Rodgerses, to be grateful to Tynan, not vice versa.

Show People comprises five lengthy profiles: an actor (Ralph Richardson), a playwright (Tom Stoppard), a TV chat-show host (Johnny Carson), 'a great comic creator' (Mel Brooks) and 'a great screen beauty' (Louise Brooks). The profile essay is a marvellous form, which Tynan used expertly. There is a line of Stoppard's here, referring to his own period as a dramatic critic: 'I never had the character to pan my friends. That is to say, I had the character never to pan my friends.' This expresses perfectly the case for not remaining a critic. In Tynan, on the other hand, it is precisely his honesty in talking about those whom he admires, including his friends,

which is so irresistible. We know that the profile of Nicol
Williamson in *The Sound of Two Hands Clapping* lost him
Williamson's friendship. One cannot feel, however, that the
friendship was betrayed by the essay.

Stoppard himself is treated to an eighty-page scrutiny in this
volume. It is the best of the pieces and will be the most useful:
it really tells you all you need to know about the man, plus for
good measure, throwing in a mini-profile of Stoppard's anti-
type, Vaclav Havel, together with a glimpse of Pinter in the
pavilion. The least happy of the pieces is the one about
Johnny Carson, although I must admit that the first time I
read it I was unacquainted with the *Tonight Show*. Last
summer, however, turning to the American Forces' Network
in Seoul, I knew at once whom I was watching, purely through
Tynan's description. (I recommend the AFN, particularly
for its public-spirited advertisements exhorting the troops not
to let themselves go utterly to seed.)

Tynan gives an elaborately full account of Carson, but the
subject seems hardly worthy of the attention or the respect.
One gets sentences like this: 'Other than a married couple
who act as housekeepers, the Carsons have no live-in servants.'
(That should read: the Carsons have two live-in servants.) Or
this one: 'The year 1977, for Carson-watchers, was one in
which the *Tonight Show* while retaining all its sparkle and
caprice, gained not an inch in intellectual stature.'

One hardly associated it, from what Tynan had hitherto
told us, with any such thing as intellectual stature. But enough
carping. This is an excellent book. Tynan is sometimes compared (exaggeratedly, in my view) with Hazlitt. His own
rating of himself was more modest. 'When Lamb is at his most
whimsical,' he says, 'I sometimes feel I could go a couple of
rounds with him and not make a total fool of myself.'

Indeed he could.

19 October 1980

The Romans in Britain *(OLIVIER)*
Enjoy *(VAUDEVILLE)*
The Potsdam Quartet *(LYRIC STUDIO)*

What I call the Amadeus defence works in the following way: you are concerned to forestall criticism of the strikingly bad play you are about to write; so you make the work as obscene as you can, with the result that any critic who objects to it lays himself open to charges of puritanism and narrow-mindedness. The aim is to make the general public say to himself: 'If we are having a perfectly horrible time, this must be in the cause of Great Art.'

What I call the Brenton Variation throws in left-wingery and the Irish dimension, so that the audience should feel: 'If, when we are not bored rigid by this play, we find it utterly repugnant, that is because we are imperialist pigs who do not care two hoots about the crimes the British Army is committing in our name.'

Neither the Defence nor the Variation should be effective against a little calm self-questioning. Ask yourself, in Howard Brenton's *The Romans in Britain*, the new play at the National Theatre which has so upset Mary Whitehouse and Sir Horace Cutler, leader of the Greater London Council, what is the purpose of this obscenity, and what is the value of this violence?

Do we, for instance, care anything about the Celtic criminal who is strung up by the feet while his throat is cut? If the odd Roman soldier sodomised the odd Druid, what is that to us? Answer: nothing.

The only interest in either case is technical: the blood must gush from James Carter's throat (in real life, the supply would be less manageable and rather more plenteous, I fancy), while Peter Sproule must appear to get it up Greg Hicks, in full view of the audience and with the pair of them bollock-naked, so to speak, excepting for Mr Hicks's preposterous wig. I have not seen that much anal rape in real life, but I imagine it to be rather more messy than what we were shown.

Where my own experience does become relevant to my estimation of the play is in the Northern Ireland scenes (hang on: you thought we were in Ancient Britain; this is true, but the play chops around between 54 BC, AD 515, and 1980).

It should have been obvious, both to Mr Brenton and to the director Michael Bogdanov, that if an army finds a man hiding in a field in sniper country, and they tell him to stand up slowly and put his hands over his head, they will not immediately allow him instead to put his hands casually into his trouser pockets. Soldiers in general do not like the idea of being killed.

The man in question (Stephen Moore) is a disguised British officer who is waiting to assassinate a man called O'Rourke. In due course, he gets picked up by the IRA, who suspect his membership of the SAS. Mr Moore, somewhat surprisingly, confesses his identity and purpose; O'Rourke (James Hayes) believes his story and decides to have him shot. At the last moment Mr Moore pulls his gun, but is riddled with bullets.

As it happens, I was once apprehended by the IRA on precisely the suspicion of military espionage, and I can assure Mr Brenton that the drill is somewhat different. Once again the first thing the IRA do is search you very thoroughly. They don't want to be killed, either. And once they have searched you they take you somewhere where they can question you at leisure. After all, if you are a member of the SAS, you will have vital information which they wish to extract from you. In my case, I'm happy to say they desisted, and I was let go after questioning by the late Maire Drumm. But the case of Captain Robert Nairac would suggest that the next stage after questioning is torture.

I supposed that Mr Brenton reckoned that the squeamishness of the audience might just baulk at the sight of the good old rebels torturing the nasty imperialist officer, but if we are going to make such an exhibition of our political and sexual realism, we should not be afraid to show a little mutilation on behalf of the Republican cause, should we?

I may say that Mr Moore's depiction of a practised killer arrested by practised killers is distinctly unconvincing. But a great deal of the fault lies with the script.

The directing is quite deficient in its grasp of reality. We are shown a man standing over a diseased corpse, which stinks so foully that it makes him retch. But at the end of his retching the man continues to stand right over the corpse chatting away about this and that. This indicates to me that the director has had the luck never to smell a corpse.

This play is a nauseating load of rubbish from beginning to end. It is written in a ludicrous pseudo-poetic yob-talk; such themes as it possesses are banal beyond belief; and the intended bravery of the acting company amounts to no more than an embarrassing exhibitionism.

It is advertised as unsuitable for children. It is unsuitable for anyone. If I were Sir Peter Hall and had instigated such a production, I would take myself out to dinner and very tactfully but firmly sack myself over the dessert.

That said, I should make it clear that I in no way support either those who wish to use this production as an excuse to cut funds to the National, or those who on hearing the word 'nudity' will at once dial 999. Not that I think that the police should not go to the National. I think that the police should throng to the National, every night of the week.

And I strongly recommend that they should see Michael Gambon's performance in *Galileo*, which is quite the best thing in town. Mrs Whitehouse should stop persecuting the police. She should not force them to sit through *The Romans in Britain*.

There are two marvellous performances in Alan Bennett's semi-fermented new play, *Enjoy* (Vaudeville). Colin Blakely, with scarcely any more visible aid to transformation than a moustache and a pair of strong glasses, turns himself into a decrepit old man with a steel plate in his skull, and the consequent tendency to come over all funny – which he does, before our eyes, with devastating effect. In a typical line, his wife tells him: 'As a victim of a hit-and-run driver, I think you're entitled to put your feet up.'

136

The wife is played by Joan Plowright, in a performance which uses this actress's brilliant eyes to brilliant effect. Both of these old people have surprising reserves of intelligence and strength, despite almost conventionally dotty appearances. And within the play, there are more than enough funny lines to provide them with a conventional two-handed comedy.

But it is evident by the end of *Enjoy* that Mr Bennett was nauseated by the knowledge that, if he wanted to, he could preserve this aged couple in the amber of conventional drama. It seemed to the playwright that there was something grotesque and intrusive in such an act. Instead of doing so, he therefore constructed an unconventional and highly confusing work in which his own nausea and self-accusation is presented on stage: the son who swears to his mother that he will never put her in a home turns out to be a playwright; the museum for which he has destined his mother is none other than this play.

The over-all result is sentimental, embarrassing and bad: bad from a combination of strong talent and little faith in the value of art. It is true that there can be something unpleasant in the actual art of turning one's relatives into art – but nobody is obliging Mr Bennett to be a playwright, or to be that kind of playwright. I felt most strongly that the problems raised in this play, and its awful self-accusations, should have been resolved by the author before the work reached rehearsal. There is only one question to answer: Does Mr Bennett believe sufficiently in his art to proceed with it? If he does not believe in it, nobody else will. If he did believe in it, the badness in this present work would disappear at the flick of his fingers. We would be left with the comic masterpiece Mr Bennett was afraid to write.

At the Lyric Studio, Hammersmith, there is a substantial new play by David Pinner. *The Potsdam Quartet* shows a string quartet comprised of Clive Swift, Frederick Jaeger, Peter Eyre, and Jerome Willis, arguing backstage about their own personal futures, while in the Conference Chamber the world is divided up between Roosevelt, Churchill and Stalin.

The problem with such historical plays (a problem not entirely avoided by Mr Pinner) is to make the characters illuminating but not too illuminating about the contemporary circumstances in which they find themselves. This was the classic discovery of nineteenth-century fiction: the historical character must share his ignorance with us, just as much as his knowledge. A string quartet, employed to provide background music while the world's leaders relax, would certainly be aware of the 'historic' nature of the moment they are witnessing. But, as Mr Pinner rightly shows, their view of the chief participants would be no better than any public view of the period. It is extraordinary how often playwrights ignore this important elementary truth.

The main interest of the play, however, is not the division of spoils between the conquerors, but the struggle among the members of the string quartet over their future together, a future which is put in hazard by the news that one of them has Parkinson's disease (yes, I know, another play about a musician with a wasting disease, but I hardly think Mr Pinner is to blame for the coincidence), and by the determination of one of the homosexuals in the quartet to destroy the group at the first opportunity, using scandal as the means of destruction, if necessary. This leads to a passionate defence of their musical co-operation, delivered by Clive Swift. The ending is an example of Nunn's Manoeuvre (named after Trevor Nunn): the audience will leave the theatre happily if you give them a good song-and-dance routine in the final moments. If you wonder how a song-and-dance routine is introduced into a play with four main characters, and written within the realistic convention, the short answer is: by the scruff of its neck.

I saw this piece late in the week, after it had received mixed notices. There were not many people in the Studio, which seemed a great shame considering the quality of the acting. But I should add that there are mistakes of timing, and moments when the pace seems to go a little awry. (For instance, a monstrous insult to the sick musician, calling his Parkinson's the Devil's Disease, is taken up and comprehended almost before it is delivered. But the thing about such appalling insults is that they so surprise you that it takes a moment or two for them to sink in.)

Among the most effective passages is a dialogue between nerve-racked, pill-popping Peter Eyre and a non-English-speaking Russian soldier played by Tim Charrington. I have followed the whole of Mr Charrington's acting career (that is to say, this is his second appearance on the professional stage). Here, he offers a sustained study of mute ignorance, not without some passion. It is highly intriguing to watch him form his preferences and strong aversions in relation to the other actors on stage. He becomes a kind of exclusive interpreter of the non-verbal activity taking place before our eyes. The directing is by David Giles, and the intelligent design is by Michael Edwards.

19 October 1980

The Emperor Jones and The Chairs
(ROYAL EXCHANGE, MANCHESTER)

In *The Emperor Jones* (Royal Exchange, Manchester), the runaway criminal who becomes the hated despot of a West Indian island has put the word around that he can only be killed by a silver bullet. The only silver bullet on the island (or so he thinks) is in the sixth chamber of his gun. Jones has his escape route planned, in case the despised natives should turn nasty, which they of course do, as natives will, at the beginning of this one-act play.

So the gorgeously-apparelled Jones must flee through the jungle, pursued by the sound of drums, and on his way he must shed his hat, his spurs, his patent leather boots, and all the items which have reinforced his godly image in the eyes of his subjects. One by one the chambers of his gun are emptied in the direction of the accusing shadows of his past, shadows which join in the sinister pursuit. When the silver bullet goes, Jones's luck goes with it. Enter a witch doctor. The play draws to a close.

This is a stock magazine adventure story, out of which Joseph Conrad might have made something profound. But Eugene O'Neill is not in that class, as he shows only too plainly in this piece. For once, he does not labour each point to death, but when he does not do so the points nevertheless establish themselves with all the remarkable ease of cliché. If the play has a virtue today, it is simply that it provides a rare opportunity to give a black actor a major role.

Errol Jones left the Manchester production at the last minute. Peter Postlethwaite blacked up and took over, and gave an excellent impression of an opportunist on the run. Albie Woodington played the Cockney Smith, another stock figure from the pulp literature of the period. Carl Campbell as the witch doctor choreographed his own dance, which was highly effective until the Emperor himself was drawn in, when

140

for a short while it appeared hilarious. Richard Negri's production showed off the resources of the theatre, and there were moments when it and Peter Bennion's design came near to achieving something exciting. But by the end of the evening the technical virtuosity of the theatre had become a distraction. The shallowness of the play could not be saved by the profundity of the sound effects.

Part two of the evening, Ionesco's *The Chairs* (starring Gwen Nelson and Frank Thornton), was a big mistake. This is a pretentious and sentimental work, which presumes upon the patience of the audience, putting across a minimum of comic material at interminable length.

The essence of the Absurd is that its metaphors should seem to offer meaning, but that the meaning should be withdrawn at the very moment that it is grasped. It should engage but never satisfy. This is the effect which Kafka introduced into the mainstream of our literature. With Ionesco's play, the metaphors throw themselves at you quite shamelessly. They pester you. They won't go away. They announce platitudes as if they were revelations. Compare the effect of a tiny passage of Kafka (for instance, his intriguing short play *The Warden of the Tomb*) with *The Chairs* and you will see what I mean.

The Kafka takes up only the briefest time – but it grows afterwards in the mind. The Ionesco looks like a neglected soufflé.

26 October 1980

The Crucible (COTTESLOE)

Who writes as well as Arthur Miller? Second question: who has ever written so well for the stage in the language of a different period from his own – a language to all intents and purposes invented by the author to stand for the common speech of seventeenth-century Massachusetts. It is hard to think of a parallel for *The Crucible* (Cottesloe) because the majority of plays composed in such a manner have sunk without trace.

What people write in the language of the past, or in the language of the future (which for some odd reason, usually amounts to the same thing) is almost certain to date, to turn fustian more rapidly than any other kind of writing. It is like those Victorian paintings of medieval England, in which one sees nothing but the period in which they were painted. But the language of *The Crucible* does not seem to date in such a way, just as Miller's plays do not seem to date.

By all rights, according to the logic of fashion and the transience of taste, *The Crucible* should be passing through an eclipse. It should be hard for a generation fed on warmed-up Brecht (ready-Brecht would be a suitable trade-mark) to perceive the merits of this completely alien tradition of left-wing writing – a tradition rooted in morality and the individual.

The secret of the play's effectiveness may lie in the indirect-ness of its method. It is not strictly speaking a political allegory, by the way. You can understand it perfectly well as an account of the way witch hunts actually worked. If Miller chose to present the story of the Salem witches because of the way it shed light on McCarthyite America, he nevertheless – this is the crucial point – chose first to present the story, to create that other world, wholly and in all its moral complexity.

Every artist seeks the perfect conditions for free movement and I suspect that Miller found that he could move more freely

142

in the seventeenth century, at that particular time, than in the twentieth. One senses this release in the language itself – it can be as rich, twisted, or metaphorical as its author pleases.

Whether Bill Bryden's production at the Cottesloe is marvellous or merely very good indeed I do not know. The trouble was I found myself too engaged on the play's behalf, mentally cheering it on from the touchline, and anticipating each development. Once one is in such a mood it is impossible to gauge one's own reaction. There were faults: there is comedy in the play, but not of the kind that allows laughter in the midst of the most dramatic scenes.

The piece of comic business worked out between the clergyman (Dave Hill) and the deputy governor (Tony Haygarth), where the former keeps leaning on the latter's shoulder in court, seemed to come from a quite different sort of drama and to reduce two otherwise fine performances. Mark McManus takes the hero Proctor's role, and Dinah Stabb is his wife; these two stood out as the most powerful portrayals, although the competition was strong. James Grant needed a little more salt: as the Rev. John Hale he must surely participate more in the hard fervour of the religious period. He it is, certainly, who must change his mind effectively, but he must first have been rather more of a bigot. Valerie Whittington and Caroline Embling are the leading girls, and very chilling they are.

2 November 1980

Richard II, Richard III *(STRATFORD)*
Storm *(PICCOLO TEATRO, MILAN)*

Alan Howard divides opinion like no other leading actor in Britain today, divides it so sharply that one suspects even his worst detractors of paying a certain tribute to his stage presence. It is axiomatic that an actor needs presence. But as soon as one defines those qualities which contribute to presence, one finds that one is describing, not what all great actors share, but what distinguishes one actor from another. A definition of great acting as written by an admirer of, say, Olivier, aspires inevitably towards a definition of Olivier. Even the most seemingly-essential features (piercing eyes, for instance) may prove non-essential. If an actor with no eyes at all stepped on to the stage and proceeded to convince us, we should rapidly incorporate 'lack of eyes' into our definition of greatness.

Mr Howard is in possession of a pair of eyes, but they are hardly his most remarkable feature. Tap those eyes with a teaspoon, and I suspect that the merry chink of metal against glass would ring out through the auditorium. If I try to picture that face now, as I write, I find that my memory endows it with a kind of puffiness, as if Mr Howard had been woken from deep sleep and summoned straight on to the stage. Now the eyes narrow, the mouth falls slightly open, and the actor's general demeanour indicates a striving to work out just what the hell is going on.

What is going on? It is the two-day marathon with which the week opened, in which Terry Hands directed Mr Howard in the major roles of Richard II and Richard III at Stratford-on-Avon. By the end of the week, much of the excitement which Mr Hands whipped up has faded from the memory: to rely, as this director typically relies, on sheer pace, is to concentrate on the most transitory of responses. When we step off the switchback, we may feel somewhat shaky on our pins, but by the time we have left the fairground, the equilibrium is restored.

What stays in the mind, then, either as a virtue or as a fault? From *Richard II*, I retain a clear impression of the quality of kingship: the king as the sun, the source of light; the king as the isolated man-god; and the pathology of kingship. Mr Howard displays a hysterical bifurcation: on the one hand, all is well, and nothing can stand in the way of royal good fortune; on the other hand, all is lost. There is no intervening mood. Consequently, the dandyism of the court has a certain strident splendour, exceedingly well indicated both by Farrah's designs and by the demeanour of the actors. The court must either be utterly splendid or it is nothing.

To what extent can such a pathological view of the king be rescued, in the second half of the play, and brought to some kind of dignity in misfortune? I see no objection in principle, but I do not think Mr Howard as yet plays it right. In the first half, it is noticeable how faithfully he sticks to the verse-line, and how well the poetry repays him for that faith. In the second half, where a devastating effect is sought, the poetry is shattered and dispersed. Once that happens, the attention wanders.

If *Richard II* has a glaring fault, it is the staging of John of Gaunt's death. One moment the old boy seems as right as rain. The next moment, we learn that he has croaked it. By contrast, in *Richard III*, we are left in no doubt at all as to the poor state of King Edward's health: David Suchet's head, under the make-up, looks like a lump of peppermint toffee that has been chewed up and spat out. This is ghastly, a dismaying contrast with the same actor's marvellous Bolingbroke.

Richard III is a much less successful production all round. Its chief ideas are shallow and distracting. For instance, when Hastings's time is up, Ratcliffe and Lovell stick daggers into his back like piçadors, before dragging him off for decapitation. This kind of idea is the directorial equivalent of the people one sees in televised street interviews, waving to mother from the back of the crowd. 'Hi there, Mom,' it seems to say, 'it's me, Terry.'

145

The next scene, when Gloucester effects his final ascent to kingship, takes place on a hastily-erected stage from which dangle puppets of Adam and Eve and the devil. The line 'Tut! I can counterfeit the deep tragedian', is taken as the cue for a play. Once again, however, the idea makes no sense excepting as a piece of directorial intrusion, and the puppets make no sense at all. Mr Howard's performance and interpretation depend upon the crippled condition of the King, but there were so often passages in which the King was obliged by the director to perform feats of extraordinary agility that the idea of his being crippled was also senseless. The withered hand (through which a dagger is stuck, in order to make the point that it really is withered) remains a powerful and useful limb.

Strindberg's *Storm* has been broadcast in England, but not given a major stage production. This is a crazy state of affairs in a period when chamber plays are all the rage. Giorgio Strehler's production, which I have just seen at the Piccolo Teatro in Milan, is technically exquisite: you feel that the laws of nature have been suspended in the region of his stage – so that at one moment we see rain pouring down on one side, and a split second later the park bench several yards away is dripping wet. Some of the characters are only glimpsed through smoked glass, or by flashes of lightning; at one point, a fully visible girl is given an unobtrusive double. This was a terrific production which further convinced me that we should see more of Strindberg.

9 November 1980

Nicholas Nickleby *(RSC, ALDWYCH)*

One weeps buckets, of course. At the Aldwych Theatre they actually pass the buckets along the rows, for the convenience of the spectator, and there are Kleenex dispensers where the opera glasses used to be.

But such measures prove woefully insufficient. The woman behind me wept so vigorously it was as if a double-barrelled water-pistol was playing on the back of my neck. At the death of Smike, I added my own contribution. A torrent of tears, erupting from the theatre, carried off a whole column of traffic, sweeping it down the Aldwych and back along the Strand as far as Charing Cross. If the GLC closes the show down, as seems likely from the latest protests of Sir Horace Cutlet, it will be on the grounds of breach of flood regulations. Already David Threlfall (who plays Smike) has been helping police with their inquiries.

The occasion, in case you're not with me yet, is the return of the RSC's *Nicholas Nickleby* to the Aldwych. I watched the two parts again a week ago, watched them with a passionate admiration which does not diminish with the days. If anything, the replacements to the cast are an improvement on their predecessors, while the production itself certainly yields more on a second viewing.

It is directed by Trevor Nunn and John Caird, and it would be a rash critic who claimed to be able to distinguish the work of the one director from that of the other in such a co-operative effort. Nevertheless let boldness be my friend. From Mr Caird's last solus production, *The Caucasian Chalk Circle*, I retain one particularly vivid impression of a moment when the company (behind the scenes) made a series of noises in order to depict the burning down of houses. The quality of the sound was extraordinarily precise, although it was clear that this was a depiction of burning (not the thing itself).

In *Nicholas Nickleby*, again and again, the company must

147

solve this question of depiction. Because of the large number of scenes, it would be out of the question actually to build, say, a gaming-house on the stage. A gaming-house must simply be indicated – it must establish itself, then dissolve before one's eyes, with great speed. There is a group around a roulette table. We hear the wheel spin round and the ball come to a halt. But when the group dissolves, there is no table and no wheel. Instead, a gent with a large football rattle is glimpsed making off into the wings.

Such happy inventions come thick and fast. It is not that I attribute them all to Mr Caird. I merely associate such an inventive pleasure with his style of directing. The coach must leave for Yorkshire, the omnibus for the East End, the cabriolet for Sir Mulberry's home, the horses must rear up – but there is no coach, no omnibus, no cabriolet, and there are no horses. Again and again, a scene would establish itself in the space of two seconds in all its brilliant complexity. When it dissolved one might ask oneself: what was it made of? What were the props? I remember on one occasion the answer was two chairs, nothing more.

In France, where theatre is so much more of a conjuring trick, there are directors who could match Messrs Nunn and Caird in the mere matter of prestidigitation. In Jean-Louis Barrault's recent *Zadig*, for instance, one merely had to blink at an empty stage – and a whole glittering court appeared out of nowhere. But Barrault's directing, astonishing as it is, does not put itself at the service of a realistic style of acting – it imposes itself on every one of the stage's achievements. In *Nickleby*, all the technical brilliance of the stagecraft has a purpose, namely to present Dickens's story as truthfully as possible.

For this purpose, the acting style must emulate Dickens's range – it must vary from the boldest caricature to the most faithful realism. And if there is one quality to the whole day's show which, above all others, I associate with Mr Nunn, it is this range. Contained within one show is all the intense intimacy of *Three Sisters* (almost all of whose cast are to be seen on stage) counterpoised against the vast busy-ness of *Once in a Lifetime* (Mr Nunn in his out-Broadwaying-

Broadway mood). It is a question of speed, speed, speed – interspersed with moments of daring slowness and calm. Everything may come to a halt, if needs be, as long as it is clearly understood that when the pace resumes, it really does resume.

After my first viewing I wrote mainly about Roger Rees's performance as Nicholas (which is even better than before) and David Threlfall's extraordinary depiction of Smike. Both of these portrayals redeem for the modern audience the parts of Dickens's novel over which one would have expected the production to stumble. They do not traduce Dickens – no, they take his values absolutely seriously – but they purge him of all sentimentality.

Beyond these two central performances, it is impossible to do justice. But since I have already mentioned those three sisters, one might as well have a look at what became of them when they left the world of Chekhov and made their way, not to Moscow but to London. Emily Richard has just stepped into the most difficult part in the whole story, taking over as Kate Nickleby, a pallid figure in the original and one who must play some of the most cloying scenes. Miss Richard brings a degree of extra articulation to this part, and she is at her best when she is able to show spirit, when she is roused from innocent virtue to protest.

Janet Dale makes a career for herself as Miss Knag, the malicious assistant to Madame Mantalini. I had forgotten how funny this performance is (or perhaps it has developed), particularly the irritating habit she has developed of echoing what her interlocutors are saying, as it were trailing after them conversationally, a habit which leads her into a spectacularly comic double-take, when a terrible insult is delivered to her face.

Everybody in the company (and this is immensely attractive) is prepared to perform the widest range of tasks, from exalted to menial. Suzanne Bertish has perhaps the best deal of the lot. She is an actress who has suffered in my eyes from one honourable disadvantage – namely, that her performance in *Three Sisters* keeps recurring in the memory and interfering with the receptors. Here that problem does not arise:

149

she begins in a broad Yorkshire with hideously refined pretensions as Fanny Squeers; she continues as Miss Snevellicci with a brilliant version of Dorothy Tutin (the mysteriously French accent that comes from Teesside); she ends under heavy make-up in the Stygean gloom of Peg Sliderskew's hovel, with a thick Glaswegian accent. She obviously relished these transformations, which she carries off marvellously.

30 November 1980

Hiawatha (OLIVIER)

This is the third time that the ghost of Henry Wadsworth Longfellow has appeared on the London stage in the last six months. In Athol Fugard's *A Lesson from Aloes* the poem 'The Slave's Dream' was sent up rotten by the white hero and his coloured friend. More obscurely, in Sam Shepard's *Buried Child*, the underlying story according to which the maize miraculously sprouts in the garden where a child has been buried is adapted from the Indian aetiological myth told in the excellent Fifth Book of *Hiawatha*. Now, *Hiawatha* in Michael Bogdanov's production for children, which my eight-year-old companion described simply as 'brilliant'. Longfellow, then, is still a poetic presence. What sort of poet was he?

The answer for the most part is, that he was bloody awful. There are a few fine examples of good–bad versification – the anti-slavery poems, 'Paul Revere's Ride', 'Excelsior' – the last of which has been smartly sent packing by a classic parody:

> The shades of night were falling fast,
> The rain was falling faster,
> When through an Alpine village passed
> An Alpine village pastor.

Good poetry has nothing to fear from parody. 'Excelsior' cannot survive a moment's irreverence.

But there was a worthwhile element in Longfellow's work. The project of his poetic career – to search European poetry for forms which could thrive in America – was fine and ambitious. It is rightly argued that in this quest he pre-dates Eliot and Pound. 'The Grave', a translation from Anglo-Saxon, is the forerunner of Pound's 'Seafarer'. And Longfellow anticipates *The Waste Land* in writing an extended poem whose chief inspiration comes from anthropology, more precisely from fertility myth and stories of

151

renewal. That poem is *Hiawatha*, which may stand with *Sohrab and Rustum* from England and *Taras Bulba* from Russia as one of the best primitive poems of the nineteenth century.

What you should look for in *Hiawatha* is not the beauty of the individual line, but the beauty of the story – and this is what comes over so well in Mr Bogdanov's production. Hiawatha sets out to kill his father, the West Wind, to avenge his mother's death, and the West Wind is delighted at his son's courage. Who could fail to be interested in the idea of patricide as the first step in manhood? (*Hiawatha* was completed in 1855, a year before the birth of Freud.)

Who could fail to be stirred by the journey the hero makes into the belly of the sturgeon, whose great heart he stops? Then he must wedge his canoe athwart the innards, and wait for the sea-gulls to peck their way through the fish, until the ribcage is exposed, and he is able to call for help.

Most of Hiawatha's exploits involve killing, and yet there is no finality in death according to the Indian legends. The sturgeon is killed in the Eighth Book. In Book 22, the last book, it still leaps from the lake. Pau-Puk-Keewis, the Storm Fool, takes the shape of a beaver. He is killed. So he takes the shape of a swan, to fall from the sky to a second death. And even when Hiawatha has finally disposed of him, it is only in order to turn him into an eagle, just as in the legend I have already referred to, he killed the great friend of Man, only to turn him into Indian corn.

The rebellion of Pau-Puk-Keewis is perhaps the finest passage in the story – evil arises out of nothing more than a boredom with the wise rule of Hiawatha. So the hero must kill the rebel, must kill his old friend who danced at his wedding. If there is an echo here from the treachery of the Arthurian court, it derives, like so many of the echoes, from the archetypal material which Longfellow used. If the transmogrified Storm Fool reminds us of Proteus, if Hiawatha's canoe reminds us of Odysseus's raft, if the prophetic passages bring echoes of Virgil, this is not through conscious emulation on Longfellow's part, but because when this highly educated man looked at the Indian legends his cultivation taught him to discover such things in a new, exciting and largely uncharted imaginative world.

That is the great interest of *Hiawatha* as a poem. Except in the occasional moments of preaching there is nothing ersatz about it; nor should it be patronized by tin-eared critics. It is a uniquely successful American epic. That is why, if you take your child to see this splendid production, you yourself will not be wasting your time.

14 December 1980

The Revolt (NEW END. HAMPSTEAD)

The Revolt, by Villiers de l'Isle-Adam, receives its London première at the New Theatre in Hampstead, 110 years after its original, unsuccessful Paris production. Because the play concerns a woman who leaves her husband and young child, comparison has been made between this work and Ibsen's *A Doll's House*, which Villiers anticipates by about a decade. And on such a comparison, Villiers must inevitably fall down; he becomes a barely competent realist: there is no great sense of the society in which his figures move; their house has no neighbours. It is said to be an old town house, but it seems to have been placed under a bell-jar of the author's imagination. Now the air is pumped out of the jar, and the characters suffocate before our eyes. No sound travels through a vacuum, and we may suppose that the conclusion of the play has left its two characters in complete silence.

Perhaps I have already said enough to indicate that realism is the wrong concept, and Ibsen the wrong comparison. The essence of realism is context; remember *Juno and the Paycock*, with all the sounds of the tenement block seeping into the flat – that is realism. And think how in Ibsen's realist plays, even in a studio setting, the imagination expands upon the action – expands in the direction of other houses, other lives, expands to include whole landscapes, populated or haunted. Such a sense you will not get from *The Revolt*. The escaping wife talks of having purchased a lonely house in 'Norway, Sicily, or Iceland, no matter where'. The peculiar order of these countries is significant – she is not thinking of real places, but of an abstract loneliness and a solitude in nature.

The realist says: you may not present an abstraction on the stage; everything must be specific, concrete, individual. That is his programme, but it is not a programme which all the world is obliged to follow. *The Revolt* does not anticipate

Ibsen – it anticipates Strindberg, and it does so with such striking accuracy that if the play had been presented as one of his lost works, I feel sure that it would have been generally accepted as authentic. There is a way Strindberg's characters have transparent skin, like babies in incubators. Indeed, there is a way in which the tops of their skulls have never closed up, so that looking in, one may perceive their pulses and their passions. They do not revel in the indirectness of normal conversation. They have an abnormal ability to go straight to the heart of the matter.

That is what the two characters in this extraordinary little play possess in abundance. They are quite unable to beat about the bush. The husband's thought is entirely dominated by a financial logic, which cannot help but dictate its aesthetic considerations (it might be worthwhile to go to the theatre, since one makes useful contacts there, etc., etc.). But the husband is not an abstraction of capitalism (which would be extremely boring): we see, through the workings of his mind and heart, capitalism as a masculine principle, a delusion of administrative self-sufficiency.

An authority on Villiers, whose work I have consulted, thought that this play would not succeed because the husband is never given a chance – he is so humiliated by the argument that the audience might end up with an inappropriate sympathy for him. One must ask oneself, however, whether *The Revolt* is simply a play about the humiliation of woman by man, or whether, equally topically for its period, it might not be about the humiliation of man by woman. (This is the great theme in Strindberg.) The woman proves herself a better financier than the man. She informs the man, in no uncertain terms, of his shortcomings. She will leave him, she says, in order to seek poetry and her true self which he has always denied her.

Without denying or avoiding any of the accusations levelled against the man, one may quite legitimately ask just how admirable the goal of the woman is. It is the pursuit of a dream in the direction of death. It naively conceives poetry to be a world of its own, divorced from society. Its belief in the natural life is juvenile, and completely unserious – the notion that Sicily and Iceland may be in some sense equivalent is an entirely frivolous kind of abstraction. Finally, the revolt fails – it fails, says the woman, because she has already been defeated by her husband: 'I am chained to a hateful man who has destroyed me. A man more dead than alive has crushed the life out of me.' But perhaps the revolt fails because it is stupid. And perhaps the hatefulness of the man is a dishonest alibi.

This is not Simone Benmussa's interpretation in her production, but it is surely what the play shows, whether deliberately or inadvertently. Olivier Pierre plays the man, with a degree of foolish self-love, but without the willingness to follow the character wholeheartedly into humiliation. Susan Hampshire is the woman, and it is the elegance and sincerity of her performance which make the play so very well worth seeing.

21 December 1980

Galileo (OLIVIER)

John Dexter's production of *Galileo*, which I revisited at the National Theatre last week, remains for me the most exciting theatrical event of 1980 – and does so by virtue of one central performance. Other actors have scored great personal triumphs – I think of Jonathan Pryce in the Royal Court *Hamlet*, Roger Rees and David Threlfall in *Nicholas Nickleby*, or James Aubrey in *Doctor Faustus* – but none of them had to convince me of the intrinsic worth of the play he was in.

After *Galileo* on the other hand I was forced to change my mind on three points. I was obliged, by the production and particularly by Jocelyn Herbert's design, to abandon a dislike of the theatrical architecture of the Olivier Theatre itself. After a series of pompous and lifeless designs, here at last was a production which seemed to revel in the space that was put at its disposal. Secondly, I had at least to modify an intense artistic and political antagonism to Brecht. The third change was something more in the nature of a dramatic upward revision.

I had previously very much admired Michael Gambon as a comic actor of a mournful disposition. He has the ability to create an aura of conspicuous stillness around his features, so that when he does move each facial muscle is eloquent. If one thought of Mr Gambon in a typical costume, as it were in his motley, one would think of those complicated macintoshes with flaps and straps and buckles – garments that appear both quintessentially modern and dreary. It would be no bad thing if Mr Gambon gave up the motley for a season or so. In the eyes of all who have seen his Galileo, he has taken such a decisive step forward in the direction of great tragedy.

So I returned to the National in the hopes of working out just what it is that he does in order to establish that devastating transformation we witness in the play. I had imagined it as

157

something that must take place backstage in the interval – but in fact it happens in full view of the audience. He turns his back on us during a scene shift, and keeps it turned for a while. When his features become visible again, they are ravaged by the combined effects of disease, indulgence and intellectual disgrace. It is not a question of make-up. It is something he has done to his brain. As one director puts it: 'He has killed off those brain cells which are normally destroyed at 60 and at 70.' It is quite useless to return to the play in the hope of working out what the trick is. What the trick is must be . . . great acting.

If the play itself is rightly described as great, it seems to me that it snatches its greatness from the jaws of a massive defeat, and it is for this defeat that I blame Brecht strongly. As a poet and a playwright he could not resist selling art's most precious quality, its freedom and independence – and selling that freedom to a cause for which he was unwilling even to declare himself. All his equivocations about Communism, and about Stalinism in particular, seem to me completely unlovable. To join in a movement and work for it is one thing. But to refuse to join a movement but send your *art* out to work for it – that I think vile. It is like sending your little daughter down the mine.

Even in *Galileo*, Brecht's sense of history is deeply tendentious: one feels strongly that every moment glimpsed, every action observed, is rigorously put at the service of the argument. Indeed, this is not surprising, since more than most plays *Galileo* is a great argument, one which proceeds more or less without interruption throughout those fifteen scenes. But the consequence of this is that, at a certain stage, we lose interest in the pretensions of the play in so far as it is supposed to show Galileo himself. We become exclusively interested in what the author is saying about his own contemporaries and his own world.

This strikes me as a limitation. The reader will no doubt object that there is no novelty in such a limitation: Shakespeare's history plays show a vision of history just as tendentious as that of Brecht. Or do they? As far as I know, Shakespeare's version of history simply shares the shortcomings of his period. It does not conspicuously preen itself over the superiority of its philosophy to any rival in the ring. Shakespeare is not forever nudging his audience into line.

But there is a difference between a play and a history book? Yes, indeed, I judge a play by no grander criterion than to ask: what does it pretend to achieve, and does it achieve it? If a man walks on to a stage and says: 'Here we are in Rome', I'm quite happy to take him at his word and see what happens. It might be an imaginary Jacobean Rome. Or it might be historical. Now consider what happens at the National; a slide is flashed on to the screen, with the inscription 'Rome 1616'. In fact the slide depicts Florence. That is a mistake in the production – but it is only a mistake because a claim has been made that the slide shows Rome.

In the same way, if you compare the Galileo of the historian with Brecht's hero, the only contradictions that arise will be in the area where history and drama are seriously competing for our allegiance. Brecht's Galileo conducts a battle against secular power as personified, paradoxically, by the Church. (Brecht argued that the play should not be seen simply as anticlerical, although he did not mind relying on a few good laughs at the expense of the Church.)

Now compare this figure with the Galileo presented by Stillman Drake in his useful monograph recently published by Oxford University Press in their Past Masters series. Here we have a historical Galileo fighting primarily against the entrenched interests of philosophy in his day: the philosophers are the villains, and at a certain point on in the game they unscrupulously bring in the Church. The involvement of the Inquisition is seen as accidental, not historically determined. Galileo himself is viewed as a pious man who reacts with horror against the improper intrusion of theology into scientific disputes, not because he fears for science so much as that he fears for the good name and for the future of the Church.

Professor Drake's pious Galileo is obviously a figure who would be of no use to Brecht, since he contradicts Brecht's idea of history all along the line. To the extent that the playwright is keen to sell us the wisdom of his history (this is, after all, a didactic play), the superior knowledge of the historian can indeed damage him.

But much remains even after such damage has been done. Most of all, the powerful conception Brecht has of his hero's contrasting greatness and weakness – this has nothing to do with any theory of the tragic flaw. It is a perception from the author's own painful experience. A character flaw such as physical fear or self-indulgence may remain quite inert and unimportant during periods which do not make great demands on the individual. But at the decisive turning point of history, while such a flaw may remain what it always was, while it may not grow out of proportion to the character's virtues, what the age demands may throw that flaw into a terrible relief.

Something trivial and normally benign, such as a fondness for goose liver cooked with apple, may come to represent everything that is wrong about a man, everything about his betrayal, about his age. Brecht knew only too well that most terrible of sensations – the fear of history. It is that fear which Mr Gambon's Galileo so movingly embodies on the stage.

In the penultimate scene, when his former pupil, Andrea, tries to recover his respect for his old master, Galileo insists on the correctness of the young man's disillusionment. He is indeed a traitor to the truth. He is indeed a criminal in the eyes of history – in the eyes of that terrible judge whom Brecht himself had every reason to fear.

28 December 1980

Man and Superman *(OLIVIER)*
Naked Robots *(WAREHOUSE)*

I owe an apology to the National Theatre for having inadvertently walked out of *Man and Superman* at the end of the sequence in Hell, five minutes before the interval. It was not boredom. I *was*, at that particular moment, profoundly bored, but not to the point of malice. Rather, I needed a reward. The Platonic idea of one of the National's coffee ice-creams (the ones with the grounds mixed in) loomed so large in the mind that it blotted out all other considerations. In other words, I was driven from the theatre by greed. I apologise.

Four and a half hours is not a long time to spend at the theatre these days, particularly if that includes a half-hour interval; and the National habit of presenting full texts seems to me to be admirable – with one provision, namely that the director who chooses to present a full text shows us just why he felt that his production would make this possible to take. If Christopher Morahan wanted to begin with a dramatisation of Shaw's preface, continue with a complete reading of John Tanner's revolutionist's handbook, and then present us the complete play, so that the event took a couple of days of solid viewing, I would be delighted to try it out. Once. But there would have to be some pretty convincing device, so that one was indeed able to take the argument in, aurally.

As it is, Beerbohm's original judgement, that this is not a dramatic work but a dialogue in the tradition of Plato, Lucian and Landor, is not dispelled at the end of an evening at the National – nor can one see how Mr Morahan thought it *would* be dispelled. If one disagrees with Beerbohm, it is only over the value of the dialogue. It has no dialectic. The specific way in which it taxes the very great skills of Daniel Massey is revealing as to its limitations.

Mr Massey (as Don Juan in Hell) overworks the attitude of

161

wild exasperations with his interlocutor. He is never in the position of defending an argument that has been astutely attacked, only of expounding further a preconceived argument which his interlocutor has been too stupid to follow to its logical conclusion. This is the source of the tedium. It is not that Mr Massey fails to put the argument across. He understands the argument perfectly, and I have seldom heard a more intelligent, sustained performance.

The trouble is that the argument is not good enough – not concise enough, important enough or sufficiently well articulated to merit its length. It has an unpleasant reek, like the reek of those little cafés near the British Museum. It reeks of crankiness and faddism. It must go on, this argument, because it has no home to return to, only a miserable bedsit. Time lies heavily on its hands. It is inexorable.

Worst of all, its author imagines that by pointing out what a gas-bag his contemporary hero John Tanner is, by underlining the inexorability, he will make it somehow comically acceptable. But this is artistic treason, not comic technique. Artistic treason goes in for cheap laughs. Note for instance Shaw's 'jokes' at the expense of Milton, that *Paradise Lost* goes on so that few people have ever read it to the end. As a matter of fact, Milton never blathers in the way that Shaw blathers – certainly not in his poetry. It is also famously true of Milton that he could forget his beliefs for long enough to think himself, to feel himself into the role of the great Adversary Satan. In *Man and Superman*, by contrast, there is no Adversary.

On either side of the Don Juan scene a passable play about a political activist yielding before the designs of his attractive ward is enacted to considerable effect before our eyes. This is due to Mr Massey's wonderfully vivid loopiness, which enlivens the stage from his first entrance, and to Penelope Wilton's marvellously funny and determined performance as Ann Whitefield. Arriving on stage in full mourning, Miss Wilton wears an expression which made me burst out laughing the moment I saw it. The fact of her father's recent death and her assumption of mourning had meant to this character that she had the absolute right to be the centre of attention –

and by Jove, she would exploit that situation for all she could get out of it.

From that moment on (with the exception of a few passages in the tedious third act) Miss Wilton lays bare the workings of her mind and will, that will which must triumph in the end – from the first sight of her this point is never in doubt.

At the Warehouse John Caird directs *Naked Robots*, a play by Jonathan Gems which is one of the best pieces of new writing to have been seen at this theatre for quite a time. It has been accused of formlessness and lack of control. I didn't see this at all. What I saw was a study in which very specific characters, in a quite specific period and world, were allowed undogmatically to work through their changing relationships. It took its time, and quite rightly so. The degree of latitude in the plot was a result of that lack of dogmatism in the conception.

The generation under surveillance moved in the world of pop music and its accompanying elaborations of style. Failure for them would be a failure to live up to the style, to live through the style, to dictate style. One (Raad Rawi) is an African Asian, for whom success in London as a designer of space-age clothes is an alternative to the memory of failure and anonymity in Mombasa. Two of the girls come from middle-class homes – their present poverty has a certain charm as a flight from wealth, although it is clear that the world in which they aspire to move will exact its toll in ways which they would do anything rather than admit.

One is reminded of their backgrounds by the most surprising traits. For instance the pop-singer Desna (Trudie Styler) shows an unexpected competence when faced with a man with a head-wound, while both she and Gemma (Catherine Hall) make a very good job of putting an overdose case (Lynda Marchal) back on her feet. At such moments, when rising to meet the occasion they become unselfconsciously their mothers' daughters.

The rest of the time they take their style from their quite amazing clothes (designs are by Ultz, fashion consultant is Jean Seel and credit is given to Clothes for the Future by BASTET). Philip Davis, fresh from the Royal Court, plays

163

the Cockney pusher, a character doomed to failure in his most cherished projects – the drugs deal which will secure him independence, the securing of Desna's love. All the characters are beautifully observed – it is an excellent company.

25 January 1981

Virginia *(THEATRE ROYAL, HAYMARKET)*
Present Laughter *(GREENWICH)*

Maggie Smith's chief task is to avoid what the audience expects from her. There are moments in *Virginia* (Theatre Royal, Haymarket), when the tart comedienne we all know and love reaches out to the audience and effortlessly plucks a laugh. Recognition is instant. A little signal is given – by an ironic twist of the body, or a nasal twang in the voice. At once we are reminded of everything this actress must forgo in order to tell us something new, in order to tell us something about Virginia Woolf.

There is a moment, too – a single moment – when she tells us of her coming out in society, and executes a hectic little dance around the stage, when her limbs behave like those of a new-born calf. She has tremendously comic limbs: it is hard for her to mime that moment when Virginia was the victim of her half-brother's sexual insult; she is too brilliantly able to see the joke.

For the rest of the time, though, she stands tall and thin (at least she seems tall), as in that famous photograph of Virginia Woolf and T. S. Eliot, in which Eliot's first wife seems to collapse in the presence of such elegance and brain. When she falls into madness, she takes us far – but not too far beyond the world of style. I think that madness is more sordid than this, a greater humiliation. Miss Smith's performance shows us the terrible possibilities of transformation – where love changes to hatred at no more than the flick of a wrist. But we are spared the very worst.

Perhaps it is not explored in Edna O'Brien's sagging script, which comes to us as very little more than a monologue, diluted by Virginia's father, her husband Leonard, and her lover Vita Sackville-West. These extra figures are scarcely more than mannequins on the stage. It is Virginia who occupies the author's exclusive attention.

165

One affectation has not been avoided: Miss Smith tackles the text by systematically altering its punctuation, so that in the long stretches of monologue no sentence ends with a full stop. There are lots of full stops, but they all come in the middle of phrases. Once you begin to notice this, it is impossible to avoid. It is as if the punctuation of the text is out of register – as in a cheap colour photograph.

Life must have been tough for leading figures in the theatre during the period of *Present Laughter* (Greenwich), when hearth-rug auditions were constantly being sought for aspiring actors and actresses.

In Coward's play, the famous actor Gary Essendine (Donald Sinden) is pestered by a kind of Mrs Worthington (Jill Johnson) on behalf of her reckless niece (Belinda Lang). During the ensuing audition scene, I was reminded of a passage in James Agate's diary for 1944: 'Excellent lunch, after which I am persuaded to interview a boy of 20, Don Sinden, who . . . has some notion of acting. Will I say whether, in my opinion, he should go on the stage or stick to cabinet-making, to which he has already served his apprenticeship? Murmuring "Stick to your fretwork, young man!" I prepare to go to sleep.'

But Agate relented and heard Sinden as Wolsey and Buckingham, and in a scene from *On Approval*. Noting (as well he might): 'Vowels not common', Agate told Mr Sinden to 'Stick to Shakespeare, beginning at the bottom of the ladder. Which advice may ruin his career. The giving of it certainly wrecks my afternoon.'

And now here is Mr Sinden, in Alan Strachan's production, impersonating to his evident pleasure the greatest romantic comedian of his time. One thing he can't do is play the piano at all convincingly. Left alone of an evening for once, he tickles the ivories so nervously he seems to expect them to burst into fits of uproarious laughter. Quite whether the audience is supposed to join in the laughter, we were not sure.

That technical defect apart, if I was ever apprehensive on Mr Sinden's behalf, it was over his future as a tragedian. If you disliked his recent Othello, you may enjoy seeing some of its

166

best moments torn to pieces at Greenwich. If, like me, you thought he carried off that difficult 'Goats and Monkeys' exit line extraordinarily well, you will be alarmed to see it sent up as the most disgusting piece of ham acting.

Despite such alarm, it is impossible not to enjoy this comic performance and production. Gwen Watford plays the loyal secretary of long standing, who gives as good as she gets. Dinah Sheridan is the elegant and understanding wife, Polly Adams the predatory woman. Three strong performances, with Miss Adams quite marvellous opposite Mr Sinden in the Act II seduction scene, a masterpiece of Coward's affected/natural dialogue. Julian Fellowes plays a mad aspiring playwright, with hideous vividness and agility, like a frog out of Hell. Terrific.

1 February 1981

Rosmersholm
(ROYAL EXCHANGE, MANCHESTER)
Suburban Strains *(ROUND HOUSE)*

Even in great drama, as in great painting or as in practically
every tapestry of a certain age, a particular element can fade –
the red turns to pale orange, or the greens are eliminated from
the colour scheme – leaving it up to the imagination to supply
the deficiency. In Ibsen's *Rosmersholm* (Royal Exchange,
Manchester) the hidden psychology of the characters remains
as striking as ever – more striking perhaps, since the play was
prophetic in its very conception of psychology – and its effect
when first performed was baffling. What those early Norwegian
audiences would have understood perfectly, however, was
the political context of the struggle between liberalism and
conservatism.

This is the colour which has faded from the scheme.
Norwegian politics of the period seem from the outside to be
petty, crusty and provincial, but conducted in terms so amazingly lofty that we find it hard to imagine their English equivalent. Certainly not in contemporary terms. In contemporary
terms, a figure like Roy Jenkins may be described as a man of
principle, an idealist. In Ibsen's world, had Mr Jenkins dared
to set foot in it, he would have been denounced at once as a
sensualist, a libertine and a rogue. These conceptions of
principle do not appear to survive long outside of the context
for which they were designed.

In *Rosmersholm*, Rebecca West (Celia Gregory) attempts
to push and cajole the man of principle, Pastor Rosmer
(Christopher Gable) in the direction of apostasy. Rosmer has
lost his faith and is about to announce this and his support for
the liberals. What he does not see is the completeness of the
rejection which will follow. Ibsen's world is dangerous, as
dangerous as that of the Shakespearian court or that terrifying

atmosphere of the classical Spanish play, in which one foot wrong means a sword through the guts. The causes of death may have changed. The upshot is the same. What we see is a life-and-death struggle conducted on the psychological plane.

I could have done without the first-night audience at Manchester, particularly the snorting buffoon behind me who communicated to all around him the fact that he had ceased to take the play seriously, greeting each new development with a nasal explosion. But there was one particularly exciting moment, after the audience had begun to titter, when they were brought back to an awed silence by the reappearance of Espen Skønberg.

You didn't know there was a character in *Rosmersholm* called Espen Skønberg? Quite so. This is the name of the actor, one of Norway's leading players, who has been brought over to Manchester to play Ulrik Brendel, Rosmer's former tutor, now an intellectual vagabond of advanced years. It is a part which, in the Norwegian theatre, is traditionally reserved for the Ralph Richardson of the day, and this is precisely what Mr Skønberg appears to be. He possesses all the Richardson qualities, with an irresistible ability to destroy the distinction between comic and tragic, so that one is both vastly amused and rendered incapable of laughter, fearing to miss a moment's magic nuance.

Whereas with Sir Ralph there must always be an element of great familiarity which he brings on to the scene, with an English audience Mr Skønberg had quite the opposite effect. A foreigner, he seemed to step out of an imaginary Norway, precisely the Norway of Ibsen's poetic vision, a Norway in which the elemental was at war with the ideal.

Alas, when he left the stage a degree of levity returned to the audience. Why? Some blame must go to Caspar Wrede's production, which bound the chief characters too literal-mindedly to the lines they were obliged to utter. Christopher Gable's Rosmer needed an element of counterpoint. He could have relaxed far more, without subverting the intensely high-minded spirit of his speeches. Had he gone further in portraying the implicit weaknesses of Rosmer's character, he would paradoxically have made him seem much less of a cipher.

Celia Gregory, memorable as Cassandra in *The Greeks*, had much to offer. But she was nervous, I thought, in the opening scene and allowed a flatness of delivery to spoil the meaning of some speeches. The over-all effect was of an unfinished performance which needed greater emotional commitment at the high spots, and elsewhere simply a little more confidence. Miles Anderson's relatively brief appearance as Peter Mortensgaard, the free-thinking editor, was most striking.

Alan Ayckbourn's company returns from Scarborough to the Round House, this time with a musical written by Ayckbourn in collaboration with Paul Todd. *Suburban Strains*, which follows the break-up of a schoolteacher's marriage, her liaison on the rebound with a sadistic doctor, and her final . . . happy ending comes over like a demonstration of the virtues and flexibility of theatre-in-the-round.

All this technical inventiveness, in my case, had a counter-productive effect, just as the interwoven time-scheme of the piece, in which parallel scenes took place simultaneously on stage, made any emotional involvement in the characters' lives very difficult to maintain.

Mr Ayckbourn some time ago hit a rich vein of humour, in observing the lengths to which friends can go while not listening to a word the other is saying. This vein is far from exhausted, but that other rich Ayckbournian seam (his ability to take the audience individually on one side and say: 'Isn't life awful . . . yes, yes, I know . . . I understand') gives me the pip.

If a seam can properly be said to give a chap the pip.

8 February 1981

Jeder Stirbt Für Sich Allein
(SCHILLER-THEATER, WEST BERLIN)
Wallensteins Tod
(DEUTSCHES THEATER, EAST BERLIN)
Die Ausnahme und die Regel
(BERLINER ENSEMBLE, EAST BERLIN)

Obliged to return to Berlin to give evidence in the appeal of a young neo-Nazi who had attempted to bury a broken bottle in the skull of a friend of mine, I took the opportunity to look at a new theatrical spectacle set in the days of the Third Reich. Peter Zadek's *Fallada revue, Every Man Dies for Himself* (*Jeder stirbt für sich allein*) has already been attacked as a tasteless and trivial waste of a great deal of money. It marks the opening of Boy Gobert's regime as artistic director of the newly renovated Schiller-Theater.

'A great deal of money' in this case means £360,000. The spectacular lasts five hours, with a full chorus of striptease artists, Hitler Youths, tap-dancing Führer look-alikes, blood, leather, feathers and fans. It sounded like just the sort of thing I most detest. Actually, I found it tremendously impressive, and while it is true that the outer limits of tastelessness are very thoroughly explored, it seems to me that they are explored to some purpose.

Hans Fallada is the pseudonym of the German writer Rudolf Ditzen (1893–1947), who achieved world fame in the 1930s with his novel *Little Man, What Now?* He was not the most attractive of characters, either as an artist or a man. The son of a respectable lawyer, he spent a lachrymose childhood failing to live up to his parents' expectations. In his late teens, he made a pact with his best friend. They fought a duel. Whether it is true, as Fallada later confessed, that he snitched the bullet from his friend's gun, we do not know. Fallada shot the other boy, who begged to be put out of his misery. So

171

Fallada shot him again point-blank through the heart. Then he attempted to kill himself, but was less brilliantly efficient. His mother's reaction on hearing of the scandal tells us everything we need to know about the period: 'Thank God', she said, 'that it was nothing sexual.'

Fallada's existence in early manhood alternated between aspiring artistry (imitation Expressionist novels), desperate odd-jobbing, sickness, morphine addiction, prison for embezzlement and, worst of all perhaps, journalism. In mid-life, however, he hit lucky as a novelist in the left-wing 'Neue Sachlichkeit' mode. Unfortunately, at precisely the same moment, Hitler hit lucky as a Führer. At once Fallada changed his tune. The next novel was seasoned with Nietzsche, and there was a cringing foreword in which the author 'bit into the sour apple' and made the requisite nod in the direction of the Nazis.

He spent a comparatively quiet Third Reich, but in the end fell out of favour as an author. He published regularly until 1943. At the end of the war, he was quick to welcome the Russians who, recognising a true Vicar of Bray when they saw one, appointed him Mayor of Feldberg. In a short while he had a job in East Berlin. *Every Man Dies for Himself*, his last novel, was written in twenty-four days in 1946. Quick work in every sense, it was a tribute to the German resistance to Hitler, a story derived from the Gestapo archives, about an old couple who, on losing their son early in the war, begin to leave postcards all around Berlin, denouncing both the leadership and the war.

On Zadek's stage you are shown the tale of such heroism (the couple will suffer execution on discovery) as told by such an opportunist. For long stretches, you have straight drama as derived from the book, beautifully conjured up scenes in Berlin rooms, effects of wide open spaces in which the large stage is left almost empty, while the monumental scale of the city is indicated with a vast granite plinth. There is also some extremely effective use of painted backdrops.

In general, the designs by Dieter Flimm and Johannes Grützke are superb, and they made me wish, not for the first time, that the painter's art was put to more effective use on the

172

British stage. Zadek himself clearly has a painter's eye: the composition was perfect throughout some sixty scenes, and the directorial technique was breath-taking. If the story had been told on its own in this way, it would have made a telling but sentimental piece of normal length.

Instead, presented as a spectacular revue, the story comes with its own critique incorporated. Zadek is at his least good when he is presenting Nazism as a sexual fantasy (simply because much that can be said, although true, is a cliché). He is at his best in developing a critique of the sentimentality both of the Nazi ethos and of the author. Fallada's choice of an old man as hero gave him the opportunity to present the ability to resist Fascism as a lovable, eccentric and doomed quality. An old man, with his life as it were behind him, is a possible hero for the sentimental and ambitious author, who would have had considerably greater difficulties in imagining his hero as, say, a writer at the height of his powers, such a man as for instance the Hans Fallada of 1933, whose immediate instinct was for personal survival.

In the same way, it is sentimentality which makes Fallada have his Gestapo officer commit suicide out of remorse at having successfully tracked down this aged resistance fighter. In general, the Nazis did not commit suicide out of remorse, nor have the torturers and camp officials been crowding to the psychiatrists, tormented by their past crimes. It is the surviving victims of those crimes who remain haunted by their experiences.

As for the sentimentality of Nazism itself, it is satirised accurately, but the response which the satire evokes from the audience struck me as sometimes too superior, too much a question of fastidiousness of taste. Indeed, the audience reaction was most interesting. When they booed vigorously, I thought Zadek had done pretty well. At the end of the first spectacular revue sketch, 'celebrating' the fall of Paris, I thought: Well, that wasn't as shocking as I had expected. Then the audience burst into appreciative applause, and my stomach turned over.

In East Berlin at the Deutsches Theater, I saw a production of Schiller's play, *Wallenstein's Death*, a production which one could hardly believe was seriously on offer, so bad was it. The actors often needed prompting (not surprisingly, since there are seventeen other items in this theatre's repertoire for February). The make-up people had thought it would be interesting if every man on stage had a bright blue chin and a yellow forehead. Abysmal.

At the Berliner Ensemble, Brecht's lecture against capitalistic justice, *The Exception and the Rule*, was performed with great truthfulness by its main actors, Michael Gerber and Hans Joachim Frank. We were told at the end not to accept as normal the present state of affairs (meaning capitalist justice). Boarding the train for West Berlin, I could not help but feel the force of this propaganda diminished, as the soldiers came with their tracker dog, to scent any possible fugitives who might be hanging from the undercarriage.

15 February 1981

A Month in the Country (OLIVIER)

Turgenev's *A Month in the Country* (Olivier) provides the brilliant exception to the rule that, in the age of realism, drama lagged decades behind the novel. It was written between 1848 and 1850. Flaubert completed *Madame Bovary* in 1857. If you think of Turgenev as a novelist, he is one of several leading European figures. If you think of him as a dramatist, he is quite alone. He anticipates Ibsen, for instance, by thirty years, Chekhov by half a century.

The programme at the National suggests that had it not been for theatrical censorship, Turgenev might well have become known to posterity primarily as a dramatist. But censorship is only a part of the story. This impact of realism is far greater in the theatre than on the printed page, and that is why the theatre had to wait. It was one thing to read *Bovary* in the 1850s, on one's own, as a scandalous book. It was quite another thing to see a play about adulterous love, in company, at the theatre.

Nor was Turgenev in advance of social mores alone; he was also in advance of theatrical practice. To write a realistic play in 1850 was like composing music for an instrument which had not yet been invented. Only in one technical aspect (its extensive use of the soliloquy) does *A Month in the Country* show its age. Otherwise, it is as startlingly not of its time as, say, the work of Büchner.

Peter Gill's first production on the Olivier stage communicated some of the thrill of psychologically realistic writing. 'I have never taken ideas but always characters as my starting point,' wrote Turgenev (a formulation to be echoed by Ibsen). In the scene where Natalya, the lady of the house, decides to dismiss the young tutor, Aleksei, with whom she has fallen violently in love, there was a magnificent sense of a conversation getting quite out of control, and events racing along faster than Natalya could control them. The very idea of dismissing the young man is blurted out before any of its consequences have been weighed up.

Natalya is played by Francesca Annis. She has a commanding presence, and one can sympathise in the play both with those who love her and those who are desperately afraid of her. I must say however that I thought she had been quite misdirected by Mr Gill. She had been encouraged in a musical drawl which strung all her words together, like vivid pink swags of Bubble-Yum. There was an emotional over-articulation, as one often hears in radio plays, when the actor is trying to compensate for loss of vision. The consequence was that the sense of her putting on a performance blurred many of the moral questions.

There was no sense of household intimacy, from the start to the end of the production. The Olivier stage had been tastefully floored by Alison Chitty. The sparing application of Colron wood dye imparted a greenish tinge to the ambience, and there was an independently floating roof, which became a louvred shutter. The action took place always, therefore, in what appeared limitless space. This looked terrific, but the looks served that tendency in the production which directly subverted the best possibilities of the text, as when what was obviously a confidential chat had to be shouted across the acres.

The company, which included a large number of former Riverside stalwarts (many of whom one had hardly noticed until they rushed on to the stage for applause at the end), has that striking and lively figure, Nigel Terry, cast against type as the live-in lover, the trusted family friend who keeps Natalya amused while her husband (Robert Swann) runs the estate. It is the arrival of Aleksei (Ewan Stewart) which turns all female heads. Mr Stewart has a charming line in bashfulness, and his first encounter with Natalya was marvellously performed by both actors. Michael Gough is the worldly doctor, Caroline Langrishe the ingenue.

22 February 1981

The Best Little Whorehouse in Texas
(THEATRE ROYAL, DRURY LANE)

If there was a brothel, such as *The Best Little Whorehouse in Texas*, in which the girls all positively liked their work, and in which the management insisted on the highest standards of cleanliness, where drugs were absolutely banned, where every employee could count on the personal friendship and understanding of the Madame – what would be the objection to such an establishment? This is the question innocently raised by the bright new musical at the Theatre Royal, Drury Lane. And if you put it like that, it is already slightly harder to answer than otherwise, since the brothel you have described is a fantasy.

Don't get me wrong. I am not saying that brothels cannot be cheerful, friendly places. Indeed, for several weeks I actually lived in a brothel – not out of greed, out of poverty. It cost $1 a day, and I can't remember having had a single complaint. Even the cockroaches had taps in their heels, and always a Country and Western song on their lips. But to be realistic about brothels one has to admit that the girls who work in them, one way or another, have missed the boat. Successful prostitutes do not work in brothels. They become society hostesses. We all know this.

A Japanese friend of mine gave me a piece of advice, which I should like to pass on to the general reader. Never, he said, go for the most beautiful girl in the brothel; avoid the best rooms – the ones on the first and second floors; the beautiful girls are irritable and greedy – they will certainly swindle you; always go to the third floor, where the plain girls will be much more pleased to see you, and consequently give you a better time. This friend of mine knew what he was talking about, since it was in such circumstances that he first met the woman who later became (cue for violins) his wife.

I always try to include a fascinating fact in each column.

Fascinating fact No. 4,329: The German for a brothel, rather confusingly, is *Puff*; the word for a Madame is *Puffmutti*. End of fascinating fact. Now back to Texas.

It is a measure of the general unshockability of the West End audience that the most successful jokes in *Best Little Whorehouse* were the dirtiest ones, and the ones which most blatantly offended against the decorum of a first night. Great gusts of laughter swept across the sea of dinner jackets at the mere mention of venereal disease. Confronted with a spectacular tableau of tastefully simulated sex scenes, the audience quite clearly congratulated itself upon having made a good choice of an evening out. They even hissed the villain, the TV crusader who seeks, in the name of public morals, to close the brothel down. They laughed the idea of decency out of court, and they put themselves squarely on the side of the frank pursuit of sexual gratification, not to mention the commercial exploitation of sex.

Which gave one the opportunity to reflect once again on the failure of audiences to make any connection between what happens on stage and what goes on in their daily lives. At the Riverside Studios recently, the audience listened enthralled while a cultural emissary of East Germany told them to trust the wisdom of the Communist Party. Because this was done in the name of art it was not considered in the least intolerable. And because, at the other end of town, all this mockery of Christian sexual morality was packaged as entertainment, I very much doubt whether even the Christians in the audience were much offended.

If this sounds like a prelude to an attack, it is not. The programme note explains that the story is taken from history. For a century and a half, there was a splendid country brothel in Texas, which a TV campaign closed down. 'Everything in the play is true. Except what we made up,' says the note. Quite so. What they made up included the idea of the perfect brothel. But this does not matter, since what the musical proposes, in effect, is true: if there were an ideal brothel in Texas, public morality would close it down, and not even its favourite customers would come openly to its defence. Thus the fantasy has an unhappy ending, and the girls disperse, to face a much less happy sort of life.

And thus too, the audience disperses into the real world of London, where nobody I've ever met, apart from the odd Member of Parliament, frequents brothels.

It's a noisy, vulgar, always amusing and sometimes very funny musical. The book is by Larry L. King and Peter Masterson, the music and lyrics by Carol Hall, who must take the credit for one of the most attractive aspects of the evening, namely that it is strongly in favour of women having a good time. A talented cast includes Carlin Glynn as Puffmutti, Henderson Forsythe, Fred Evans, Sheila Brand, Betsy Brantley and Miquel Brown. A success? I should say so.

1 March 1981

The Faith Healer (ROYAL COURT)
Goosepimples (HAMPSTEAD)

On a dozen occasions at the Royal Court we are reminded that the Faith Healer of Brian Friel's title is, metaphorically speaking, an artist. This kind of nudging insistence is excessive. If a man writes a play about an Irish faith healer, he should just give his audience enough time to have a think about faith healing, before he introduces its figurative significance. The primary meaning should be allowed its day in the sun.

Mr Friel's faith healer, an Irishman working in exile around the small towns and villages of remotest Scotland and Wales, is single-minded in his devotion to his gift. For the sake of the gift, the healer will suffer, his wife will suffer, his Cockney manager will suffer a way of life in which comfort, personal friendship, the very self is subordinated to the great Goal. Those who seek the help of the faith healer are the very ones who dislike him most, since the fact that they come to his 'performances' is proof of their desperation.

The healer spends his life working on the fringes of the Celtic world. In Ireland itself he will not work, for reasons which become clear when, after it seems that his gift has deserted him, he returns to County Donegal. One night in a pub he is inspired to work a cure on a crooked finger. His success leads to a celebration, and the celebration is a prelude to defeat. There is a young cripple called McGarvey, whom he is asked to cure. The landlord warns him that McGarvey and his friends are savage and bloody men; he will fail in his cure, and they will kill him for his failure. But the faith healer knows all this. He goes out to meet McGarvey and is indeed killed.

Meaning: Ireland hates the artist for his gift; the artist has no power to cure the ills of young Ireland; if he goes out to confront the sickness, he will undoubtedly be destroyed.

And this is no doubt true of the kind of artist who considers himself a faith healer. Those who challenge the metaphor, however, will find this an unsatisfactory play. For myself, I cannot believe in salvation through art, and I think that those who do hold such a belief are almost bound to produce bad work. Mr Friel's play was impressive to sit through, partly because it was pretty hard to follow, and yet convincingly delivered in a series of four monologues spoken by three actors. Patrick Magee takes the title role, Helen Mirren is the suffering wife, Stephen Lewis does a very welcome comic turn as the Cockney manager. Directed by Christopher Fettes, this company works accurately, whole-heartedly and well. I felt at the end: that was quite a play, but I must now read it. If a play leaves one with such a feeling, I suppose this is already a sign that something is amiss.

The trouble stems from Mr Friel's choice of form, a series of dramatic monologues. The term 'dramatic monologue' is normally used to refer to a piece of verse or prose, written from the point of view of a character, either fictional or historical. Browning's 'My Last Duchess' is a good example. The word 'dramatic' attaches itself to the description because the author forsakes his own voice to a great extent and imitates another; he will give the reader the impression of events taking place, in such a way that the drama can all be inferred. This kind of writing is self-sufficient. You read 'In a Spanish Cloister'. You are at once transported to such a cloister, and required to see it through the eyes of one of its inhabitants. The writing does everything.

Now if you put a dramatic monologue on stage, it ceases to be dramatic in this sense. You take from the imagination the task of supplying both actor and scene. In a normal play, in true dramatic writing as opposed to 'dramatic monologues', the text is absolutely not self-sufficient in this way. The spoken text is only a part of what the audience takes in – and the great skill of the dramatist is that he never forgets this. The dramatist does not have much leisure for explanation, in the novelist's way, or for description. He is concerned with presentation of primary material.

If you read Mr Friel's text it gives you absolutely everything you need to know. If you see it on stage, you get considerably

181

less from it, partly because it is not always possible to remember what the story was, and who exactly is who. While the work is incomplete in the imagination, it has a great deal of vibrancy. But a reading sets that vibrancy at rest. One notices how very badly written the wife's soliloquy is (with its corny repetition of sentences beginning with 'and', and with its occasional echoes of Molly Bloom). Nor can one avoid feeling a certain distrust of Mr Friel's tendency to self-projection. The artist, he implies, is a miracle-worker. I beg to disagree.

At the Hampstead Theatre, Mike Leigh is presenting his latest show, *Goosepimples*, devised from improvised work by Jim Broadbent, Marion Bailey, Paul Jesson, Jill Baker and Antony Sher. The resultant play bears many superficial resemblances to a West End farce; with this excellent but fundamental difference, that whereas in a farce things begin fairly realistically, only to get out of hand, in *Goosepimples* the realism is achieved only in the later stages of a highly improbable journey. People begin as caricatures. They have funny voices and peculiar walks. There is something systematically odd about their behaviour. Yet the odder they become, the more truthful is the characterisation.

Events are set in the flat of a car salesman, whose plans for the evening include a dinner for a colleague and his wife, with whom the protagonist is conducting an affair. The lodger, a girl croupier, brings home a non-English-speaking Arab whom she presumes to be an oil-sheikh. The Arab presumes that he is in a brothel, and that, for instance, the cocktail bar in the corner is, precisely, the kind of bar where one pays. The motive force in the play, plotwise, is the complete inability of the two cultures to communicate. Retrospectively it all makes sense. At the time it seeks to make no sense at all.

At the centre, there is a quite brilliant performance by Antony Sher as the Arab, a performance so perfectly imagined that it physically transforms the familiar features of the History Man in such a way as to render them quite unrecognisable. It is terribly funny, but at the same time immensely distressing, as we come to see the flat through the Arab's eyes as a dreadful, inescapable Hell, the fulfilment of

all his worst fears. Marion Bailey, the girl who has picked up
the Arab, becomes more and more hysterically distressed as
she fails to make him conform to her dreams.

8 March 1981

The Cherry Orchard
(BOUFFES DU NORD, PARIS)
The Triumph of Death
(BIRMINGHAM REP STUDIO)

Meyerhold complained about the Moscow Art Theatre and its early productions of Chekhov. He detested the assumption on which the naturalistic approach to production was based, the assumption that the audience was incapable of bringing its own imagination to bear upon the production in question. The naturalistic theatre, by fussily supplying every element in scenery and sound effects, 'was consistent and resolute in banning the power of mystery from the stage'. And he quoted Schopenhauer: 'A work of art can influence man only through the imagination. Thus art must constantly arouse it.'

It is a safe bet that Meyerhold would have been delighted with Peter Brook's production of *The Cherry Orchard*, which opened in Paris last week at the Théâtre des Bouffes du Nord, and in which the only setting was the theatre itself. This is an abandoned vaudeville house, which Brook's company have set to rights but never redecorated, so that its blackened walls supply a constant reminder of past splendour.

The house is alive with possibilities. Mme Ranyevskaya goes to bed somewhere behind the dress circle, from whose balcony she leans down, with an awareness of all the romantic associations of balcony speeches, to dispense a largesse which is quite beyond her means. And when those means are finally exhausted, and the house is to be abandoned, the whole of this triple-galleried height is brought into action, in the search for Trofimov's galoshes, and the attic is ransacked for luggage.

Two things are significantly missing from this theatre: curtain and stage. For the most part, the action takes place at ground level, on an area strewn generously with Oriental rugs

184

and carpets. Those who saw *The Conference of the Birds* in the same theatre will remember that a Persian rug provided the sole background to the action in that case. I suppose it is part of the delight of Oriental rugs for Mr Brook that the language of their design has proved truly international, spreading over the centuries throughout Europe, Russia and the East with a success unrivalled even by the elements of Greek architecture. In this production, the same carpets, which in Act One provide the domestic element in the design, will become, for the purposes of Act Two, formal representations of flowered fields.

The design and costumes, by Chloe Obolensky, give no sense of austerity or asceticism. Quite the contrary. There is even a feeling of wicked extravagance in the beauty of Mme Ranyevskaya's costume for Act Two. This central role is taken by Natasha Parry (Mrs Peter Brook), and it was the really memorable feature of the evening.

Such great roles can be like hidden reefs on which great talents wreck themselves. Drawn to the role precisely because of its greatness, the actress can all too easily satisfy herself by giving an impression of what it would be like to be a great actress, so that what the audience observes is a tiresome and self-involved 'beauty', strutting up and down, forever attempting to glimpse the effect she must be making as she turns prettily around. Thus the audience is cast in the role of the tame domestic sycophant, or worse still, the dressing-room mirror.

The character drawn by Chekhov is certainly not free from self-love; but she continually surprises us with her self-awareness. The theme of the play is pride. The landowner and her brother know perfectly well what is happening to their inheritance, but their pride forbids them to make a rational compromise with circumstances. They must feign awareness, but as Meyerhold points out, the central motif of Act Three is Ranyevskaya's awareness of impending misfortune. What Natasha Parry gives us in full measure is the sense of a character who has suffered in the past and is suffering still. This entails no sacrifice of charm or coquetry – indeed it guarantees the effectiveness of that charm and beauty which Miss Parry possesses in such abundance.

The brother is played by Michel Piccoli, as a study in evasiveness which hides, when necessary, behind a much colder snobbery than the sister ever assumes. This is not a tremendously weepy, hopeless Gayev, but an airy character whose feet never seem to touch the ground. By contrast Niels Arestrup is solidity itself as the up-and-coming purchaser of the orchard. This is a wonderfully lively company, which plays with a great sense of tempo. There is no interval, but no sense of strain either. The story bowls along, beautifully, amusingly, affectingly. It is agile, but it is not obnoxiously athletic. It is Chekhov without chairs – informal, fast, and great, great fun.

Those who liked *The Romans in Britain* will adore *The Triumph of Death*, David Rudkin's new play at the Birmingham Rep Studio. It's terrible. We begin with the Children's Crusade, after which a matriarchal, potato-eating community is founded somewhere in Mummerset, dedicated to the worship of Christ in his manifestation as the Great God Pan (complete with prosthetic whang). This identification of the two shepherd gods derives from English Renaissance poetry (see Milton's 'Ode on the Morning of Christ's Nativity'). The rest of the conception makes no sense at all, historically, anthropologically, philosophically, or artistically.

There is a eucharistic celebration at which Christ/Pan forgets himself to the extent of committing the sin of Brenton with one of his flock, who comments: 'Thy stretching of me feels so black, thy cock is crowned with thorns.' The established church decides to put a stop to all this and arrests Jehan, the matriarch, who goes on trial in Act Two under the name of Joan . . .

Before she is burnt at the stake (which we watch, and after which she is somewhat hilariously reduced to a neat pile of ashes, like Harriet and the Matches), she gives birth to Martin Luther, who enthrals us with a long description of defecation, and ends up quoting L. P. Hartley. This is not so odd, since it transpires that Luther is an asylum inmate of the present day.

The play ends with a surprise dig at capitalism and humanism . . .

Did I say 'play'? This is not so much a play as a cry for help. Indeed, in his last two pieces, Mr Rudkin has given the impression of an artist who has quite lost his way in the woods, and who desperately hopes, by making as loud a noise as possible, to attract the attention of some passing forester. Good luck to him. Bad luck to this piece, with its ill-fated attempts to revive the iambic pentameter as a dramatic measure, with its dreadful grammar, its half-hearted use of archaisms but above all its absence of any intellectual or artistic discipline.

15 March 1981

Mike Leigh in Retrospect

This week I treated myself to a Mike Leigh retrospective. First, I returned to the play, *Goosepimples*, which is currently such a success at the Hampstead Theatre, and which will shortly transfer to the Garrick. Next, I took in a few television plays, *Abigail's Party*, *Grown Ups*, and *Nuts in May*. Then I saw about eight more Mike Leigh films. Then I went home and listened in complete privacy to the banned radio play, *Too Much of a Good Thing*. Then I went to bed.

The radio play, incidentally, was banned by Ian McIntyre, Controller of Radio Three, on the grounds of its banality. I am glad that banality was the only objection, since the play happens to include a prolonged sex scene of a highly explicit nature, very carefully and cleverly observed. You might have predicted that radio sex, like radio ballet, would prove rather dull fare – but not a bit of it. Mr Leigh keeps one's attention constantly engaged by asking the blind listener to decide for himself just exactly who is doing what to whom, and how far have they got. Seldom have the virtues of stereo transmission been shown off to better effect. Mr McIntyre is a big man. By changing his mind on the fate of this play, he could prove himself a great man.*

When Mr Leigh directs, there really is a distinctive acting style. It comes across on radio, in the performances of Philip Davis and Lesley Manville, as the driving instructor and his virgin pupil. These performances are built out of speech mannerisms: the instructor, for instance, has a subtly ingratiating nervous patter – he never imposes either on the pupil or on her father, but he is careful never to let the silences get him down. Words bubble out of him.

The father (Eric Allan) is a rat-catcher, and there is a dialogue in which Mr Davis tries to think of the odd question about the state of rat-catching today, while contriving not

* Mr McIntyre did not take up this suggestion.

to insult the father's profession. The basis of the whole comedy is the contrast between the extreme modesty of the instructor's mannerisms, and the expertise of his seduction. The story-line is deliberately banal in the way that most seductions are banal to those not involved in them. But the characterisation is anything but banal.

The comedy of mannerisms – a phrase which glibly offers its services as a description of Mr Leigh's work – is, however, only the starting point. Funny accents, peculiar walks, extraordinary speech habits, these are the first tell-tale signs of one of Mr Leigh's productions. In a surprising way, they keep a sense of aesthetic distance between the spectator and the actor, and they are responsible for an effect which I have observed more than once this week – namely, the oddly long time required before one permits oneself to take a Mike Leigh character entirely seriously.

One critic of *Goosepimples*, whom I ran into at the Hampstead, complained that Mr Leigh always made his cast act badly because he filled them with hatred of the characters they were portraying. One frequently hears the word 'patronising' used against such work. It is true that Mr Leigh has no sentimental feelings for the working class (most theatrical representations of workers are overwhelmingly sentimental), and that he gives his lower orders a very rough time. For my own part, I find this savagery both honest and exhilarating. But there is always a stage beyond the savagery, a stage at which Mr Leigh and his actors make psychological discoveries of a quite unparalleled force and profundity.

I'm thinking of such creations as Brenda Blethyn's extraordinary performance in *Grown-Ups*, the recent TV play set in working-class Canterbury. Miss Blethyn was the older sister who persecuted the newly-wed couple with her kindly attentions, and who eventually sought refuge in their newly-acquired council house. This was a depiction of an overwhelmingly powerful instinct for self-preservation, expressed in a neurotic passion for cups of tea, taking refuge in the loo, knitting, chatting, making sure that she was never alone for a long time.

As the pace of the film speeded up, it was clear that we were being offered not so much a character as a pathology of desperation. With half her brain, Miss Blethyn knew what was happening to her. The other half was completely taken over by instinctual forces. Thrown out of her sister's house, she must find a new home at once. Taking refuge with the next-door neighbour, her sister's old schoolteacher, is the brilliantly embarrassing solution to her problem. Not only must she take refuge there, she must immediately make the house into her home: as soon as she sees the wife's knitting lying on the chair, she is impelled to take it up – to become a part of the household. In a matter of minutes, she must become one of the family.

In *Goosepimples*, which with *Grown-Ups*, I would rate as the best of the things I have seen this week, there is a similar sense that what we arrive at is a pathology. One sees it in Jill Baker's performance as the greedy wife – greed being the foundation of the characterisation, the bold preliminary brushwork in the portraiture. Then we must ask, what is this greed about? What we interpret at first as an antagonism between Jim Broadbent and Miss Baker is seen to be a cover for their love-affair. But there is a hitch here. In order to put the suspicious husband off the scent, the lover must pretend to humiliate the wife. Challenged as to whether he is having an affair, he puts all the disgust he can into his reply: 'I wouldn't stoop so low.' As it turns out, however, there is no difference between pretence and reality, when it comes to humiliation. What Miss Baker so memorably portrays is a woman trapped in an inevitably humiliating passion. That is what her greed is about.

There is an element of the pathological, too, in Marion Bailey's depiction of the girl croupier who is torn between her intense desire for money, and her perfectly genuine sexual fear of the Arab she has brought home. The terror she shows at the idea that her Arab might not be the oil-sheikh she has imagined, her brave attempt to reconcile a cosmopolitan with a distinctly suburban conception of morality, her inability both to get what she wants and to be the kind of person she would respect – well, if such perceptions derive from a hatred of a character, then hatred cannot be too bad a thing.

But for my own part, I do not think that *Goosepimples* is vitiated, as a work of art, by the quite proper disgust it evinces for the behaviour that it portrays. It amply repays a second visit, incidentally, and will prove a very nifty sort of Trojan horse, whereby this exceptionally talented director will conquer the West End.

29 March 1981

L'Amour de l'Amour
(THÉÂTRE DU ROND-POINT)
Britannicus (THÉÂTRE DE L'ODÉON)
The Wild Duck
(THÉÂTRE DE LA VILLE)

Jean-Louis Barrault has a new theatre in Paris. The Théâtre du Rond-Point, on the Avenue Franklin Roosevelt, occupies the shell of a former skating rink. The wooden interior of the old Théâtre d'Orsay has been unscrewed and re-assembled on the Right Bank; it opened on Friday last, with *L'Amour de l'Amour*, an account of the legend of Cupid and Psyche.

Paris for me is the theatrical centre of the world, the city in which the actor's and director's skills are most variously and generously on display. The Renaud-Barrault Company, with its vivid rhetoric based on the art of mime, makes a major contribution to that greatness. I'm thinking of the last two important shows – *Zadig*, in which Voltaire's story was richly depicted in the visual language of a Persian miniature, and the revival of Claudel's complete, and immense, *Le Soulier de Satin*, in which the world of the Spanish Empire was spread out before our eyes.

Things happen on this stage with an inconceivable speed. You blink once. An imperial court has appeared. You blink again. There is a shipwreck on the high seas. Design can be brilliant, but it is the actor's body which emerges as the hero of each show. One feels that there is no experience which the body cannot express.

In the latest show, however, I felt that the director had put his theatre at a disadvantage by the combination of film with stage action, so that we saw a number of scenes against a projected background of marine life, or so that a character might be speaking from within the coils of a photographically living snake. This introduction of film made the language of

192

gesture seem that crucial bit less vivid. What actor could compete with a gigantic projection of an octopus?

Then there was a failure of design – a failure to find a way of bringing the ancient Greek world to life without reminding the spectator of some modern version of Greek style. It is a notorious problem: you set out to provide a few tasteful elements of the Hellenic visual world; you end up with something which looks like a florist's window-dressing. The classical world has been too often plundered for ideas. Those who nowadays return for more must set themselves in competition with all our cultural history.

What to do, then, with a play like Racine's *Britannicus*, in which the seventeenth-century viewpoint depicts Rome under Nero? In the production at the Odéon, designed and directed by Gildas Bourdet, we find ourselves in what appears to be Versailles under Louis XIV. It is dawn, the shutters are closed, and the superb antechamber is quite dark. The production exploits beautifully the unity of time, so that the play's ending takes place in a similar twilight. In the interstice, the representation is faithful to the seventeenth-century classical style, save for a very few subversive details. There are elements of the furniture and the decoration of the room which post-date the costumes, and if one looks closely there are radiator vents under the windows, and plastic discs under the legs of the tables and chairs.

What we are offered, in other words, is a play set in a paradoxical present day, a costume drama mysteriously taking place in a museum. At the height of the action, there is one deliberate and shocking solecism – a man actually removes his wig and proceeds to commit suicide before our eyes. Thus action finds its way on to a stage where verbal rhetoric had previously enjoyed its austere monopoly. There is a tremendous feeling, throughout this production, that both director and company have an absolute faith in Racine's text and in their approach. There is no swerving, no misplaced nervousness on behalf of the audience. The reception was exceedingly enthusiastic.

The company in question, incidentally, is the Théâtre de la Salamandre, which operates from an old cinema in Turcoing, near Lille in the north of France.

Another great success is Lucian Pintilié's revival of *The Wild Duck* at the Théâtre de la Ville. Here a problem is solved which defeated our own National Theatre: how to play Ibsen's domestic tragedy on the large, open stage. In Paris, the approach is boldly anti-naturalistic from the start. The design takes its cue from the fact that young Ekdal's trade is photography.

In the first act, the dinner party is seen through a vast two-way mirror, mottled with what seemed to be damp spots; the effect is that the actors half materialise like images on a plate and that with a slight change of lighting the whole action can dissolve away. The chamberlains are grotesquely made up. They watch a lantern slide show after dinner, gasping at the illusions which are projected over their heads while a solemn voice announces the names of Italian cities.

For the remainder of the action, the rooms of young Ekdal's house have been, as it were, unpacked on to the large stage. The attic, instead of being a poky little hole, is as large as it must appear in the imaginations of the father and the son. Indeed, it comprises the whole of the back wall, with ladders and gantries going right up on to the roof.

When a shot is fired into this vast and wonderful space, a flutter of birds ensues, and an egg falls on to the living-room floor. This happens twice, to comic effect. On the third shot, we expect something similar. But nothing happens, for there follows that passage of dramatic irony, when Gregers Werle imagines that he has persuaded Hedwig to sacrifice her pet for the sake of her father. Then, as the characters realise that something has gone wrong, they rush up towards the roof of the theatre, to an immense commotion of disturbed birds. As they reach the roof, Hedwig herself (or what looks alarmingly like her) falls the whole height of the theatre on to the stage.

Bold as he is with his staging, M. Pintilié is the great unfolder of Ibsen's text. You emerge from this production physically shocked, and yet also exhilarated. You feel that the original force of the realism has been conveyed by this truly spectacular and quite idiosyncratic production.

5 April 1981

Don Juan *(COTTESLOE)*
The Seagull *(ROYAL COURT)*

What happened to Don Juan in the end? One of the earliest versions of the story has him murdered by outraged Franciscans, while another imagines him to have publicly repented his sins and retired to a monastery. For Camus, in his essay on Don Juanism (in *The Myth of Sisyphus*), the latter fate seemed particularly appropriate – to mock the doctrines of the Church from within the cloister, to contemplate the absurdity of existence from the confines of the cell.

In Molière's play, the villainy of Don Juan reaches its climax at the moment of his feigned repentance. Of all the sins he has committed, hypocrisy is seen as the very worst, and there is a marvellous speech in which he argues that in becoming a hypocrite he is only following the example set by his age. A director has two questions to ask of his text: What does it mean to us now, and what did it mean to its author and his period? In Peter Gill's production of *Don Juan* (Cottesloe), it is the second question which receives its answer during this speech; the worst villain in the world, says Molière, is not as bad as the man who hides his misdeeds behind a sanctimonious front.

Retribution follows: the trap door, perhaps the most famous trap in the history of theatre, opens. But note how few lines Molière devotes to the disposing of his hero. It is as if he had sent the man down to Hell only as a way of rendering his major theme acceptable to the censorship of the day. All right, if the man is a villain, he must be punished . . . but by that time the damage has been done.

The damage, by the way, is the mere raising of the atheist's question: if God does not exist, by what law shall I live? To Don Juan, the non-existence of God is self-evident, and the only philosophy he lives by is the self-evidence of arithmetic: $2 + 2 = 4$, that is all he believes. He lives, therefore, only for

195

pleasure. But pleasure, he discovers (in anticipation of Schopenhauer), is not a positive but a negative quality. It consists in the removal of an obstacle, the banishment of pain. Confronted with a woman, Don Juan must seduce her. But at the moment of victory, he is condemned, infallibly, to be bored by his conquest.

This is the modern, or the forward-looking, element in the play and it is this quality which Nigel Terry most beautifully captures. His Don Juan is the victim of his own clarity, the philosopher who has seen through everything. No wonder then that he seems unable to concentrate on the action which he maliciously provokes. Deprived of ethical significance the world in which Don Juan moves is liable to lose altogether its grip on his attention. He judges reality by one criterion alone: does this provoke my desire? But reality must inevitably disappoint him, since he never encounters an object capable of resisting that desire.

This is an exciting production. As unveiled on Tuesday, it seemed insufficiently rehearsed, so that some lines were quite wrongly delivered, and many others could have been smoothed over. But the central performance was so good that the slightly unfinished quality was in a way an added attraction. You felt the play reaching out and testing its own strength. This is the great attraction of seeing a work by Molière, who is hardly central to our own theatrical tradition. Vast areas of European theatre still remain closed to us. There are wonderful discoveries to be made. In the comedy, the nearest we get to the kind of comic business to be found in Molière (even in this deeply serious play) is the Punch and Judy show.

Mr Gill has allowed a certain symbolic presence of slapstick in his production, but one does not feel that he is asking us to laugh like children. John Fowles, who provides the translation, has pointed out any possibility of sexual innuendo. But this, though it earns laughs, is hardly a very interesting area of investigation.

Mr Fowles must take some credit for the fact that the play works so well. But I think that the earlier scenes could have been better done, and that the Mummerset idiom for Pierrot and Charlotte is a fairly boring rendition. Ron Pember plays Sganarelle, Don Juan's servant. The point is, surely, that this figure is several generations earlier than Figaro, and that the master–servant relationship is consequently the more tightly ordered: Sganarelle really does have no alternative but to obey his master and therefore run the risk of hell-fire in his company.

Michael Gough plays the Don's disapproving father, and carries the part off admirably, bringing an immediate gravity to the stage, and articulating excellently his long reproving speech.

At the Royal Court, *The Seagull* has been translated by Thomas Kilroy, and set in Ireland, in the Anglo-Irish society of the last century. This is a very good idea, for which a note in the play text (jointly published by Methuen and the theatre, at 80p instead of a programme) argues most convincingly. At a stroke, you remove from the play that quality of ethereal 'Russian-ness', which puts such a false romantic gloss on our reading of Chekhov and his contemporaries. One could remove this quality with violence: for instance, if the word samovar was translated as tea-urn, we would always be brought down with a bump when the item was mentioned. Samovars are, after all, fairly prosaic pieces of equipment.

The Kilroy approach, which finds a historical equivalent in the doomed world of the Anglo-Irish, performs the task much better. This translation is not an act of violence, but is a work of illumination. The central feature is that it gives us a way of understanding the gap between the summer visitors to the Irish country house, and those who are obliged to live there all the time. It is a class gap and a cultural gap. There is a peasantry. That problem, which always arises in an English-language Chekhov, disappears at once.

Above the peasantry and household servants, there is the professional and managerial class whose fate is intimately linked with the fortunes of the land. And above them floats the doomed class, those who do not understand agriculture, who cannot see what is at stake when a patch of fine weather gives an opportunity to get the harvest in.

Curiously enough, the programme note tells us that Turgenev, the founder of this dramatic tradition, owed a literary debt to the Anglo-Irish: 'I could never have written about the Russian peasants as I did, had I not read Maria Edgeworth.' Chekhov's own great debt in *The Seagull*, of course, is to Shakespeare: the play elaborates a parallel with Hamlet and Gertrude in the relationship between the actress mother and her aspiring writer son.

Anna Massey plays the mother, and if there were no other performance of any value in the production one would still recommend it on the basis of this vivid, comic but most touching depiction. The difficulty of playing an actress on stage derives from the easiness of the task. Any actress can play an actress. But to say that is no more than to say: any actress can act badly. To play an actress and make one actually care for the character – that is quite something. The son is Anton Lesser, and the girl he loves (Nina in the original) is Harriet Walter.

I hope one day to find a way of describing Miss Walter's virtues as an actress; to say that she is completely natural is both true and false, since the more one sees of her work the more careful differentiation one notices. She is the only actress I know who can play a boy (in *Cloud Nine* and *Nicholas Nickleby*) without making me throw up. If that is natural, then everything for her is natural. She is naturally excellent, and a fine match for the romantic Mr Lesser. I might mention also beautiful performances from Veronica Duffy and Alan Rickman as the original Marsha and Trigorin.

12 April 1981

The Merchant of Venice (STRATFORD)

Consider *The Merchant of Venice*, which opened at Stratford this week in John Barton's new production, from the point of view of the merchant himself – that is to say from the point of view of Tom Wilkinson's Antonio. He's the one who sets the play going, with his confession of melancholy, a melancholy brought on by the prospect of his friend, Bassanio (Jonathan Hyde) marrying Portia (Sinead Cusack). If Bassanio wins Portia, Antonio loses his only love. It is to prove his love that he undertakes what an early commentator called his 'extravagant and unusual kind of bond'.

For this extravagant act, Antonio is often considered a fine, selfless sort of fellow. Mr Wilkinson, as I understand his performance, thinks otherwise. There is something deeply unpleasant in this ambition of a friend to insert his own death between Bassanio and his mistress, to engineer a way of saying to Bassanio: 'You may have your love, but it is paid for with my life.'

And Antonio does indeed, to a great extent, engineer the conditions. It is he who insists to Shylock (David Suchet) that the bond between them, since it cannot be a bond between friends, must be a bond between enemies. Shylock understands Antonio perfectly, and offers him, instead of a high rate of interest, the famous arrangement of the pound of flesh. When he hears the offer, Mr Wilkinson is genuinely delighted, while Bassanio is horrified. Mr Wilkinson has found the one way of upstaging Portia. If he defaults on the agreement, and it comes to judgement, there is no way that her wealth or beauty can save him from death and his revenge. That is his subconscious motivation.

There is no love lost between Antonio and Portia. Her first question in court ('Which is the merchant there, and which the Jew?') comes over as a quite delicious snub.

From Portia's point of view, her task in the trial is to thwart two kinds of revenge: Shylock's upon Antonio, Antonio's upon her. From Antonio's point of view, it is an attempt to dress up suicide as judicial murder. At this point, the role is as taxing as any in Shakespeare: the actor must be a man about to die, but he must not show an excessive degree of self-awareness. When he is saved from the knife, Antonio does not consciously see his ambition as having been thwarted. The motivation lies deeper than that. If suicide is murder at one remove, and this is suicide at one remove, then the relation between motivation and action is bound to be in some parts obscure.

I found myself watching Mr Wilkinson closely, as his supposed death drew nearer. He was drinking quite heavily, but without showing the effects – in the manner of an experienced heavy drinker. When it came to the moment of baring his chest for the knife, and he was obliged to remove his necktie and shirt, I could not help wondering at the meticulousness with which he pocketed a stud or tie-clip, as if reserving it for future use.

Would a man behave like this, in the last moments of his life? In all probability, yes. It is like the key moment in Orwell's description of a hanging when the man on the way to the gallows sidesteps in order to avoid a puddle. Such trivial actions are the final assertion by whatever remains of our will to live. A tie-clip itself is no longer of importance to us. But to treat a tie-clip as if it were important – that is what matters.

A moment later, when Portia played her winning card, the Stratford audience responded with obvious relief. There was no doubt that the confrontation had been most effectively played, by Miss Cusack, by Mr Suchet, and by Mr Wilkinson. It was for me an apt climax to an affecting and consequently deeply disgusting exposition of Christian society at work. Now Shylock was cornered and his final humiliation could be achieved.

We remember, from the beginning, that Antonio had conceived the bond as a contract between enemies. Portia's justice is not his justice. He and Shylock understand each other perfectly. So that when, after a brief hysterical reaction of relief, Antonio recovers to find that he has not given his life for his friend, it is not out of character for him to take his frustration out on the Jew. If there was one reaction which impressed me in the Stratford audience, it was the horrified sucking of teeth which greeted Antonio's insistence that Shylock become a Christian. That really told you something about the Venetian state religion. For the merchant of Venice such vindictiveness was utterly in character.

26 April 1981

The Forest (STRATFORD, OTHER PLACE)
The Book of Sir Thomas More
(YOUNG VIC)

Splendid! A new Russian classic enters the English repertoire with all the elements that a Russian classic should possess. *The Forest*, by Alexander Ostrovsky (Other Place), has a land-owning widow who lives by selling off tracts of timber, forever at the mercy of the rising merchant class. And if you think that is a bit fishy, I might add that in another of Ostrovsky's plays, there is a heroine whose name means 'the sea-gull', whose life has been destroyed 'by a passing lady-killer'.

Ostrovsky (who died in the year that Chekhov embarked on serious drama with *Ivanov*) survives in the international repertoire on the basis of *Thunder*, which Janacek turned into *Katya Kabanova*, and as author of *The Snow Maiden*, which both Tchaikovsky and Rimsky-Korsakov set to music. *Thunder* was translated into English in a useful but rare Penguin Classic, *Four Russian Plays* (1972), by Joshua Cooper. In other words, Ostrovsky, like Victor Hugo, is familiar as a playwright, but not among the English theatre-going world.

That state of affairs will now change. Jeremy Brooks and Kitty Hunter Blair have produced a new translation of *The Forest*, which in Adrian Noble's production is both as exciting as this director's recent *Duchess of Malfi*, and also consider-ably less bloody. The comedy is boldly conceived, and the production takes a delight in mixing a natural style with the most vivid caricature. Caricature is often used as a pejorative term in criticism. But true caricature is a most difficult and rewarding art, requiring absolute accuracy and continual strength of line. I knew that I was going to love this production when Eve Pearce flitted across stage as the eavesdropping housekeeper, drawn inexorably to the scene of any possible scandal, and possessed of an ability to become invisible to the

202

characters on stage while remaining, in fact, in full view. Wide eyes darting to and fro, a face across which it seemed impossible that a smile should flicker, she looked like a Russian version of Mrs Danvers in *Rebecca*.

The housekeeper is right-hand woman to Barbara Leigh-Hunt, the land-owning widow, a character of fundamentally malicious disposition. There were occasional moments of slight panic when I thought that either Ostrovsky or Miss Leigh-Hunt was going to attempt to redeem this figure in our eyes, and display some element of fine feeling. But no, thank heavens. She kicks off hypocritical, continues as scheming, selfish and cold, and brings the portrayal to a wonderful climax of meanness, at a moment when a less whole-heartedly nasty character might have seen the opportunity for a grand public gesture.

She reminds us of an evil stepmother from a fairy story, and that, precisely, is what she is. Janine Duvitski plays the impoverished niece, betrothed against her will to a good-for-nothing for whom Miss Leigh-Hunt nurses a secret passion, Paul Whitworth. Miss Duvitski is a goodie – natural, loving, passionate, but with a morbid tendency to think on suicide. Mr Whitworth is shallow, affected, cowardly, with his eye on the main chance, and with a comical faith in his ability to come across as a swell. How could true love light upon such a character? No, Miss Duvitski's affections are elsewhere, and a glance at the cast list is enough to tell you where. True love is Allan Hendrick. True love is always Mr Hendrick. He's the only one who can do sincerity. But how to get the dowry necessary for the betrothal to Mr Hendrick?

It is here that the two comic master-strokes of the piece are played. Along through the forest, hopelessly down on their luck, come a tragic actor (Alan Howard) and an old vaudeville player (Richard Pasco), who, having met by chance, decide to try out their fortunes chez Mr Howard's mean aunt (Miss Leigh-Hunt).

Mr Howard is as mad as a meat axe: when he thinks of the way the acting profession has degenerated and been handed over to university men and puny tenor voices, when he thinks of the fine qualities of his own bass voice, when he contemplates his fallen splendour – well, you feel that anything could happen. And that, too, is what the nervous Mr Pasco feels, as he inquires in awestruck tones: 'Were you . . . very good?' It is a line which produces one of the best laughs of the evening, as these two of the season's heavyweights display all their skills for our amusement.

Mr Pasco matches Mr Howard's tendency to grand gestures with a wonderful display of broken-spirited servility. At the great house, where Mr Howard passes himself off as an officer in order to impress his aunt, Mr Pasco is cast in the role of Sganarelle, a role he understands perfectly. He must serve, but he must finally rebel. For that fatal tendency of Mr Howard's to indulge in the grand gesture will ruin both their futures. We see in the dénouement how his romantic nobility of spirit has brought this actor down.

The work is rewarding for all the players – for Dennis Clinton as the servant, Hugh Ross and Raymond Westwell as the rich neighbours and for Paul Webster as the timber merchant. I do not think there is a weak spot in the whole company. As for Mr Noble, who must just be recovering from the extravagant praise heaped on his Webster production – it would be very suspicious, would it not, if Mr Noble were to be walking into the main house one day, when a gigantic flower-pot was dropped on his head, and one of our other bright young directors was seen scuttling away over the rooftops?

Very suspicious indeed.

A really surprising play, partly about London xenophobia, is *The Book of Sir Thomas More* which the Poor Players presented this week at the Young Vic as a neglected piece of Shakespeare. I doubt the attribution. The hero quells a race riot with an eloquent plea against enforced repatriation:

> Imagine that you see the wretched strangers
> Their babies at their backs and their poor luggage
> Plodding to the ports and coasts for transportation,
> And that you sit as kings in your desires. . . .
> What had you got? I'll tell you: you had taught

How insolence and strong hand should prevail,
How order should be quelled; and by this pattern
Not one of you should live an aged man. . . .

3 May 1981

Total Eclipse *(LYRIC, HAMMERSMITH)*

Christopher Hampton's play about Rimbaud and Verlaine, *Total Eclipse*, was first produced in 1968. It returns now to the Lyric, Hammersmith, in a revised edition, directed by the writer David Hare. It is a fine play and a distinguished production which draws on the full resources of theatrical illusion. Hayden Griffin supplies a design which exploits a mobile stage, combined with a series of paintings as backdrops. These tableaux (executed by David Lawes) are effective in proportion to their stylistic resemblance to the art of the period. If they remind us of the avant-garde of the 1870s, they perform economically a vital and complicated task. Most directors seem to hate the idea of the painter's art being employed on stage. They want architects and sculptors for their designs – but painting, which is the designer's art par excellence, they detest. It is too competitive.

Mr Hare, on the other hand, is a cool customer. He encourages his designer to supply scenes complete with human figures, so that in the last episode, a whole mirrored café is presented with its clientele. It is a beautiful effect, the more delightful for the fact that it bursts on to the retina after a Black Forest (conceived literally), which relied entirely on Rory Dempster's lighting. During the court scenes, the lighting gave us perfect vignettes from Daumier. The costumes are by Carol Lawrence, and if I mention all these features first, it is not out of neglect for the actors, but because I believe most strongly in this kind of design, which has been asked to play an integral and creative role in the production. The incidental music, by Nick Bicât, is also tantalisingly good. Scored for string quartet and synthesiser, it has a similar function to the paintings, appearing to represent extracts from some great, melancholy masterpiece of the period.

Simon Callow, who plays Verlaine, is an actor with the will to commit himself entirely to a performance. If I have disliked some of his past work, it is because he occasionally shows us the commitment in advance of the performance itself: what one sees is the effect of the adrenalin, the pure energy, the sweat, the saliva; the commitment advertises itself to the detriment of the content.

On this occasion, he articulates every thought and response of Verlaine, from the moment of his first sight of the 16-year-old Rimbaud (whom he has invited to Paris after reading his precocious poems, but whom he had believed to be 21), to the last scene of decrepitude in which he looks back on his love-affair with the poet and imagines that it was always happy.

The truth was that for Verlaine, the affair was a deep humiliation, which ended in his imprisonment. Mr Callow has put on weight to an alarming degree: the profile of his stomach is a warning to us all. His Verlaine is a weak and self-indulgent man, prone to acts of extreme violence, which he immediately follows up with cowardly apologies. One does not get from the play, either as written or as performed, any great sense of the manner in which Verlaine might have been an influence on Rimbaud, nor of the source of his attraction for the younger man.

This Rimbaud, as Mr Hampton portrays him, is all coldness and scorn. Only once does he cry out as if nervous of being abandoned. In Enid Starkie's biography, which Mr Hampton cites as a source, and which he follows in most respects quite faithfully, the bad behaviour begins as soon as the young man senses hostility to his appearance. One imagines someone more vulnerable and more alert to the impression he is making.

It was a bewildering impression. One observer was moved to a comparison with Christ among the Doctors. Another coined the phrase 'Satan among the Doctors', and it is this ambiguity which Hilton McCrae puts across. He is beautiful, strong, and vicious. He does not yield an inch. His only moment of real tenderness comes in that final passage which, as we then know, Verlaine is inventing as a comfort to his wounded memory.

The upshot is that we tend to see the whole play as an account of Verlaine's experience, and to view Rimbaud more from the outside. It is a deeply affecting work, simply and directly expressed in a language which does not need to strive to achieve its poetic effects. I should mention a really striking performance by Lynsey Baxter as Verlaine's tight-lipped, long-suffering wife – a performance which does ample justice to its historical original.

10 May 1981

Cats (NEW LONDON THEATRE)

One of the encouraging things about T. S. Eliot as a poet, from the point of view of any aspiring author, is his ability to write drivel. He is not the sort of poet who reaches the stage of maturity, after which everything he composes has a certain quality. One day he writes a masterpiece. The next day he is doodling.

In Mrs Eliot's fascinating edition of the *Waste Land* manuscript, you can see the process at its most astonishing. Following the advice of Ezra Pound, Eliot cut out the drivel and simply published whatever remained. This was like publishing a very old Aertex vest, a paint-rag. Not surprisingly, the public was very surprised.

Even among the *Collected Poems*, compact as they are, the standard varies wildly. In the charming section entitled 'Minor Poems' there is hardly a dud line: there are highly original landscape poems, beautiful lyrics and an amusing pastiche of Edward Lear. For the bullying Anglicanism of the subsequent section, 'Choruses from the Rock', there is nothing good to be said. As for the plays, the unfinished *Sweeney Agonistes* is a masterpiece of poetic drama. But the other plays. Oh, heck.

In *Old Possum's Book of Practical Cats*, one of the most successful children's books of the century, Eliot is doodling. The prestige of the author blinded a generation of parents to the inexcusably low quality of the writing. A loyal readership grew up comprised of that horrid kind of child who knows how to affect a literary taste which will impress and do credit to his family. To be 'on Eliot' at the age of three – that was something!! 'Mama,' said these Midwich cuckoos as they tripped off to bed, 'now that I've finished Old Possum, mayn't I be entrusted for the night with Papa's copy of *Knowledge and Experience in the Philosophy of F. H. Bradley?*'

Cats, at the New London Theatre, is the price we have to

pay for Andrew Lloyd Webber's nursery proclivities. Oh, it's a smash hit, by the way, and one of the few hot tickets in town. And even as I write, I can hear Elaine Paige's song 'Memory' drifting in through the windows, from the monumental mason's across the road. The first-night audience behaved as if they had all staked their shirts on the musical's success. A chap beside me kept climbing on to his seat. I got the impression that he had been hired in order to make an ass of himself.

Hysteria is always off-putting. Judged by the standards of the West End, there is no doubt that *Cats* contains marvellous things. I'm thinking particularly of Gillian Lynne's choreography – the way she gets dancers to do things one had naively assumed to be physically impossible, and the way she manages to insinuate designs into an apparently random collection of animals. Wayne Sleep, in his solo routine as Mr Mistoffelees, memorably combines a swift and impressive dance with a series of conjuring tricks. Throughout the evening, Mr Sleep is most successful at putting across a feline personality. He is always worth watching; the pleasant singing voice is more than one has the right to expect.

Then there are comical turns. Paul Nicholas as an outrageously bewigged rock star, Bonnie Langford and John Thornton as Mungojerrie and Rumpleteazer. The whole company dances at the audience in a way which demands one's enthusiasm. If you went for an evening's dancing, you couldn't be disappointed.

But if you judge the piece by the standards which Trevor Nunn, the director, has set for himself, then you must ask just how successfully the musical puts across the book on which it draws? What you miss entirely from this production is the feeling you get from so much of Eliot's poetry – the feeling of pre-Blitz London, the London which was still intact as a city, with its churches and its clubs, the squares, the houses with their railings and area steps. This is the world the Practical Cats inhabit.

John Napier's design, which chooses to convert the New London Theatre into a spectacular rubbish dump, does away with all possibility of calling this capital back to life. As a result, several of the numbers entirely lose their savour. There is no feeling of club-land. There is no sense of the luxury of railway travel (the scene in which a train is assembled before our eyes is very poorly staged). And the best of the poems, 'Macavity: the Mystery Cat', while it is given a tremendous build-up, falls flat as a presentation of the cat's character (a derivative of Mack the Knife).

'We had the experience but missed the meaning'; I think that Brian Blessed actually sang this passage from the 'Four Quartets', as an opener to Act Two. It is certainly a good motto for the show. A large-scale musical needs a climax, and there is no climax in *Old Possum*, so a climax had to be imported from elsewhere. What you get is an awful ceremony in which the cat of easy virtue (Miss Paige) goes up to heaven to be given a second chance, while Mr Blessed sings a perfectly fatuous setting of 'The Ad-dressing of Cats'.

One leaves the show with a sense of having been spiritually got at, as if this were the Westminster Theatre. When invention has given out (which it does during the second half), this kind of spiritual pretentiousness takes over. The finale is quite ghastly, and left me with a profound depression.

17 May 1981

A Note on Metre

When it comes to the discussion of Shakespearian metre, the *Observer* television critic Clive James is a most notorious quack. Berating the cast of the BBC's *Antony and Cleopatra* last week for 'murdering the verse', he cited the following example. The half-line 'Age cannot wither her' had been delivered with the emphasis on the word 'age', as if, Mr James commented, something else could wither her.

Well, there are many other things – childbearing, famine, those long hot summers – which tend to wither the Egyptians. But this is not the point of the line in question ('Age cannot wither her nor custom stale') in which a distinction is being drawn between age and custom – two words which must be given due weight. Interestingly enough, it is physically impossible to pronounce the word 'age' without giving it emphasis. Once again, the *Observer* is demanding the impossible.

Mr James goes on to dress the cast down for their tiresome attempts to 'delve for the deeper significance'. 'In Shakespeare,' says this enviably wise man, 'there are no hidden secrets; the profundity is transparent all the way to the bottom. The rhythm of the verse tells you all there is to know, and it is much more than any director, actor or critic knows.'

In saying this, Mr James commits precisely the same solecism as those who argue that one should go for the meaning at the expense of the 'poetry'. He imagines that poetic rhythm can be understood without regard for meaning, that the rhythm is somehow detachable from the words. There is a kind of verse of which this is true. It is known technically as 'doggerel'. But the Shakespearian line works differently from doggerel.

Its working can be briefly explained. There is the basic metrical pattern of five tee-tums, with two standard variations – an extra syllable at the end of the line, and a reversal of accents in the first foot. Thus, instead of every line beginning tee-tum, some lines begin tum-tee. This is how the word 'age' can come at the beginning of the line. Shakespeare was not obliged to put it there, he could easily have written: 'No age can wither her, no custom stale'. He varied the rhythm precisely because he wanted to throw emphasis on the word 'age'.

As against the metrical pattern (which is unvaried), there is the shape of the individual line, which aims at uniqueness. In the majority of iambic pentameters, you will find that there are four natural conversational stresses – not five, four. One of the metrically accented syllables is deprived of emphasis. In the line under discussion, the word 'her' is metrically accented, but might well not be emphasised. On the other hand, if it is emphasised, the likelihood is that less weight will be placed on the word 'wither'. There is a trade-off.

The essential key to the rhythm of the individual line is the meaning of the words. Emphasis is always a matter of meaning. And the genius of the iambic pentameter derives from the easy relationship between the metrical pattern and the individual possibilities in performance. With a longer or shorter line than ten syllables, metre must assert itself or be lost altogether. But it is precisely the unassertive quality of the iambic pentameter which gives it its strength as a vehicle for dramatic discourse. The line offers you five possibilities for emphasis, of which you should normally take up four. But if you wish, for a specific purpose, to emphasise every syllable in the line – that is your right as an actor. On the other hand, if you emphasise every syllable of every line in the play I think we are entitled to walk out.

24 May 1981

Britannicus *(LYRIC STUDIO)*

Two guards (Herzel Jacoby and Hossein Karimbeck) are passing the time of day in a brick-floored waiting room. We know that it is a waiting room, since there are copies of *Country Life* on the benches. We know that these men are guards: their dark glasses and leather uniforms tell us as much; the automatic weapons merely underline the point. But of course the weapons do not belong to the same waiting room as the copies of *Country Life*. We know that we have entered a paradoxical space, a paradoxical time.

This is Nero's antechamber. This is Rome. But it is the Rome of the seventeenth-century Frenchman Jean Racine, as conceived by the director Christopher Fettes and the designer Candis Cook. The play is *Britannicus*, the theatre is the Lyric Studio, Hammersmith. Now the guards draw down the metal shutter and the action begins.

Perhaps action is the wrong word. Just as there is no point in travelling around the world unless you are prepared to abandon the customs by which you live, the categories of your everyday understanding, so there is no point in entering the world of Racine unless you actually enjoy the prospect of a drama constructed on principles that flatly contradict all the assumptions of our native theatre.

Dramatic action, in the sense that we understand it, is rigorously excluded. We like to see a good stage-fight. For Racine, such a thing is unthinkable. Nobody dies on stage. As Roland Barthes points out (in his delightful little book *on Racine*, from which I shall be borrowing several observations), one does not die in Racine, because one spends the whole time talking. To be banished from the conversation – that, for these characters, is death. To become a Trappist monk, that would be suicide.

But although all dramatic action takes place exclusively within the speeches, this does not mean that nothing happens.

214

Racine's theatre, as Barthes has it, is a theatre of violence; violence, rather than love, is the true theme of this play. Nero and Britannicus love the same woman, June (the Penguin translation pushes its luck when it anglicises this name). June lives for Britannicus alone. Nero has absolute power. Britannicus is the sole threat to his power. But although he can destroy Britannicus, the price Nero must pay is that he earns the hatred of June.

At the climax of the play, June does indeed become a Trappist monk. That is to say, she enters the order of the Vestal Virgins, and the playwright underlines the character of this aggressive suicide: 'Now, without dying, she is dead for him.' Nero is left all-powerful except in what he most desires. In the eyes of Rome, June will continue to exist. But for him she will not exist, and he knows it. This is what will turn him into the most notorious tyrant in history. The end of the play is the beginning of the tyranny.

Nero (Jonathan Kent) begins the play as an innocent, a benevolent despot whose reign has so far been entirely just. But he is not yet free from the power of his mother Agrippina (Siobhan McKenna), the woman who has put him on the throne in preference to the rightful heir Britannicus (Garry Cooper). In order for Nero to become fully powerful, he must also overthrow his mother, and in doing so take upon himself her guilt. At the beginning of the play, Agrippina is a criminal. At the end, she has become strangely innocent. She and her son have swapped places.

To put this play across, the company were obliged to invent an acting style which would correspond to the heroic French model. That this has been achieved is extraordinary, and it is extraordinary that the effect is both true to the original and absolutely modern. The translation by John Cairncross is an accurate aid to study, but not so helpful in performance.

The cast is never less than excellent. Valerie Sarruf plays the confidante, Alan MacNaughtan is the good soldier Burrus, Donald Pickering the insinuating adviser Narcissus (he gets what he deserves, being torn to pieces by the Roman crowd – in the last moments of the play, one of the guards drags him across stage, contained most sinisterly in two black plastic bags), and Elizabeth Richardson is impressive as June. The chief contest though is between Mr Cooper and Mr Kent, two really powerful performances. The production is more disciplined, over-all, than Mr Fettes's *Doctor Faustus*, and I think it an even more remarkable achievement.

31 May 1981

The Doctor's Dilemma (GREENWICH)

What is the Doctor's Dilemma? Shaw's play, which opened in Greenwich this week, asks us to imagine a brilliant physician with the ability to cure tuberculosis, but with a strictly limited numerical capacity to his medical unit. He can cure ten patients at a time. Well, stretching a point, he can cure eleven. In order to decide whom to cure, he must have a criterion; he must ask himself, 'Is this patient worth curing or not?'

The analogy offered is that of a raft to which ten men are clinging for dear life. If the admission of an extra man would jeopardise the lives of the ten, what would you do? The dilemma expressed by the analogy is a real one – one indeed which is so familiar to anyone who has been anywhere near one of the world's great disasters that its invocation in a facetious context can only be painful. As for the medical profession, the modern comparison would be with a kidney transplant or some kind of expensive cancer treatment. The newspapers are full of stories which stem from such real dilemmas.

In my experience, medical people or relief workers who have a limited amount of aid to offer will indeed frame for themselves some set of criteria to decide whether an individual is worth saving. They must adopt such criteria in order to stay sane. But they do not imagine that the judgements they employ reflect any kind of justice. An overworked field surgeon may look at twenty emergency cases and quickly decide that it is worth concentrating on three of them. But he doesn't fool himself that the moral value of the characters comes into it. He chooses the people he has the best chance of saving. The fact that he must make such a choice is a tragic circumstance of his life, something with which he will always have to live.

In Shaw's play, this fearful dilemma is frivolously handled. The doctor falls in love with the wife of a great artist. The

217

great artist is dying of tuberculosis, but he also happens to be a most terrible bounder. It suits the doctor to hand the case over to an incompetent colleague, a man who stands a fifty-fifty chance of killing off the artist double-quick. By now we have said goodbye to the original dilemma. For however serious a view we take of the artist's moral shortcomings (he borrows money unscrupulously and is a bigamist), they hardly amount to capital offences. Nor is the doctor a court of law. The doctor, as it turns out, takes it upon himself to murder the patient. Do we have any dilemma in condemning him?

And what do we feel when confronted by the death-throes of the artist himself – immensely prolonged as they are, although deprived of the true sordidness and terror of a death from TB? The category 'black humour' might be invoked in defence of the scene. As it happens, I strongly admire several examples of black humour – it is the kind of humour that expresses a rage against existence. If the humour comes across as the authentic expression of rage, one admires, precisely, that authenticity.

There ain't much rage in this play. To be frank, it's feeble. As paradox succeeds to dreary paradox, you are hardly surprised when the actors have difficulty in remembering the lines. 'Life does not cease to be funny when people die,' says Shaw, 'just as it does not cease to be serious when they laugh.' But in *The Doctor's Dilemma* life does not begin to be serious. Alan Strachan directs this production. Poppy Mitchell has designed it. It's got some good things. James Cossins is a good thing. Maria Aitken is another.

7 June 1981

The Shoemaker's Holiday (OLIVIER)

You only need to know a couple of things to understand the general drift of *The Shoemaker's Holiday* (Olivier). The first is that the shoemakers of Olde England (besides being the salt of the earth) were a dab hand at the 'three-man song', the contemporary equivalent of the barber-shop trio. The second is that people from the Low Countries were unable to understand English, besides being inordinately fond of butter.

Had you dropped in on a London shoemaker's shop half a millennium ago, you might have heard this satire on the Flemings being given in close harmony.

> Rutterkin can speak no Englishe.
> His tongue runneth over like butter'd fysshe
> Besmeared with grease about his dysshe,
> Like a Rutterkin, hoyda, hoyda.

And had you felt so inclined you might have joined in the Chorus:

> Hoyda, hoyda, jolly Rutterkin,
> Hoyda, hoyda, like a Rutterkin,
> Hoyda, hoyda, hoyda, hoyda,
> Like a Rutterkin, hoyda!

thereby sending up the Flemings something rotten.

All right, so the joke has worn pretty thin over the centuries, but in Dekker's day (that is, around the year 1600) it was still good for a giggle. Bring the two ideas of the 'gentle craft' of shoe-making and the butter-loving foreigner together, as in the line 'A Fleming butter-box a shoemaker?' and you were fairly sure of a laugh. Today, the difficulty with Dekker is that he loved the slang of his time and exploited it with such verve that a single speech may attract explanatory notes like flies to a dunghill.

But the notes are not necessary for a general getting of the hang. Simon Eyre, the shoemaker made good, is the Elizabethan equivalent of Barrie Mackenzie, never at a loss for a phrase: 'Away with you Islington whitepot, hence you happerarse, you barley pudding full of maggots, you broyld carbonado, avaunt, avaunt . . .' He can go on like this for ever. He does. One hardly needs to know that the citizens of London enjoyed a trip to the country suburb of Islington, where they would eat a dish made of cream boiled with eggs, or that a 'happerarse' is one whose breech sticks out like a hopper.

You can find these things out but you're not obliged to. The point is simply to enjoy the command of invective. That means, by the way, that we must always be able to make out what Eyre is saying: 'Peace, midriff, peace' is an odd way to address one's wife, and might get a good laugh if heard.

John Dexter has directed this production, one of the few major revivals the play has had. Alfred Lynch gives an amiable Simon Eyre, but he could afford to enjoy himself more in the part. Brenda Bruce is his wife, and makes the most of her transformation through steadily more elaborate costumes as family fortunes increase, with all the concomitant difficulties, such as absurd shoes and wide skirts.

The story of the two young men and their cross love-affairs derives, curiously enough, from the legend of Crispin and Crispian. Peter Løvstrøm is Rafe: he goes to the wars and returns minus one leg, to provoke the most moving scene of the evening and also to provide Mr Dexter (so he *is* a sadist) with the opportunity of having him knocked over not once but three times. This was hard on the audience and is no doubt tough on Mr Løvstrøm. Michael Thomas is Rowland, the young nobleman who does not go to the wars but spends the course of the play pretending to be a Dutch cobbler. This he does well.

But the surprise and delight of the evening is the last act, in which David Yelland appears as a send-up of the Olivier Henry V, a performance that gets more laughs than any other.

The design by Julia Trevelyan Oman has masses of excellent detail, but the stage architecture looks ersatz, and the wreath of plastic flowers in Act One seemed to have been stolen from a cemetery.

21 June 1981

London International Festival
of Theatre

At the Tricycle Theatre last week you could see a chap simulating that thing that people do – with a live goose. The production was Goethe's original version of *Faust*, as performed by Die Vaganten, a group based in Cologne. Here is an extract from the programme note: 'Die Vaganten consider the shock element vital to their theatre. Accordingly they present drastic images which provoke the fantasies of the audience. They suggest that one of the functions of their theatre is to break through taboos in order to confront the public and make them voyeurs, then, in turn, to attack their voyeurism.'

This is all too typical of what passes for thought in the theatre, and the production itself was typical of the hysterical approach to the classics which one finds in West Germany. Remember that in West Germany there is no genuine capital, and every city competes to become the metropolis. In every city there are subsidised companies with ambitious directors. When a play becomes fashionable, as for instance *Antigone* became fashionable a couple of years ago, one might find major productions of it springing up all over the Federal Republic. But every production has to be different. It must compete for attention at the national level. Hence the hysteria, hence the fear of the text. The text, after all, is the one element which, if given its head, might make one production resemble another.

Die Vaganten is a small group working on the studio scale. The *Urfaust* is a small-scale play, ideally suited for such a company and, since it is a draft of a play rather than a finished work, one could hardly object to a free treatment of the text. What you actually find, on the other hand, is a brave attempt at a complete demolition of the piece, a complete subversion of the original.

222

What tyrannises the theatre in Germany is not the corrupt taste of the bourgeois audience, but the corrupt taste of the directors and the theatrical elite. The unfortunate goose, in this context, falls victim to a desire on the part of the company to compete on a low budget with more highly subsidised companies.

I very much doubt whether many fantasies were aroused, or whether much voyeurism was rebuked. But it did, for a brief moment, look extremely funny, as the actor gasped in simulated ecstasy and the goose was obviously doing its best to close its eyes and think of Germany.

The occasion for this company's visit is the London International Festival of Theatre, whose first year this is. Everyone is congratulating the organisers on having managed, starting with no resources other than their determination, to supply something which has been lacking in London for the last six years. Nine foreign companies are involved and there is a week of the festival still to go. For my own part, although I welcome any opportunity to see foreign theatre, I should have been much more encouraged by the festival had the choice of work not been so narrowly antitextual.

From looking at the programme, you would get the impression that we live in a world without playwrights; nothing is brought on the grounds that it is an interesting new play from a writer from such and such a country, and there is (with the exception of the dreadful *Urfaust*) no single item from the international classical repertoire. This last is a waste of an opportunity, since it is one obvious way of crossing the language barrier.

But there are compensations, including one production which alone would give the festival organisers cause to congratulate themselves: *Macunaima*, by the Brazilian Grupo de Teatro Macunaima, which is at the Lyric, Hammersmith. This is an epic tale, with all the trappings both of modern life and of the primitive world of the Amazonian jungle. The hero Macunaima leaves his tribe on a series of adventures involving a lost talisman. He goes to the great cities, Rio de Janeiro and Sao Paulo. He changes from loincloth to snappy, white suit. He moves indiscriminately among contemporary and legend-

223

ary figures. And he is always blundering into the unknown.

The production uses simple resources but builds up its own distinctive visual language. A large range of animate and inanimate objects are suggested through the medium of newsprint. Newspaper animals of extraordinary sizes and shapes pass inexplicably across the stage. Fruits and flowers of crumpled newspaper blossom and are consumed. From time to time, the jungle is blasted with white noise, as a threatening contraption passes through spreading poison.

This is the world of 'Tristes Tropiques', the world of systematic physical and cultural annihilation. When a man leaves such a jungle he must cross millennia in order to enter the city. When he tries to return to the jungle, it has already been destroyed for him. It is no longer his home.

That is the outline of the play. But there are innumerable scenes and characters, and the production rises to its most beautiful effects in the evocation of city life. Sometimes it looks like a magnificent ballet in the making. It often resorts to music and to mimic effects. But one is finally frustrated at not being able to understand not merely Portuguese but its Brazilian variants.

Language is an inescapable problem with such a festival and no single solution is satisfactory. To turn one's back on words in the theatre is to ignore the evidence of evolution: there are things words can do which nothing else can. Simultaneous translations are a distraction (and anyway are not here available). A brilliantly gifted company like Het Werktheater can perform well both in German and in English, in addition to their native Dutch. But for the two Polish companies we have seen this week the attempt to speak English was disastrous.

The Theatre of the Eighth Day, from Poznan, and the Teatr Provisorium, from Lublin, both sounded marvellously convincing in their own language, but had both decided quite recklessly to perform sections of their work in English, a language which left them expressively crippled. The translations they used were also to blame, but worst of all was a revelation of the banality of much of the material.

This was a kind of theatre which alluded to the greatest themes without apparently having the ability to explore any further than the initial allusion. The Theatre of the Eighth Day told us (in the New Half Moon Theatre) that God was dead. The Teatr Provisorium told us (in the ICA) that we should turn to the crucified Christ. These messages sounded oddly similar, earnest and desperate. There were many lines which, quite plainly, would have had resonances in a Polish context which the translation simply destroyed.

Here is the last passage of the play by the Theatre of the Eighth Day: 'Ladies and gentlemen, let me tell you our tragic story. We are dispossessed sons. I think we understand each other here. We come from the same father. We are oppressed by the same shoe. But we have the right to speak and you have the right to listen. We all have the right to disagree, with this.'

9 August 1981

Much Ado About Nothing *(OLIVIER)*
The Mayor of Zalamea *(COTTESLOE)*

The key to *Much Ado About Nothing* is the character of
Claudio. If we are to believe the play, we must understand how
it is that this conventional enough young lover is impelled to
such extremes of cruelty in the church scene, where he springs
his accusations upon his former bride-to-be, Hero.

To understand, in this case, is not at first to forgive. The
play requires that Claudio pays his penance for this behaviour.
But it also requires that he should be forgiven after the
penance. And that period is not long. This is not *The Winter's
Tale*. It is a matter of hours, not years, and within the terms of
the penance lies the promise of eventual forgiveness. Claudio
must behave terribly, but he must not be a terrible man.

Not long ago there was a production of *Much Ado* in which
the nastiness of the church scene was taken as the clue to the
whole moral world of the play. The humiliation of Hero was
seen, not as a terrible consequence of human fallibility, but as
the natural behaviour of the society portrayed. And, as a
result of this there leaked a poison from this one scene which
infected not only one's view of the play but also, uncontroll-
ably, one's view of the actors themselves. The whole company
gave me the creeps, in a way which was certainly not resolved
by the end of the evening. The familiar comedy had turned
into a horrible event.

In Peter Gill's new production at the Olivier, Claudio is
played by Tim Woodward, an engaging young actor whom
those who saw the film of *The Europeans* will remember as the
artist brother of Lee Remick. He's a chap of charm. Sincerity,
generosity of spirit, youthful passion – he might with justification list these among his special skills in the way that other
actors mention their fluency in French. If we do not follow
him quite the whole way in the church scene, it is because he
remains a shade too considerate. We cannot quite allow that

226

he would have let matters reach this pitch.

And here's an odd corollary: Caroline Langrishe, who plays Hero, does not seem to suffer more than the partial humiliation offered by Mr Woodward. She faints, of course, as required by the plot, but when she recovers her senses she also recovers her composure – and this seems quite wrong. An unjust accusation of this kind is a terrifying experience, not least because, however much one may know one's own innocence, a scene like the church scene is enough to convince one of a mad possibility of guilt. Protesting innocence, one must convince not only the world but also oneself.

What of Benedick and Beatrice? Michael Gambon has encumbered himself with a very peculiar accent. It's hard to know where it comes from, not hard to tell him what he should do with it. He seems to be aiming for a ludicrous portrayal of Benedick in the opening scenes, in order to have something new to spring on us when he shows us the romantic and responsible Benedick of the second half. But of course the accent stays with him.

With Mr Gambon playing opposite Penelope Wilton there is bound to be a great deal to enjoy, the puffy-lidded melancholy of the one, the vivid and passionate interior life of the other. When Miss Wilton knows where she is going, she jolly well knows. When she sees what she wants, she goes for it like a bullet. When she is transparent the effect is irresistibly funny, and when she is confused, as in the early scenes, she can be most moving. I wondered, during the crucial exchange in which she asks Benedick to kill Claudio, whether she did not once give the wrong signal to the audience and ask for their laughter when she should have been thinking of other things. I should like to see both of these performances again in a few weeks' time, when I've had a chance to get over my first-night nerves.

Mr Gill's production has fine touches, including a masked ball of strange beauty, and including some fine music by George Fenton. The design by Alison Chitty contrasts oak-panelled interiors with Tudor brick exteriors. The costumes reinforce the sense of period, but other details confuse and subvert it.

227

Worst of all, the green floor, which for outdoor scenes suggests grass, when combined with the panelled interiors gives an irresistible impression of wall-to-wall carpeting. The scene-changes are long and complicated, with occasional comic business that does little to help the play itself. We are asked to take the low-life comedy on the nude merits of the text.

This means that the scenes with Dogberry and the watch pass swiftly, more swiftly than in most productions, but they hardly raise a great number of laughs. It appears that the director has despaired of injecting great humour into the low life. One might sympathise with such despair, but it is hard to admire it.

In general, from the point of view of production and design, *Much Ado* shows the effect of a growing awareness on the part of Mr Gill that the formula which succeeded (or sometimes succeeded) at the Riverside will not work at the Olivier.

Those elegant rudimentary sets beautifully placed in a great parkland of empty floor so that the actors were obliged to indulge in a long-jump sprint in order to get on or off stage; those 'texts laid bare'; that refusal ever to enclose the action or to wrap an environment around the play, so that, while a great play looked good, a lesser work might bleed to death before the audience's eyes; what was distinctive, in short, has now become insufficient to meet the demands of the situation. One might add that what worked in the past cannot be expected to continue to work indefinitely. Success exhausts a good idea, but the demands of art continue.

Everyone knows that there is a wealth of classical Spanish theatre, but nobody puts it on the English stage. Why? The chief reason seems to be that there are no really good translations. The verse-line is short and I had imagined that it would not adapt at all well if imitated directly into English. But Adrian Mitchell's translation of Calderón's *The Mayor of Zalamea* follows its original very closely and comes across extraordinarily well at the Cottesloe Theatre. There are rough rhymes and insistent rhythms, which English actors are not used to dealing with (our classical drama tends to dispense with rhyme and to subdue poetic rhythm to the pattern of conversational speech), but as soon as the audience gets the hang of it, the tragi-comic possibilities of the form display themselves.

The sub-title of the play ('The Best Garrotting Ever Done') will give an indication that the values displayed are not, to put it mildly, those of this day and age. But the success of the piece is that it shows an intricate moral problem developing, and offers a solution as neat as the cutting of the Gordian knot. The mayor's dilemma is this: he is brought to the point where his honour requires that he avenge himself on a nobleman, but at the same moment, being elected mayor, he is made custodian of the law. How can he reconcile his two duties?

The answer is: he just can. By the end of the evening we are very glad that Michael Bryant, the mayor, has found a way of putting to death Daniel Massey, after the way Mr Massey has treated the innocent and virtuous Leslee Udwin. These central performances, together with that of Basil Henson, give the emotional charge to the evening. Clive Arrindell puts over the character of the son, moody, passionate and basically (like so many characters in Spanish drama) as mad as a meat axe. The production by Michael Bogdanov is by no means perfect, but its imperfections are uninteresting in comparison with its great virtue, that it takes a marvellous play and puts across its essential qualities.

16 August 1981

Edinburgh Festival 1981

The Grand Inquisitor made his appearance twice this week on the Edinburgh stage. In the first instance, he sent Jesus Christ to burn at the stake. In the second, he would have done much the same with Candide, had the innocent young man not run him through with his sword.

To take the second instance first: in Voltaire's story, however far-fetched the plot may be, the psychology of the key moments is always convincing. This realism is the source of the book's humour, the contrast between what philosophy claims and what experience teaches us. In Leonard Bernstein's musical, *Candide*, for which the book was written by Hugh Wheeler, what was once a reflection of true life becomes either fantastic or sentimental. In Voltaire's day, such perils as the press-gang and piracy were real. Lisbon was indeed destroyed by an earthquake, and it is true that in the immediate aftermath of the destruction, the streets of the city saw an outburst of religious zeal which would have been terrifying to any Protestant member of the foreign community there.

Voltaire destroys Lisbon in a paragraph, in much the same way that earthquakes destroy cities in a tremor of seconds. His first witness of the destruction, an experienced sailor, sees at once the prospect of personal gain: 'The sailor immediately rushed into the midst of the wreckage, braved death to find money, found some, took it with him, got drunk, and, after sobering up a little, bought the favours of the first willing girl he met in the ruins of the destroyed houses, amid the dead and dying.'

That sentence is typical of Voltaire. It shows his ability to be, at the same time, both calm and angry, objective in manner, sensational in impact. He does not raise any objection to the behaviour of the sailor; it is Dr Pangloss, not the author, who says, 'You're behaving badly, my friend: you're

230

not respecting universal reason, you've chosen a bad time for this' – and who, for his pains, receives a stunning rebuke.

Voltaire can be exceedingly funny, but he does not strive to be funny. Candide may be naive, but he is not slow to defend himself against the Jew, whom he kills, simply, frankly, and instinctively, in much the same way as he first made love to Cunegonde. A few sentences later, the Grand Inquisitor arrives at the scene of the crime. This is what goes through Candide's mind: 'If this holy man calls for help, he'll certainly have me burned, and he may do the same thing to Cunegonde. He's had me whipped unmercifully. He's my rival. I've already begun killing. My course is clear.'

In the musical version, which Birmingham Repertory Company staged at the Assembly Hall, neither the Voltaire of Nickolas Grace nor the Candide of William Relton could have been capable of such 'swift, clear-cut reasoning'; the one was forever ingratiating himself with the audience, the other behaved as if butter would not melt in his mouth. Everything about the musical showed the signs of a fussy concern that the audience should be having fun every second of the action. Wit went out of the window, and Voltaire's ability to shock was carefully smothered. The prancing nuns in the number, 'Auto Da Fe (What A Day)' were certainly in bad taste. But the Catholic Church itself is in worse taste than Broadway or Birmingham could imagine.

Dostoevsky thought somewhat along these lines. At least, in the story within the story of *The Brothers Karamazov*, when Christ appears in the city of Seville, the Grand Inquisitor makes his famous speech explaining why the Catholic Church has gone over to the Devil, why this was necessary, why the Inquisitor will not tolerate Christ's reappearance on earth, and why, in the Last Judgement, God will be obliged to forgive the Church for the complete revision of his doctrine which it has undertaken.

It is a daring and complex piece of reasoning, which has previously been used as the basis for a drama on its own. But in the version by Richard Crane of the Brighton Theatre, it is truncated to a series of paradoxes. For my own part, I was not familiar with the novel before seeing the play, and I found the

231

latter wilfully obscure. To tell such a story in two hours, with only four actors, you have to have thought of some device so ingenious and compelling that it will silence the obvious objections. There was no such device.

Instead, there was an added element of confusion as the role of the father was passed from actor to actor, and as the point of some of the material became distorted in the process of truncation. The acting company, however, was most striking, being made up of Bruce Alexander, Alan Rickman, Stephen Boxer, Peter Kelly. But it was hard to focus on the production, let alone (for many members of the audience) to see it.

On the official programme, undoubtedly the finest work was the Théâtre de la Salamandre's *Britannicus*, which I reviewed previously when it visited Paris. This was a beautifully designed and directed piece (both credits go to Gildas Bourdet, with Alain Milianti also directing), set in what seemed to be Versailles of the seventeenth century, but must in fact have been a present-day palace (with central heating, Perspex labels under the oil paintings, and electric plug-sockets if you cared to look closely), in which Racine's drama was paradoxically being re-enacted.

Also from Birmingham Rep came an immensely elaborate *As You Like It*, with costumes which seemed to belong to *My Fair Lady* and heaven knows what else. It was indeed far too strivingly luscious a production, directed by Clive Perry, but it featured two fine actors; David Rintoul, whose strong and fine voice filled the Assembly Hall with ease, played Orlando, and Lynn Dearth gave a continually lively Rosalind.

From the Balkans came a most mysterious production by the National Theatre of Romania, which we were informed was Terence's *The Girl From Andros*, and that 'language was no barrier'. Something, I'm afraid, was a very big barrier indeed. If it was not language, it must have been quality.

23 August 1981

Macbeth (OLD VIC)

'Were such things here as we do speak about?' asks Banquo, 'Or have we eaten of the insane root/That takes the reason prisoner?' Somebody, I guess, has been handing out the insane root at the Old Vic, where Peter O'Toole's *Macbeth* opened this week to titters from the audience and the worst reviews of the year.

Don't trust those reviews. The spectacle is far worse than has hitherto been made out, a milestone in the history of coarse acting. It moved the *Daily Mail* to giggles, and I was in such difficulties that I often wondered whether it would be better to leave the theatre and explode outside. But something froze the laughter on the lips. It was the premeditated awfulness of O'Toole's performance. There was no question of risks taken, or brave attempts which had simply failed. This was the kind of awfulness which could have been seen a mile off.

Brian Grimwood's poster, with its sweet little owl and its dear little bat with knitting needles, was awful in a way which promised a children's picturebook version of the play. On the other hand, Keith Wilson's set appeared to have been loaned by a minor public school, with a special vote of thanks to the masters' wives, who did such sterling work in cobbling together the costumes from a heap of old drawing-room curtains, and who slaved away behind the scenes to produce such authentic effects as, for instance, the cloud of dust which billowed from Macbeth's tunic when Banquo clapped him on the shoulder. (A stock joke in coarse acting shows.)

The production was notable for the incomprehension with which lines were delivered and for the most wild moments of 'interpretation'. In the second scene, the King pointed to an apparently half-dead figure on the floor and said, 'What bloody man is that? He can report,/As seemeth by his plight, of the revolt/The newest state.' But the poor Captain seemed

233

in no state to do any such thing. The second witch went into a paroxysm of agony before delivering the lines 'By the pricking of my thumbs/Something wicked this way comes.' Brian Blessed, as Banquo, said, 'Look to the lady,' and actually threw Lady Macbeth (Frances Tomelty) to the nearest by-stander. You could see what had been going through his mind. He was thinking, 'That Lady Macbeth, she's a rum sort. I wouldn't trust her as far as I could throw her . . . come to think of it, how far can I throw her?'

This reminded me of Mr Jonathan Keates's long-projected version of *Othello*, in which the Moor comes on stage carrying an enormous flat fish and says, 'Perdition. Catch my sole! But I do love thee' while tossing the fish to Iago. In Bryan Forbes's version of *Julius Caesar*, I expect Mark Antony would deliver an involuntary belch before saying, 'Oh, pardon me! Thou bleeding piece of earth/That I am meek and gentle with these butchers.' (While we are off the subject, here is the first Shakespearian knock-knock joke. 'Knock, knock.' 'Who's there?' 'Mandy.' 'Mandy who?' 'Man delights not me, nor woman neither, though by your smiling you seem to say so.')

But let us get back, if we can bear it, to the Old Vic. Miss Tomelty has a voice which, when it drops a little, sounds exactly like Margaret Thatcher, so that lines like 'Naught's had, all's spent./Where our desire is got without content,' come across like Conservative pep talks on the economy. Now anyone who has been anywhere near Mrs Thatcher will also know that the woman absolutely exudes sex appeal. She has a way of quite undressing one with her eyes, and I can think of few Conservative politicians with whom I would rather . . . hello, hello, this is getting out of hand. The point is that when Miss Tomelty invited the spirits that tend on mortal thoughts to unsex her, she made the invitation quite the most provocative thing in the world; so far from being unsexed, she was all over her returning husband, and he all over her, like a rat all over a drain.

My colleagues have commented on the Knightsbridge witches, the sword that bent in the duel, the classic gaffe when Macduff announced that 'Macbeth was from his mother's womb untimely ripped', the laughter in the audience when Mr

O'Toole arrived drenched in gore and announced after an age-long pause that he had done the deed (had he not told us, we might have supposed that some discontented members of the cast had placed a bucket of blood over his dressing room door); the moment when the Macbeths walked straight into the scenery, and a hundred or so other minor points which a little time (a century, for instance) might straighten out.

As to Mr O'Toole's performance, it was deranged. 'I have', says Macbeth, 'a strange infirmity which is nothing/To those that know me.' At first, I thought that this must be a portrayal of drunkenness. It had a slurred slowness, like that of the drunken driver who imagines he will go undetected if he sticks to the kerb and never exceeds ten miles an hour. Later, I began to wonder whether the boorishness and imperception of the delivery might not be better explained if one thought of a Macbeth who was in the habit of getting stoned out of his mind, so that his brain over the years had turned to Gruyère cheese. Finally, I was forced to reject both theories in favour of a worse explanation, that this Macbeth stemmed from an utterly private conception of personal glory, a conception so private and so intense that it rejected any offer of help or advice in its realisation, a conception that spurned the play, spurned the company, and spurned the audience.

7 September 1980

The Witch of Edmonton
(STRATFORD, OTHER PLACE)

In 1621, Elizabeth Sawyer was executed for witchcraft, after admitting:

> The place where the devil sucked my blood was a little above my fundament, and that place chosen by himself, and in that place, by continual drawing, there is a thing in the form of a Teat at which the devil would suck me. And I asked the devil why he would suck my blood, and he said it was to nourish him.
> QUESTION: Whether did you pull up your coats or no when the devil came to suck you?
> ANSWER: No I did not but the devil would put his head under my coats, and I did willingly suffer him to do what he would.

This was sensational stuff. In a matter of days, an account of the trial had been published. A few months later *The Witch of Edmonton*, by Dekker, Ford and Rowley, was acted at court. Now revived in Stratford's Other Place, it is 'a known true story composed into a tragi-comedy', a hybrid of journalism and pure fiction whose interest for a contemporary audience would have derived from the uncertainty at the time over the truth or otherwise of such stories about witches. Cyrus Hoy, in his commentary on Dekker's collected plays, published recently by Cambridge University Press, prints relevant extracts from the account of the case:

> And to find out who should be the author of this mischief, an old ridiculous custom was used, which was to pluck the thatch of her house and burn it, and it being so burned, the author of such mischief should presently then come: and it

236

was observed and affirmed to the court that Elizabeth Sawyer would presently frequent the house of them that burnt the thatch which they plucked off her house, and come without any sending.

The word 'presently' means immediately. On the one hand, the author of this account thinks the custom old and ridiculous. On the other hand, it works at once.

The authors of the play exhibit the same transitional mentality. At the outset, Elizabeth Sawyer (Miriam Karlin) knows nothing of witchcraft. She is unjustly treated by the villagers, and it is only when she is driven to blasphemy and cursing that the Devil (Miles Anderson) arrives on the scene. The primary motivation of the main characters is conceived in terms of material circumstance, misfortune, or unmysterious psychology. But the supernatural, when it does enter the plot, is treated as another aspect of the natural world.

This is utterly fascinating. This Devil in the form of a dog, whose arrival is so ingeniously staged by Barry Kyle, stays around long enough for us to become acquainted with his character. Visually, he is a mixture of canine and human, a cross between King Charles and a King Charles spaniel. He is temperamental, and there are parts of his job which he clearly dislikes. For instance, he does not enjoy putting his head under Miss Karlin's 'coats'. He does, on the other hand, enjoy a tickle.

Miss Karlin and Mr Anderson are responsible for the 'true story', which they carry off with bravura. The fictional plot concerns a young man (Gerard Murphy) who marries against his father's wishes and is subsequently obliged to take a second wife in order to make his own and his father's fortunes. The first wife is played by Harriet Walter, the second by Juliet Stevenson.

The reviewer of the 1936 production (in which Edith Evans took the title role) expressed the message thus: 'That the wicked are not always as guilty as the fortunate suppose, but are sometimes driven to a second wrong by the very remorse that arises from the first.' That is the case with Mr Murphy's portrayal of Frank Thorney, and one can see exactly why this extraordinary actor was chosen for the part. It is the ancestor of the role he played in *Juno and the Paycock* last year, the man driven mad by conscience.

Indeed, Frank takes to his bed just as Johnny Boyle did, and is there plagued by a vision of the second wife he has murdered. The realisation of this scene by Mr Kyle, on the basis of a few mildly puzzling stage directions from the original, gives one of the most moving moments of the evening, as the Devil engineers the discovery of Frank's crime by the sister and father of the dead woman. There is a primitive terror attached to the notion of the bloody murder weapon that will not go away. Mr Murphy invests the murderer with passion, guilt and hopeless shame.

His two wives are afforded striking and realistic scenes in which to develop their characters. Harriet Walter, in the play's first clever touch, is presented initially as innocent, then revealed as an unwilling deceiver of her husband, a woman no better than she ought to be. In the last tableau of the evening, it is suggested that, despite her plea for the spectator's sympathy, she will have little chance in the future to follow the path of virtue. Before the play began, she had already been too corrupted by poverty.

Juliet Stevenson is the passionate and entirely selfless lover. When Frank is distracted, she tortures herself with fears that her own shortcomings are to blame. When he denies this, in a marvellously unexpected touch, she suggests that he is about to fight a duel on her behalf, and begs her husband to make peace with his rival. All her guesses are wide of the mark, nor will her lover be ever undeceived. She accepts even her own murder, with the lines: 'I did not think that death had been so sweet; nor I so apt to love him.'

The world evoked in this production, beautifully designed by Chris Dyer, is one in which Puritans and cavaliers mingle uneasily, where 'ridiculous old customs' still abound, where the hobby-horse has not yet been forgotten. But we are asked to see this, I think, as a prelude to a new England, where witchcraft will be stamped out, the Morris Dance will be banned, and the theatre itself closed down. At the end of the first half, the light falls on a primitive whirligig in the shape of a Puritan. The wooden figure waves its arms around its head, mechanical and threatening. This is the best of Mr Kyle's work that I have seen.

20 September 1981

On The Razzle (LYTTELTON)

John Oxenford was an unusually gifted, self-educated man. He was the first to introduce the ideas of Schopenhauer to the British public. His translation of Goethe's autobiography is unsurpassed. He was drama critic of *The Times* for twenty-five years, and wrote over sixty plays. One of these, a fifty-minute farce called *A Day Well Spent*, has had an extraordinary career. The Austrian playwright Johann Nestroy transformed it into a famous comedy, *Einen Jux Will Er Sich Machen*. Thornton Wilder re-adapted this comedy into *The Matchmaker*, which in turn became *Hello, Dolly!* Now Tom Stoppard, who is himself an English version of a Czech original, has produced a new version of the Nestroy version, entitled *On the Razzle* (Lyttelton).

The latest of Oxenford's successors, the playwright and drama critic Irving Wardle, has suggested that it might be worth having a look at the original Oxenford play. My advice is: don't bother. It is a trivial little piece about a foreman and an apprentice who shut up shop while their employer is away and go off on a spree. Bumping into their master in the street, they take refuge in a milliner's, where, under the assumed names of Addison and Steele, they pretend to be connected with a customer. Unfortunately the customer turns up, plays them along and insists on being taken out for an expensive meal. At the inn, who should they meet but . . . etcetera, etcetera. There is one reasonable pun: discussing the blindness of love, a character exclaims: 'love is a torrent, and his blindness is a cataract.' The piece is published in number 531 of a Victorian part-work called Dicks' Standard Plays. By number 531, Dicks' Standard Plays was somewhat scraping the barrel.

Nestroy was an actor-manager-playwright in the thriving days of Viennese comedy (that is, in the mid-nineteenth century). He was always in need of a story. Once he had found a plot like the Oxenford farce, he set about transforming it to suit the talents of his company, to the extent that he actually wrote the names of the actors in the script, rather than those of the characters. The company was built around his own skills, and those of a man called Scholz. Nestroy was tall and thin. Scholz was short and thick. Nestroy acted clever, Scholz acted thick, Nestroy had a good voice, and his first appearance on stage was always marked by a musical number followed by a speech in which he outlined the theme of the play. The Nestroy characters always had a fine turn of phrase; they invented words; they loved borrowing foreign expressions; they commented astutely on the morals, although not the politics, of the day; they were the 'raisonneurs'.

To confuse the Nestroy-role with the Scholz-role is like giving Tony Hancock's lines to Sid James, or Morecambe's part to Wise. In this play, the role of Melchior was invented for Scholz, while Nestroy took that of Weinberl (the foreman who decides to have a spree). The National production gets these two absolutely the wrong way round, owing to Mr Stoppard's complete misunderstanding of the dynamics of the plot. The Nestroy-role is not allowed his songs, and his speeches are robbed of their bravura. Charming though Ray Brooks is, he is not allowed to command the stage or to address the audience in the manner of the raisonneurs. Thus one important typical feature of Austrian comedy is lost.

On the other hand, Michael Kitchen, in the Scholz-role, is in immediate command as soon as he comes on the scene and it was noticeable that towards the end of the play the audience began to applaud when Mr Kitchen spoke his own last line, imagining that once he had said his bit the proceedings must naturally be over. But Mr Stoppard had changed the ending, depriving Weinberl of his betrothal and introducing a sentimental last scene in which the two employees return to their tasks with only their memories to comfort them. In the original Weinberl's quick thinking wins him the hand of the rich widow.

This is not, then, Nestroy. How does it rate as a Stoppard play? I see from the daily notices that there was a torrent of wit. If so, I'm afraid that I am the one with the cataract. Mr

241

Stoppard has provided an enormous number of puns, a high proportion of which are bad. I like bad puns, as long as they are good. But there's all the difference in the world between a good-bad pun and a bad-bad pun (the kind which is completely over the heads of the audience).

The device of introducing Scottish Fortnight in Vienna (in honour of the play's first performance at the Edinburgh Festival, from which the national critics were pointlessly excluded) might have been expected to throw up a few good jokes. But all the Scottish jokes are based on clichés. There is no substance to them. Besides, Nestroy's play is about Vienna. It commented to the contemporary audience upon the society in which they lived. It was a play about business and about love. Mr Stoppard's play is about nothing at all, absolutely nothing. The jokes based on sexual innuendo are extremely repetitive and at odds with the original.

Peter Wood directs it, and there are inspired moments of comic business, along with an often ingenious handling of the stage. The designs by Carl Toms are extravagant and often beautiful. There are moments, however, when the stage looks unnaturally deserted. I did not admire Derek Bourgeois's music. I did on the other hand admire Mr Kitchen and Deborah Norton. Dinsdale Landen's performance and make-up is probably some kind of personal attack on Denis Healey.

If, by the way, all that I have said sounds ungracious, I have a surprise witness in favour of Mr Stoppard and the National production, in the shape of the philosopher and Nestroy-fan Søren Kierkegaard. That eccentric and delightful book *Repetition* contains a lengthy account of the experience of watching Nestroy's *The Talisman* performed in Berlin. What Kierkegaard emphasises is the impossibility of predicting one's own response, even when the play and its leading actor are firm favourites.

'To view a farce,' he writes, 'is for the person of culture like playing a lottery, except that one is spared the annoyance of winning money. But such uncertainty is not what theatregoers generally want; hence they neglect the farce, or look down on it loftily, which is all the worse for them. The real theatrical public has in general a certain narrowminded seriousness; it wants (or at least imagines that it wants) to be ennobled and educated at the theatre; it wants to have had (or at least to imagine that it has had) a rare aesthetic enjoyment; it would like to be able, as soon as it has read the posters, to know in advance how the thing is going to turn out this evening. Such an accord between promise and performance is impossible in farce; for the same farce may make many different impressions, and it may happen strangely enough that it has least effect when best acted.'

So, says Kierkegaard, one cannot rely on one's neighbours or upon the newspapers to know whether one has been entertained or not. 'This is a matter the individual must determine for himself.'

4 October 1981

Heartbreak House
(ROYAL EXCHANGE, MANCHESTER)

Not long ago, beautiful posters went up all over London
depicting one of those superb Edwardian hostesses with a
hairdo. The occasion was the Sargent Exhibition at the
National Portrait Gallery, but what I always thought, strap-
hanging in the Tube, was 'What on earth is Eleanor Bron up
to now?' The resemblance was extraordinary, and, if you
wished to see the resemblance in real life, I recommend the
Manchester Royal Exchange production of *Heartbreak
House*. Here Miss Bron has the opportunity – indeed the duty
– to dazzle us in her full Edwardian splendour. And oh boy
does she dazzle.

The role is first cousin to the part she played in the film of
Women in Love, but whereas on that occasion we were given a
satirical sketch (Lawrence's revenge on Lady Ottoline
Morrell), what we have here is a more intimate and telling
portrayal, one which is ultimately devastating. Mrs Hushabye
belongs to that section of British society which, on the eve of
the First World War, had the intelligence to see that something was fundamentally wrong with the world as it then was,
but which was prevented by the force of inertia from doing
anything about it.

The intellectual ancestor of the piece, as acknowledged by
Shaw in his preface, is Chekhov, and in particular *The Cherry
Orchard*. That mysterious noise which the Chekhov characters
hear (it may be a cable snapping in a mine) is borrowed by
Shaw and developed to the point of a full explanation and a
startling dénouement. When the noise begins, it is supposed
that it must be a train. In the last passage of the play, it turns
out to be the Zeppelin. The calamity of aerial bombardment
has arrived.

In a bad play this would give the characters an opportunity
to repent – to see the disaster which their chronic lassitude has

brought about. But Shaw distinguishes here between his own point of view and those of his characters, who are for the most part spared in the destruction. The war may have destroyed Mrs Hushabye's world, but Mrs Hushabye was not obliged to serve in the trenches. What Shaw gives us, therefore, is not her repentance in the face of war, but a welcoming of the war.

The bombardment is seen as an aesthetic treat. Mrs Hushabye is enthusiastic: 'Did you hear the explosions? and the sound in the sky: it's splendid: it's like an orchestra: it's like Beethoven.' And finally: 'But what a glorious experience! I hope they'll come again tomorrow night.' If the play has a single thesis it is to show how it comes about that a woman can say such a thing when the world is blazing about her.

Shaw's observations on this point are profound, and the preface to *Heartbreak House* is a fine, angry piece of writing. For once, that awful tone of narcissistic exasperation is dropped in favour of real feeling. Shaw tells us that he began the play before the war (although the latest edition thinks that this is probably untrue). It was not performed, however, until 1920, and the explanation Shaw gives is most peculiar:

> When men are heroically dying for their country, it is not the time to show their lovers and wives and fathers and mothers how they are being sacrificed to the blunders of boobys, the cupidity of capitalists, the ambition of conquerors, and electioneering of demagogues, the Pharisaism of patriots, the lusts and lies and rancours and blood-thirsts that love war because it opens their prison doors and sets them on the thrones of power and popularity.

And he goes on to say: 'Truth telling is not compatible with the defence of the realm.' This passage is expressive of his dilemma but it is self-contradictory. Were the soldiers at the front dying for the interests of their country, or were they being slaughtered for all the other reasons which he mentions? If he really believed in the latter reasons, was it not his duty to expose the war?

It is significant that nobody can now remember why the First World War was fought. Everyone has an idea of the reasons for the Second World War, but the rationale of the first has mysteriously slipped from popular memory. The important question today is: Is there a possible rationale for the Third World War – for total destruction? Moderate opinion believes that a Third World War could be justified, and that we should be moderately armed to blow ourselves to smithereens. The extremists believe that this is wrong and that we should, as a populated globe, continue to exist. The people in Shaw's play are like the moderates today, they are fundamentally out of love with existence.

This was the first time I had seen *Heartbreak House*, and I was really glad to catch it in such a fine production. Jonathan Hales directed it. The sets are by Roger Butlin, the costumes by Deirdre Clancy and the sound (which is extraordinarily good) is by Colin Duncan.

It is a play which depends on a well-balanced cast and in particular it needs intelligent and beautiful women. I have mentioned Miss Bron. Her sister is played by Diane Fletcher, who achieves a marvellously clear characterisation of a woman who has left her family milieu for diplomatic high society, but who remains drawn nostalgically to her origins. Dangerous little Ellie Dunn is played by dangerous little Lynsey Baxter (whom you will have just seen in *The French Lieutenant's Woman*). This is a remarkable trio.

The men are mostly variations on a theme of emotional enslavement. Alfred Burke is Captain Shotover, Nigel Stock is the industrialist, Norman Eshley is married to Miss Bron, Christopher Good wishes he were married to Miss Fletcher, and Peter Howell is the proud father of Miss Baxter. The burglar Richard Beale was once married to the nurse, Peggy Aitchison. There is no weak spot in the cast.

1 November 1981

All My Sons (WYNDHAM'S)

All My Sons by Arthur Miller, which opened at Wyndham's Theatre this week in a magnificent new production by Michael Blakemore, has come in, as a play, for a certain amount of critical stick. I notice that the *Listener* is worried about the narrowness of the moral argument: a war criminal is exposed before our eyes, but the criminality of the armaments industry is supposedly not examined. It is wrong, in the play's terms, to allow the profit motive to kill off your country's soldiers, but what about those soldiers on the other side? What about the Japanese?

Well, one could imagine a play which argued that it was wrong of America to fight the Axis powers. It might have been written, say, by the late Robert Lowell, who was a conscientious objector in the Second World War. But it would of course have been a different play. Mr Miller was not expressing a narrowness of vision when he chose the terms of his drama; he was arguing within the broadly accepted (and surely acceptable) beliefs about the Second World War.

He gives the greatest possible weight to the terrible aspect of war itself. His returning soldier has a simple demand to make of the society into which he has returned: if the sacrifices we made are to have some meaning, it must be that the people for whom we fought will behave differently, with an understanding of what we soldiers have been through. But this expectation is daily disappointed. America has not changed. The returning soldier feels that he has suffered in vain. More than this, he feels unable to shake off a guilt towards his comrades who have died under his command. He feels it is wrong to accept what life now offers him: everything is tainted. Even to get married would be to behave like a profiteer.

This feeling he can express well enough when he is calm. But notice what happens to his explanation at the climax of

247

the drama, when Keller, the father, tells the son that his criminal act of war profiteering was done on the son's behalf. Chris replies: 'For me! Where do you live, where have you come from? For me! – I was dying every day, and you were killing my boys, and you did it for me.'

That expression, 'I was dying every day', so typical of the kind of poetry Mr Miller searches for in common speech, is actually a hysterical reversal of the truth: what haunts Chris is that every day the men in his company died, but he did not. 'You were killing my boys –' yes, in a broad sense the father was doing so, but actually the son's own guilt about his command of an almost annihilated company is here laid at the door of the father.

The play is full of touches of this kind, psychologically profound and morally clear. One feels the force of that moral clarity all the more nowadays, when it is so rare among our contemporary dramatists. But clarity is not to be confused with naivety. Even when Chris accepts that his father is a murderer, he cannot see his way to handing him over to the police. He understands that his father is not so utterly set apart from the neighbours, whose neighbours who have actually come to respect him for 'pulling a fast one'. The only thing that pushes Chris to the limit is the discovery that his father has actually provoked his elder son's death.

This is revealed by a letter in Act III, and the *Guardian* critic, with some justification, objects to the conventional nature of the dénouement. The elder son turns out to have written to his fiancée what amounts to a suicide note on hearing that both their fathers – business partners – have been convicted of selling faulty aeroplane parts. However, it is wrong to suggest that the partner's daughter could have saved her father from jail by revealing the letter earlier. It contains no proof either of Keller's guilt or of the partner's innocence. The proof of Keller's guilt is, realistically enough, Mrs Keller's accidental remark about her husband's good health. It is not the kind of proof, however, which would stand up in a court of law.

Nevertheless, the piece is written within a convention, one which was seventy years old at the time, although rather newer to the American stage. At the Wyndham's Theatre, the beautiful design by Hayden Griffin perfectly expresses the nature of the piece. The family house is realistically built, but it is set amongst foliage which, although photographically accurate, is portrayed in two dimensions. It tells you two things at once: this is foliage, and this is traditional scenery. In the same way, the play is a conventional play, but it is also profoundly accurate.

The father is played by Colin Blakely, a powerful actor with an unrivalled capacity for making himself weak, for crumpling up under the pressure of moral argument. Rosemary Harris gives a moving portrayal of the mother, an extremely well-drawn character who possesses almost, but not quite, enough influence to keep the whole truth from coming out. Garrick Hagon and Jill Baker play the son and the partner's daughter. They have the most difficult roles in the play, roles which allow no shirking: they must act at full throttle, or the whole piece will fail. But it does not fail. It has a tremendous, plain, emotional impact.

Richard Durden is Miss Baker's angry brother. David Baron, Pat Starr, Ken Drury, and Pamela Merrick complete the team, all of whom deserve every congratulation.

8 November 1981

All's Well That Ends Well (STRATFORD)

In all probability, Shakespeare actually wrote the part of Helena, in *All's Well That Ends Well*, with Harriet Walter in mind. After years of catering for the tiresome actress-laddies of his day (their gushing mannerisms, their tantrums, their disruptive effect on his leading men), he wanted to create something entirely new: the woman of the future for the actress of the future. Certainly Helena is his best female role, and in the new production at Stratford it is Miss Walter's performance which first casts the spell.

She begins in a state of high distress, and works towards one of mysterious fulfilment. She is an actress valued for her inwardness (remember her TV performance in Ian McEwan's *The Imitation Game*), her modesty of address, her ability to suggest goodness without yukkiness (she is never, never, yukky), instinctive determination without bossiness, suffering without self-indulgence.

At the start of the play she is the poor member of the aristocratic household in love with Bertram and unable to see a way to the fulfilment of her love. Her passion is a secret, except just perhaps to Bertram (Mike Gwilym) who seems to be aware that there is something between them, something which family honour would forbid him to pursue. Meanwhile the rest of the household is under the impression that Helena is still mourning her lost father.

In her first soliloquy (Helena is unusual in being vouchsafed soliloquies) she confides the truth to the audience. With an extraordinary touch Shakespeare allows her to ask herself what her father was like, and to reply: 'I have forgot him.' This comes across with the full force of panic and dismay. One should not forget a dead parent – but one does. This is the mourner's first distressing secret.

The play shows how Helena contrives to marry and get to bed with Bertram. In order to believe it one must have a sense of two related points: the significance of the King, and the code of honour. Trevor Nunn's production and John Gunter's design offer us the last period in European history in which both these points can be convincingly established: the eve of the First World War, a period in which the code of chivalry of the officer class can be seen in a most vivid and ironic light. Modern warfare destroyed chivalry, but the tradition did not die overnight. In the First World War, when one of the most famous German pilots was killed, we are told that 'planes from every British airfield within range dropped wreaths on his base'. One believes that the officers in the French court in this production would have been capable of exactly this kind of gesture.

Seen at their best, the work of a director and designer are indistinguishable in purpose: good design is significant design, just as good directing is always aimed at the meaning of the play. The brilliance of this production derives from its exploitation of all the possibilities of the period it evokes. When the play is like a fairy story, when Helena comes to the court, cures the King of his fistula and is rewarded with her choice from among the officers, the scene evokes light opera, and our sense of idiom is satisfied. We are in a world of make-believe. But on either side of that scene, it is the reality of the society that impresses us, or rather, it is the depiction of a world which will have to come to terms with a new reality, although it can still enjoy the gloss of its traditions, its pert little armies with their goose-stepping operatic soldiers.

The framework for the set evokes the elegant white cast-iron of Great Malvern station. In a series of transformations, which are speedily and excitingly executed, this architecture accommodates the domestic scene at Rossillion, a royal gymnasium, a ballroom, a smoking room, Florence railway station, looking out to a military camp beyond, a field hospital and a wonderful café in which Cheryl Campbell gives a bravura performance as Diana, entertaining the troops with a sentimental song.

Stephen Moore, whose performance in *A Doll's House* as husband to Miss Campbell's Nora effects a notable redemption of an unsympathetic character, achieves a similar success in the crucial role of Parolles. Transformed from the swaggering pretentious officer to the revealed and reviled traitor, he picks himself up, dusts himself down and starts all over again in the role of sentimental fool. His moment of decision ('simply the thing I am shall make me live') is put over with particular skill, and his bursting into tears in the last scene is most comical.

The revelation of Mr Moore's worthlessness is important as it is the first part of Bertram's own humiliation, and it is good to see how hard Mr Gwilym takes it. He really is deeply angered and depressed, watching his old chosen companion disclosing all the military and personal weaknesses of his own comrades to those he imagines to be the enemy. The second part of the humiliation is of course effected by Diana and Helena – the revelation of the bed-trick.

I concluded from Mr Gwilym's performance that (*a*) he is indeed sincere when he says that he loved Helena all along; that (*b*) what motivates his contempt is not mere snobbery but a profound sense of loss of face. If there had been a way for their love to be realised, he should have found it. That is his problem. At the end of the action, in the words of Barbara Everett (whose Penguin edition contains a convincing defence of the play), Bertram's ordinary vices pursue him home with all the logic of a nightmare. It will be hard for him to accept what has happened. It will take time.

Peggy Ashcroft as the Countess provides a single and sufficient reason for going a long way to Stratford. Her encounters with Helena at the beginning and end of the play are of an extraordinary beauty and tenderness. Geoffrey Hutchings as the Fool, John Franklin-Robbins as the King and Robert Eddison as Lord Lafeu – all excellent work. This is an utterly, utterly, exceptional production.

22 November 1981

252

The Soldier's Fortune
(LYRIC, HAMMERSMITH)

The Soldier's Fortune at the Lyric, Hammersmith, is a distinguished rarity, a comedy by Thomas Otway composed after its author had failed to get into a good fight on Flanders Field in 1678. Resentment at the sudden conclusion of a peace treaty, coupled with the disappointment of demobilisation in London, motivates the two heroes of the play, Beaugard (Peter Woodward) and Courtine (James Aubrey), who set out on a career of adultery, fornication, and fortune-hunting.

There is a school of thought which, on approaching a text of this kind, insists on the virtues of realistic interpretation: what is valuable in Otway is his ability to convey the pungent odour of Restoration London. In Sheila Hancock's Cambridge Theatre production, although there is no mistaking the odour, the chief line of approach is to emphasise theatrical virtues.

Thus, we are given a handsome traditional set, designed by Robin Archer and painted by Chris Clark in a manner which evokes the oil paintings of the period. The painter's art, which a generation of puritan designers contrived to ban from the stage, is now making a comeback, and I strongly believe that this move should be encouraged. It is foolish to exclude the painter from the theatre, when the very problems on which his expertise has accumulated over the years (colour, tone, composition) are of vital concern in any production.

The difficulty seems to be that the modern director finds the painter-designer too competitive a figure. In the end, it is the director who must produce the animated composition that we watch. But that is no reason to dispense altogether with the resources of the painter, which are far more sophisticated than the average director seems to realise.

In the opera house, where the sense of artifice is more developed, it is not considered odd to use both traditional and

253

modern painterly techniques. What a pity, though, that you have to be as famous as David Hockney before you are invited to produce a massive painterly design – in New York. Why are there no painters at work in British theatres?

If the free, exploratory, and experimental approach to painting in the theatre belongs entirely to the future, there are nevertheless some areas in which the resources of the artist have been deployed. In his television productions of Shakespeare, Jonathan Miller has shown how the Renaissance painter can inspire composition and visual idiom. In the designs of Hayden Griffin (particularly for *The Streets of London* and, at Hammersmith, *Total Eclipse*), the unspoken rules of modern theatre design were broken to excellent effect.

In Mr Archer's designs, two of these rules are sent packing: the rule that a surface must always be hard and wholesomely textured; and the ban on painterly illusion. I particularly like the view of the piazza at Covent Garden which situated a significant proportion of the play on the site now occupied by one of our fashionable cafés, with an unbroken vista including the actors' church.

The interiors evoke the squat proportions of homespun baroque, and there is a fine conception of Sir Jolly Jumble's fun palace (now Tutton's), decorated in the very latest Pompeian manner with frescoes inspired by the Villa of the Mysteries. Sir Jolly is the go-between, a character of wonky proclivities, who makes it his business to bring the soldiers together with their sweethearts, and watch what they get up to. He is played by Hugh Paddick, who secures a high proportion of the evening's laughs; and a high proportion of the laughs he gets are inspired by his own perfectly horrible laugh.

Dilys Watling, as Lady Dunce, is married to Brian Murphy, Sir Davy Dunce, whom she persuades to act as the agent of his own cuckolding. Aware perhaps that theatrical jokes at the expense of foolish old men are beginning to wear somewhat thin over the millennia, Otway turns his foolish old man into a hypocritical villain, and has him attempt to arrange the murder of his wife's lover. He is subsequently transformed into a guilt-stricken parody of Macbeth.

The leading men perform with gusto. I was amused to notice that Mr Aubrey, when he was supposed to be fighting drunk, took the opportunity to develop his interpretation in the direction of high tragedy, where he is rather more at home. As for the maintenance of comic business and impetus, the production has many faults, and it tended to amuse rather than convulse the audience. The staging of the prologue seemed to me a mistake.

But it is worth seeing the play in this kind of production in this kind of theatre, which once staged a famous revival of Otway's *Venice Preserved*.

29 November 1981

Richard II *(THÉÂTRE DU SOLEIL)*
Peer Gynt *(THÉÂTRE DE LA ViLLE)*
Carmen *(BOUFFES DU NORD)*
The Bourgeois Gentilhomme
(GRAND MAGIC CIRCUS)

France is another country. They do things differently there.
And so well, indeed, as to make you think yourself back to
square one. If you ask yourself what is the major artistic
principle behind English productions of Shakespeare, the
answer surely must be: they seek to draw the experience
depicted in the plays as close as possible to our own.

This is a fine idea but it is not the only possible approach.
Suppose you start with the opposite intention. You say:
Shakespeare is not our contemporary, his characters belong
to the heroic past, they do not live according to the same rules
by which we live, they do not speak in the same way in which
we speak. To follow such thoughts to their logical conclusion
is to demand a style of production unmistakably different
from our own, rich tradition.

Ariane Mnouchkine has chosen *Richard II* to inaugurate a
Shakespeare season at the Théâtre du Soleil. Some season. In
addition to the opening production, she will offer the two
parts of *Henry IV*, *Henry V* and, for good measure, a couple
of comedies, *La Nuit des Rois* and *Peines d'Amour Perdues*.
The translations are her own. On the basis of the first production I should say the results will be brilliantly heterodox and
authentically Shakespearian.

The theatre itself, an enormous warehouse in the Bois de
Vincennes, has been completely redesigned. The acting, seat-
ing and dressing-room space is all carpeted with what must be
the largest doormat in history. The stage is approached,
Japanese-style, from a long raised gangway along which the
company is obliged to run at full tilt, sumptuously dressed in

256

oriental costumes and Elizabethan ruffs, to the percussive accompaniment of a Japanese orchestra.

Japanese make-up, Japanese masks for the old men, and for everybody a Japanese acting style which aims at vivid characterisation, utter precision and economy of expression, complete formal control of speech and gesture. The lines are delivered, almost without exception, directly to the audience. The groupings are linear. The voice is projected from the top of the register – the poetry is shouted out in a manner which suggests a relish for splendour.

The effect is to redeem those qualities of the play which one might, unconsciously, have made allowance for. The formality of the plays' constructions is revealed. The argument develops like a terrific algebra, a vast equation whose terms must be shifted and juggled around, according to mysteriously beautiful rules, in order to arrive at the meaning of the term kingship.

The King is a young actor of superb, hectic arrogance, Georges Bigot; his great opponent, Bolingbroke (Cyrille Bosc), has no sooner robbed the King of his superbness and his crown (leaving him only a wild pride in defeat) than the kingship turns into a shirt of Nessus. In the first scene the King leaps magnificently on to the throne, which is like a long low table. In the last, Exton (John Arnold) brings the murdered body of Richard and lays it in state beneath the table. Weary and ill, the guilty successor stretches himself out above his victim, leaving us with the image of a double tomb.

I watched this on the last night of an extraordinary week. Two evenings had been spent at Patrice Chéreau's quite different but no less spectacular *Peer Gynt*, which the TNP have just finished presenting at the Théâtre de la Ville. Here again, there is a luxurious space, and in particular the great height of the stage, which has no arch, could be employed to suggest the immensity of mountains and glaciers, or the grand architecture of Egypt.

The set combined its own monumental and brutal architecture with painted flats and drops which evoked an absolutely precise visual idiom. The scenery of Egypt suggested the lithographs of David Roberts. The sphinx when it appeared had a cut-out figure of a top-hatted man with a measuring tape, and a ladder placed against the back of its head. The actors moved among a world of illustrations – but it was a world against which they could rebel. Peer Gynt could push the encroaching crags away, and at one point he tore down a great lowering painted sky.

The decor, by Richard Peduzzi, was lit by André Diot in a manner which insolently refused to put itself at the service of the human compositions. Thus if a part of the action moved into the extreme dark, that was that – we saw no more of it. One had, though, a strong sense that direction, design and lighting were the products of powerful, independent and well-matched artistic personalities.

Peer Gynt was played by one of France's leading young actors, Gérard Desarthe. His was a performance which seemed to derive from a clinical conception of the character's mentality. When his imagination was in full flight, he would suddenly lose track of his train of thought, and wake up, astonished to find himself wherever he was, and unable to retrieve his words. The development of the role was beautifully drawn into old age. It ended, as it had begun, as a portrayal of infantilism. You felt that the hero had never been able to bear leaving his mother's arms, and that when he at last returned to Solveig (Catherine Rétoré) he was giving us the final clue to his character in his last speech:

Ma Mère, mon épouse, la femme sans péché!
Cache-moi, cache-moi, cache-moi, tout en toi!

Peter Brook's *Carmen*, which is packing that charming, tatty old musical theatre, the Bouffes du Nord, is a *Carmen* sans blague, played by a cast of six who are permitted to sing at an easeful, natural level a text by Jean-Claude Carrière which, without jettisoning all the inventions of Bizet's librettists, brings us back to the essence of the original Merimée story. The acting is astonishingly vigorous and adept. Carmen smokes a cheroot, wrestles in the dirt, has an orange squeezed playfully into her eyes, without ever being put off her musical stride.

Jérôme Savary's Grand Magic Circus is a company for whose members acting includes a whole set of skills such as juggling, tumbling, singing and playing unconventional musical instruments. Their current production, Molière's *Le Bourgeois Gentilhomme*, shows the Circus off with tremendous zest, involving as it does the most riotous turns of plot, such as the transformation of M. Jourdain's house into a Turkish court, and the subjection of the hapless hero to conjuring tricks and every possible humiliation.

At the centre of the piece, M. Savary himself gives a study of bumbledom reminiscent of Jacques Tati, to whom tribute is paid in the programme. There is the same studied ungainliness, the same fundamentally benevolent disposition, the same infinitely reduced awareness of the visible side of any situation. One is left with the image of M. Jourdain dressed in the Turkish style, with a gigantic deliquescent pumpkin for a hat, exotically clothed but failing magnificently to live up to the demands of the dress.

This, incidentally, is the kind of production that our own National Theatre was attempting to achieve with *The Hypochondriac*, and it is instructive to see how much skill is required to bring it off. These actors do not simply juggle, they juggle in a way which very vividly suggests the impossible. The skill of the actor as acrobat is as natural to him as tap-dancing would be to his American counterpart. One does not stop acting in order to throw oneself around the room. Acting, for the French, is a way of throwing oneself around the room.

27 December 1981

259

Postscript
The Right To Be Wrong

My heart sank to my boots when I entered the hospitality room of a television studio and found that I was about to discuss the role of the theatre critic with a director about whose work I had, that morning, been excessively rude (see p. 103). But Charles Marowitz is an odd sort of fish. He was relaxed and friendly, and soon put me at my ease. The atmosphere over the sandwiches was quite eerily polite.

When the cameras were on us, Mr Marowitz made his case against the critics as a group. We were, as he put it, non-entities. There was no ounce of artistic feeling in us. The great critics of the past had been artists first and foremost: he was thinking of figures such as Eliot and Pound. How did we compare with such giants?

There is no answer to this kind of point. One cannot protest, 'I'm *not* a nonentity', without looking a fool. I thought Mr Marowitz had a fair revenge.

After the programme had been made, we all began to think of the things we might have said, and here Mr Marowitz did rather less well. He asked what qualifications we had to write criticism, what preparation we had undergone. In the Soviet Union, he argued, a critic had to undergo rigorous training before being allowed to practise . . . Surely there should be some kind of system introduced in this country . . .

As if we were not to be allowed to review until we had received a diploma, and had been checked for ideological soundness. This second point contradicts the other one which Mr Marowitz had made to such effect. Neither Eliot nor Pound worked meekly within the areas for which they had received formal training. What we value in their work is written in precisely the opposite spirit: their intelligence knew no petty bounds; they invented their subjects; they put the 'qualified' critics to shame; they condemned and praised according to new standards which they themselves established.

This is the true spirit of criticism, and I may add that artistic achievement is not a guarantee of critical excellence. Not all great writers have been great critics, or even good ones. Shakespeare's own achievements as a critic are so slight as to have escaped notice. Hazlitt's reticence as a dramatist, on the other hand, does not affect our view of his criticism. Shaw, the patron saint of late developers, was a critic first, next a dramatist. Eliot and Pound are unusual in that their poetry is a kind of criticism. But nobody is obliged to become an artist, and no critic should be obliged to prove himself in any other way than in criticism.

When we write a review of a play, we are not actors, we are not directors, we are not playwrights and we are not poets. We are critics only. To say that we are bad critics *because* we are, say, failed novelists (like Shaw) is as wrong as to say that we are good critics *because* we happen to be good dramatists. Some people think that Eliot was a good dramatist. I would say that he was a great critic of Elizabethan drama, and a great poet who had every opportunity of becoming a great dramatic poet. But as soon as he began to write plays with a particular kind of production in mind he went dreadfully off the rails. The relationship between artistic and critical achievement is extremely complex.

By the way, Eliot wrote very little theatre criticism proper, and it is not at all clear that he would have been good at the job. His review of Sybil Thorndike's Medea at the Holborn Empire (reprinted in *The Sacred Wood*) comes largely in the context of an attack on Gilbert Murray as a translator of Greek verse. His obituary of Marie Lloyd (reprinted in the *Selected Prose*) is more interesting as evidence of Eliot's tastes than as an account of music-hall comedy. Eliot's great criticism is written for the reader of poetry, not for the play-going audience. It is in a quite different genre from the theatre notice.

Critics of Eliot's kind write on subjects they choose. Theatre critics must respond to other people's work, whatever it may be, as it crops up. We must work at random. They choose

261

their own terms of debate. They think in the long term. We say: 'This is on for three weeks – don't miss it.' They say: 'It might be possible to work towards an eventual reassessment of Massinger.' We say: 'Unless you see *this* Massinger *this* week, you won't know what we're talking about.' And of course they only deal with new material when they already feel strongly about it. Whereas our job all the time is to produce new responses to new work.

It follows then that the crucial task of the theatre critic is: to assess and express his immediate response. We must be true to our anger, true to our enthusiasm, true to our excitement, true to our boredom. The only point in reading our work is for the reader to find an authentically personal opinion; which means that, if we fear the challenge 'Who do you think *you* are to hold this opinion about that work?', our best course will be to resign.

The worst course (but it is extremely hard to avoid this all the time) is the kind of criticism which, instead of resting upon personal response and judgement, attempts instead to predict what the public response will be; so that the critic is imagining himself as not another individual – which would be wrong enough – but as the sum total of the theatre-going public. This is the spirit of critical timidity: *I* can't stand this new piece, but, oh dear, Johnny Public is going to love it, so I'd better watch my words.

Naturally, just as you require convictions before you can have the courage of them, so you must have responded to something before you can express your response authentically. For the modern theatre critic, who often sees five plays a week, this can be a problem. We are professionally required to extend our interest beyond our natural tastes. And we are obliged to distinguish between, for instance, a bad play and our own bad mood on a particular night; between a lacklustre performance and a sense of aesthetic exhaustion. Such distinctions are not always easy to make. If, every time I emerged from the theatre in a blind fury at what I had seen, I told myself 'Perhaps you've just got out of the wrong side of bed today', I might well save the world from some nasty and unfair reviews. But suppose I did the same with my enthusiasms:

suppose I said, 'Listen sonny, you were rather over-excited last night – it can't have been as good as all that', and proceeded to trim my response in line with the average enthusiasm expressed in the daily papers – well, who needs that kind of critic?

In order to begin work, we need the right to be wrong, the right to be unfair, the right to be overenthusiastic. Without such rights, we cannot contemplate working at all in what must be a highly instinctive art.

I have mentioned reading other notices. This is something the Sunday critic can do and perhaps should do. If some line of argument has been particularly well explored elsewhere, it is better to give another aspect of the production a little more attention. People sometimes say to me, 'Oh all you do is read the daily notices and say the exact opposite.' My reply is: *if* that is what I do, that is, in the present circumstances, not at all a bad thing. To restore the damage done by overnight reviews is a useful and distinctive function of Sunday criticism.

But there is a serious purpose behind the practice of attacking other critics from time to time. In book reviewing, this is absolutely normal. In theatre reviewing I found to my surprise that it was considered most unusual: dog was not supposed to eat dog. But one might ask, in that case, who *does* get to eat dog? Directors and actors, authors and producers are in an impossible position when it comes to replying to critics: they always seem to fear that their replies will be held against them next time around. But critics themselves are in no sense beholden to each other. An important part of their work is to disagree.

If we say as critics 'Dog does not eat dog', then we are setting ourselves up as a collective tribunal, against which there is no right of appeal. There are very few of us. We review everything that comes along. The importance of our work in relation to the theatre is far greater than that of any other criticism in relation to any other art. But we should not be perniciously solemn about our status. We are randomly selected individuals performing a task which must remain individual. I am never worried if somebody *disagrees* with what I write. I am deeply worried if some disagreement forces me to admit to myself that I didn't really mean what I said on such an occasion, or that I toned my views down, or touched them up, under the influence of some extraneous consideration. That is, if I did not act as an individual. Which is all a critic is.

Plays and Players, February 1982

Index

269

270

271